SOCCER AWARENESS

Developing the Thinking Player

by Wayne Harrison

REEDSWAIN PUBLISHING

To His Highness Sheikh Hazza Bin Zayed Al Nahyan

- Wayne Harrison

With the future perspective for the progress of UAE football in mind; and in line with promoting the professionalism of sports in the UAE, a series of related sports books have been authored.

These books are a tribute to the various clubs and individuals who strive to raise the level of professional thinking and in turn raise our future levels of achievement.

We at Al Ain Football club, based on our commitment to developing UAE sports, are proud to forward this book, in which the author Wayne Harrison; our Technical Director of Youth; presents new methodologies for building and enhancing the performance of current professional; and future professional players.

We are confident that this book will be a very valuable addition to all in the sports field.

- H.H. Sheikh Hazza Bin Zayed Al Nahyan

This book was published in association with **Al Ain Football Club** in Abu Dhabi, United Arab Emirates, where Wayne Harrison is the Technical Director of the Academy and the Football School. Al Ain is the top professional club in the UAE, winning the Asian Champions League in 2003

His Highness Sheikh Hazza Bin Zayed Al Nahyan
Chairman of Al Ain Board of Directors
Vice President of Al Ain Club
Vice President of the Honorary Board

His Excellency Mohammad Bin Thalob Al-Dirie
Member of Al Ain Board of Directors

Wayne Harrison
Technical Director Academy and School
Al Ain Football Club

**Library of Congress
Cataloging - in - Publication Data**

Soccer Awareness
Developing the Thinking Player
by Wayne Harrison

ISBN-13: 978-1-59164-109-4
ISBN-10: 1-59164-109-8
Library of Congress Control Number: 2009934357

Art Direction and Layout
Bryan R. Beaver

Photographs
Arshad Khan of Al Ain Football Club

All the diagrams in the book were created using Session Planner 2.0 software from Soccer Specific.com. This software is available for purchase and download at www.soccerspecific.com

CONTENTS

pxi / Foreword

p3 / Chapter 1 - AN INTRODUCTION TO SOCCER AWARENESS TRAINING
- THE IMPORTANCE OF DEVELOPING TECHNICAL ABILITY THROUGH LEARNING DRIBBLING; TURNING, RECEIVING AND TURNING, RUNNING WITH THE BALL; BEATING PLAYERS IN 1v1 SITUATIONS AND ONE AND TWO TOUCH FINISHING SKILLS
- AREAS OF AWARENESS
- FIRST AND SECOND TOUCH TRAINING DEVELOPING BOTH FEET
- THE IMPORTANCE OF TEACHING ONE TOUCH PLAY: IMPROVING ONE TOUCH PLAY MAINTAINING AN AWARENESS OF WHAT IS IN ADVANCE AND BEYOND THE BALL
- A PSYCHOLOGICAL APPROACH TO SOCCER
- THE DECISION MAKING THOUGHT PROCESS THE PLAYER IS GOING THROUGH AT ANY ONE MOMENT
- THE FUTSAL BALL AND THE AWARENESS COACHING METHOD
- THE COACHING PRINCIPLES CONSIDERED IN THIS PROGRAM
- COACHING METHODOLOGY AND THE PLANNING OF CLINICS
- HOW TO ORGANIZE A COACHING CLINIC SESSION PLAN
- A COACHES CHECKLIST FOR A COACHING CLINIC SESSION PLAN
- A COACHING CLINIC PLANNER FOR TRAINING
- TRAINING STRUCTURE: AN EXAMPLE OF A CLINIC PLAN FOR TRAINING
- AN EXAMPLE OF A TYPICAL AWARENESS COACHING CLINIC SESSION PLAN
- WARM UP AND COOL DOWN FOR TRAINING AND MATCH SITUATIONS
- AN EXAMPLE OF A THEME FOR THE CLINIC SESSION PLAN:AN INTRODUCTION TO AWARENESS TRAINING

p41 / Chapter 2 - METHODS OF ASSESSING AWARENESS AND INTRODUCING CONTINUUMS OF DEVELOPMENT

p63 / Chapter 3 - DEVELOPING THE LINK BETWEEN FOOT AND BODY POSITIONING AND THE AWARENESS OF OPTIONS
- C.C.1 OBJECTIVE: IMPROVING FAST FOOTWORK AND COORDINATION

p75 / Chapter 4 - AN INTRODUCTION TO AWARENESS AND INDIVIDUAL TECHNICAL SKILLS TRAINING
- C.C.2 OBJECTIVE: IMPROVING TOUCH ON THE BALL
- C.C.3 OBJECTIVE: IMPROVING BASIC DRIBBLING AND AWARENESS IN POSSESSION OF THE BALL
- C.C.4 OBJECTIVE: DEVELOPING AWARENESS IN POSSESSION OF THE BALL WITH LOTS OF TOUCHES THROUGH A FUN KICK OUT GAME WITH A BALL EACH
- C.C.5 OBJECTIVE: IMPROVING AWARENESS IN POSSESSION OF THE BALL AND DEVELOPING DRIBBLING SKILLS AT THE SAME TIME
- C.C.6 OBJECTIVE: IMPROVING DRIBBLING SKILLS: INITIALLY THROUGH PASSIVE NON – COMPETITIVE DRIBBLING PRACTICES
- C.C.7 OBJECTIVE: IMPROVING DRIBBLING SKILLS THROUGH SEMI COMPETITIVE DRIBBLING PRACTICES LEADING TO COMPETITIVE SITUATIONS
- C.C.8 OBJECTIVE: DEVELOPING COMPETITIVE 1 v 1, 2 v 2, 3 v 3 ATTACKING PLAY AND PERIPHERAL VISION
- C.C.9 OBJECTIVE: IMPROVING ATTACKING 1 v 1 AND 2 v 2 CONFRONTATIONS

p133/ Chapter 5 - THE THOUGHT PROCESSES AND PHYSICAL ACTIONS INVOLVED IN AWARENESS TRAINING AND COACHING CLINICS TO PRACTICE THEM

- C.C.10 OBJECTIVE: IMPROVING ONE AND TWO TOUCH PASSING MAINTAINING AN AWARENESS OF WHAT IS "BEYOND THE BALL"
- C.C.11 OBJECTIVE: AWARENESS; FIRST AND SECOND TOUCH TRAINING: FIRST TOUCH ACROSS THE BODY AND A DIAGONAL PASS RETURN
- C.C.12 OBJECTIVE: IMPROVING SPATIAL AWARENESS
- C.C.13 OBJECTIVE: DEVELOPING BASIC THEN PROGRESSED AWARENESS TRAINING IN THREES
- C.C.14 OBJECTIVE: IDENTIFYING LEVELS OF AWARENESS
- C.C.15 OBJECTIVE: TEACHING THE FUNDAMENTALS OF THE AWARENESS COACHING METHOD
- C.C.16 OBJECTIVE: RECEIVING, CONTROLLING AND TURNING WITH THE BALL IN FOURS
- STARTING WITH NON – COMPETITIVE PLAY
- C.C.17 OBJECTIVE: PRACTICING PASSING AND SUPPORT PLAY IN FOUR'S AND AIDING DEVELOPMENT OF AWARENESS "OFF" THE BALL
- C.C.18 OBJECTIVE: IMPROVING AWARENESS OF SPACING AND MOVEMENT "OFF" THE BALL
- C.C.19 OBJECTIVE: FURTHER DEVELOPMENT OF AWARENESS AND OF MOVEMENT "OFF" THE BALL
- C.C.20 OBJECTIVE: IMPROVING AWARENESS THROUGH A SIMPLE NUMBERS CONDITIONED GAME INTRODUCING THE THREE TEAM AWARENESS GAME
- C.C.21 OBJECTIVE: TAKING THE AWARENESS NUMBERS GAME INTO A MORE GAME LIKE ENVIRONMENT
- C.C.22 OBJECTIVE: WORKING ON PERIPHERAL VISION THROUGH THE SPECIFIC PERIPHERAL VISION COACHING GAME
- C.C.23 OBJECTIVE: DEVELOPING PERIPHERAL VISION AND AWARENESS TRAINING INTRODUCING MORE SOCCER BALLS INTO A COMPETITIVE GAME
- C.C.24 OBJECTIVE: DEVELOPING TEAM PLAY THROUGH A DIRECTIONAL FOUR TEAM AWARENESS GAME WITH SIXTEEN PLAYERS: PART A
- C.C.25 OBJECTIVE: DEVELOPING TEAM PLAY THROUGH A DIRECTIONAL FOUR TEAM AWARENESS GAME WITH SIXTEEN PLAYERS: PART B
- C.C.26 OBJECTIVE: AN AWARENESS OF WHERE THE SPACE IS TO EXPLOIT USING THE SHADOW STRIKER
- C.C.27 OBJECTIVE: A TRANSITION GAME DEVELOPING THE PLAYERS ABILITY TO RECOGNIZE THE IMMEDIATE CHANGES FROM DEFENCE TO ATTACK AND ATTACK TO DEFENCE AND TO ACT ON IT QUICKLY
- C.C.28 OBJECTIVE: COMBINING AWARENESS TRAINING WITH SHOOTING AT GOAL AS THE END PRODUCT: DRIBBLING / TURNING COMBINATION PLAYS AND FINISHING
- C.C.29 OBJECTIVE: FURTHER DEVELOPMENT OF THE FINISHING GAME USING TWO GOALS AND INCREASING THE NUMBER OF DECISIONS ABLE TO BE MADE
- C.C.30 OBJECTIVE: IMPROVING AWARENESS IN ONE TOUCH FINISHING INSIDE THE BOX
- C.C.31 OBJECTIVE: IMPROVING QUICK FINISHING INSIDE AND ALSO AROUND THE BOX WORKING ON ANTICIPATION IN FINISHING SITUATIONS
- C.C.32 OBJECTIVE: DEVELOPING PASSING AND MOVING IN RESTRICTED SPACE ENSURING QUICK DECISION MAKING
- C.C.33 OBJECTIVE: DEVELOPING PASSING AND MOVING IN RESTRICTED SPACE ENSURING QUICK DECISION MAKING IN A COMPETITIVE ENVIRONMENT
- C.C.34 OBJECTIVE: DEVELOPING THE PLAYERS ABILITY TO SWITCH THE PLAY, BE AWARE OF TEAMMATES AND OPPONENTS POSITIONING BEFORE RECEIVING AND THEN CHANGING THE POINT OF ATTACK

p261/ Chapter 6 - THE AWARENESS COACHING METHOD AND "THEMED" SMALL SIDED GAMES

- C.C.35 OBJECTIVE: DEVELOPING TEAM PLAY AND INDIVIDUAL "THEMES" THROUGH 3 v 3 AND 4 v 4 SMALL SIDE GAMES (PART ONE)
- C.C.36 (PART TWO)
- C.C.37 OBJECTIVE: DEVELOPING TEAM PLAY AND INDIVIDUAL "THEMES" THROUGH A 6 v 6 SMALL SIDED GAME (PART ONE)
- C.C.38 (PART TWO)

p281 / Chapter 7 - DEVELOPING THE AWARENESS COACHING METHOD THROUGH "THEMED" TEAM GAMES

- C.C.39 OBJECTIVE: DEVELOPING PASSING AND SUPPORT THROUGH THE DIRECTIONAL PASSING AND SUPPORT THREE ZONE GAME: PART A
- C.C.40 OBJECTIVE: DEVELOPING PASSING AND SUPPORT THROUGH THE DIRECTIONAL PASSING AND SUPPORT THREE ZONE GAME: PART B
- C.C.41 OBJECTIVE: SWITCHING PLAY AS A TEAM
- C.C.42 OBJECTIVE: CHANGING THE POINT OF ATTACK THROUGH THE DIRECTIONAL FOUR GOAL SWITCHING PLAY GAME
- C.C.43 OBJECTIVE: DEVELOPING WIDTH IN ATTACK USING THE SWITCHING PLAY GAME
- C.C.44 OBJECTIVE: TEACHING MOVEMENT OFF THE BALL THROUGH THE TRANSITION DIRECTIONAL TARGET GAME
- C.C.45 OBJECTIVE: ENCOURAGING DRIBBLING AND TURNING THROUGH QUICK TRANSITION PLAY
- C.C.46 OBJECTIVE: DEVELOPING AWARENESS USING QUICK TRANSITION DIRECTIONAL PLAY
- C.C.47 OBJECTIVE: USING A PRESSURIZING GAME TO WORK ON ATTACKING TRANSITIONS
- C.C.48 OBJECTIVE: IMPROVING ONE AND TWO TOUCH PLAY USING THE AWARENESS THREE TEAM GAME FOCUSING ON QUICK THINKING, QUICK AND EARLY FOOT POSITIONING; SUPPORT AND FINISHING
- C.C.49 OBJECTIVE: USING AN 8 v 8 GAME WITH COMPOSURE ZONES TO AID TEAM PLAY AND INDIVIDUAL PLAYER DEVELOPMENT
- C.C.50 OBJECTIVE: USING TRANSITION GAMES TO MAINTAIN SHAPE AND BALANCE THROUGHOUT THE TEAM:
- C.C.51 OBJECTIVE: DEVELOPING A TRANSITION GAME TO ENSURE MOVEMENT OFF THE BALL IN QUICK PASSING BUILDING TO AWARENESS IN ONE TOUCH PLAY
- C.C.52: OBJECTIVE: DEVELOPING AWARENESS IN MOVEMENTS "OFF" THE BALL BETWEEN THE UNITS IN OVERLOAD SITUATIONS

p351 / A SAMPLE AWARENESS COACHING CLINIC

FOREWORD BY RENE MEULENSTEEN

In my job as First Team Coach and Skills Development coach at Manchester United I am in the fortunate position that I work with some of the biggest talents and world-class players. There are many of those players who possess great awareness and understanding; such as Giggs, Rooney, Ronaldo and Scholes just to name a few. Paul Scholes is a player who I particularly admire because of his outstanding awareness on the pitch. The positions he takes up without the ball and the decisions he makes are exceptional. In my opinion, he is a great example for young players to aspire to and in his own right absolutely world class.

The Awareness Coaching method is a comprehensive book that meets the modern demands of soccer. Over the years, as we all know soccer has changed and developed in many areas ranging from the Technical, Tactical, Physical and psychological and the tempo of the game nowadays requires a high level of Technical skills, physical fitness, mental strength and tactical awareness and understanding.

The author Wayne Harrison has successfully linked all the important qualities together in the Awareness Coaching Method. He has combined theory with practical examples, which makes it easy for coaches to understand.

As mentioned by the author the level of success depends on the talent, ability and commitment of the player. It is of course important that the coach has the ability and experience to relate his training sessions to the age and the level of the players he works with. The Awareness Coaching Method has lots of challenging yet enjoyable examples of exercises to choose from to suit any session at any level.

I would highly recommend this book to any soccer coach who wants to take himself and his players to the next level.

Rene Meulensteen
First Team Coach
Skills Development Coach
Manchester United, English Premier League Champions

1

AN INTRODUCTION TO SOCCER AWARENESS TRAINING

INTRODUCTION TO THE BOOK

Welcome to the second edition of the book; **Recognizing the Moment to Play**, originally published in 2002, now renamed **Soccer Awareness: Developing the Thinking Player**.

This new book has been presented in an updated format to make it easier for coaches to follow and implement the Awareness Soccer Coaching Method. There are over twice as many pages and diagrams in this book than the first.

Many new ideas have been added to this book and all the information is presented in a new and easy to follow and logically ordered Coaching Clinic Session Plan format.

The objective of this book is to cover the Awareness Coaching Method of training from its most basic level, even before the psychological aspects kick into place, and focusing on awareness development both before the player receives the pass, as he receives it, and after he has received it, and if he has kept the ball in his possession and what he needs to do next.

THE 4 AREAS OF AWARENESS

Soccer Awareness means having an understanding of all options available, knowing what to do "before you get the ball" by looking ahead of the ball (and getting the feet in the correct position to receive the ball), and once you get the ball, to make the correct decisions. This is designed to help players keep possession with greater effect.

Possession can then be broken down into "possession with few touches" (which is epitomized by the way Manchester United and Arsenal in England play the game using lots of one and two touch plays); and possession with many touches (such as dribbling or running with the ball). Awareness before possession of the ball includes keeping the head up when preparing to control the ball, knowing where teammates, opponents and the spaces are, while at the same time keeping an eye on and possession of the ball.

On the other hand, once the player has the ball, if he decides the right option is to dribble or run with it and thus maintain possession with more touches, another type of awareness comes into play: what to do during possession and the ensuing maintenance of the ball.

We are essentially talking about dribbles and turns, and players **MUST** learn these skills. Working on the first touch, the weight, pace, timing and accuracy of it is practiced in one touch passing but it is also practiced in passing the ball to oneself, through a dribble or turn with lots of one touch control each time the ball is touched. Yes we call it first touch, second touch, third touch for clarity and to avoid confusion; but each touch is essentially a new first touch.

Hence players must develop their "first" touch through one touch passing, two touch passing (the first to themselves, the second to a teammate), three touch passing (one to control, two to set up and three to pass), and also with a touch to themselves and maintaining possession of the ball.

Learning all types of awareness takes a lot of work, practice and training. So having this awareness also means the player recognizes when and where to hold onto the ball and when to play one and two touch.

We can further break down awareness to "On the Ball" and "Off the Ball":
"On the Ball" signifies the player about to receive it or who has just received it.
"Off the Ball" refers to all the other players who are not in possession of the ball, in particular those players close to the ball who may be in the best positions to help the player on the ball with his next move or pass. They need to be moving into support positions to help the player about to receive the ball.

We are looking at 4 Areas of Awareness:

1. "On the Ball" Awareness before receiving the ball

2. "On the Ball" awareness as the player receives it and moves it on quickly using one or two touches only

3. "On the Ball" awareness if the player maintains possession of the ball using several touches, constituting dribbles, turns and running with the ball for example

4. "Off the Ball" awareness in terms of the positioning of players supporting the player "On the Ball";

This works if all players are in synch and thinking ahead of the ball.

FIRST AND SECOND TOUCH TRAINING DEVELOPING BOTH FEET

I have shown this by introducing the concept of fast footwork and coordination without the ball. Players have to **GET THEIR FEET RIGHT** before they can make a good first touch on the ball. Then by addressing basic individual technical skill training, first incorporating dribbling and turning with the head up so that players develop an awareness of their surroundings, thus knowing where teammates and opponents are as they dribble the ball or turn with the ball. This leads the coach into the Awareness Coaching aspects of the book. The players need to be able to have reasonably good technical ability before they move onto using the Awareness Coaching Method.

The book includes many coaching clinic session plans the coach can use to reinforce what we are trying to establish in the players' minds and bodies. Individual skill development goes hand in hand with this training program and time should be devoted to teaching the players important skills on the ball. These include a great first touch for a one or two touch pass, or setting the ball up with a great first touch to then run or dribble, shoot or cross, turn or pass.

I have tried to introduce an approach to soccer coaching that allows the players to develop their skills in a non – competitive environment to begin, building up to working more competitively when they are ready to progress to that stage. Initially each exercise should be practiced without opposition, building up to exercises with opposition to test the composure the players should have gained by following the program.

Once you have covered all the aspects of the coaching exercises presented in this manual you will be able to keep the training of the players in this work fresh by using different exercises at different times but still with the same results in mind: to develop composure in possession, to decrease the time and number of touches needed to move the ball. By having total awareness of all players around them, your players will be able to use their imaginations in their use of the ball and be better able to make their own decisions. There will also be developmental training for the awareness of players off the ball within the training sessions.

The idea is not to have players playing at 100 miles an hour and playing one touch all the time but to teach them to be aware of the options before they receive the ball (and have their feet positioned correctly to receive with comfort), then they can decide:
- Does the ball need to go one touch?
- Do I need to hold onto the ball until another option opens up?
- Is this the time to run with the ball, dribble with it, to shoot, to cross or to pass?

For the player on the ball, this training will allow him to be able to control it quickly one or two touch, to see the options so he does not need a 3rd or 4th touch, to see where opponents are so he does not need extra touches to get out of trouble. We are training their bodies for the footwork and their minds for the decision making.

For the player off the ball, awareness training will teach him to help the player on the ball by offering options of a free pass or perhaps a cross into the box as an example, via good positioning in different parts of the field, either in front, to the side, or behind the player on the ball. It is vital as a coach to stress the importance of this aspect of awareness training to the players. Without good movement and positioning by teammates off the ball, the player in possession, even if he possesses outstanding awareness, will be limited in his options.

The coaching ideals are designed to help the players give themselves as many options as possible and then decide which one to use at any given moment. This method is not designed to discourage dribbling with the ball or running with the ball to keep possession, but to help identify when dribbling or running with the ball would be the right option to use.

A problem I see in youth soccer is that when there is a moment to play one or two-touch, it is lost because the player isn't yet aware of this next option, does not have his feet ready in the first place, or is too busy controlling the ball and then looking to see where players are. This is too late. Good awareness involves recognizing the right time to dribble or run with the ball and this book is designed to help players decide what is needed in these moments.

Each chapter covers methods of coaching with built in progressions that complement this learning program, beginning with the most basic introductory exercises to enable players to get an easy understanding of how to gain success in their application.

As each chapter is covered the coach and the players can see that the exercises become more detailed in their content and that they encourage both the coach and the players to explore more difficult pathways providing further coaching plans to enhance their development as coaches and players. By using the exercises provided the players' decision-making and the speed of those decisions will improve.

Success is specific to the ability of the player and the amount of work and effort the player puts in. This is an ongoing self - fulfilling process that any given player must continue to explore. It is not a program that a player practices then moves on, it must be a program that the player includes in all his or her future practices indefinitely.

We are trying to establish the following in the players' make up:

A. **WHAT** do they do? (The technique or skill used / what are the options to move or pass the ball depending on the position on the field of play)
B. **WHERE** do they do it? (Position on the field can dictate this in the decision making process)
C. **WHEN** do they do it? (The timing of the technique or skill used)
D. **HOW** do they do it? (The selection of the technique or skill used)
E. **WHY** do they do it? (The tactical objective)
F. What is the **END PRODUCT**? A pass, a shot, a cross, a dribble, or a turn
G. What do they do next once the ball has left them?
   (Likely move to support in the next phase or a later phase of play, getting free from a marker to be able to be a part of the development of play again)

THE IMPORTANCE OF TEACHING ONE TOUCH PLAY: IMPROVING ONE TOUCH PLAY WHILE MAINTAINING AN AWARENESS OF WHAT IS IN ADVANCE AND BEYOND THE BALL

Linking foot preparation, body position and mental preparation to the technique involved in making a one touch pass leads us to a discussion on one touch play and its benefits. One touch play teaches the value of being able to take your eye off the ball when keeping your eye on the ball can be a disadvantage.

To make this work, players need to have good teamwork and positional sense and therefore must work hard for each other.

A Gradual Training Introduction

Introduce the training in a gradual way; don't jump straight into a scrimmage. Set it up so it is easy to do initially. For example, one touch passing in two's. Here, no great amount of awareness is needed because they are facing each other, but they must look into each other's eyes and not at the ball. This is teaching them to get their heads up, and is the first most basic stage. It is also working on the pace and direction of the pass, getting foot sensitivity started in terms of that first touch on the ball that is now in effect a pass.

Then move to groups of three where a little more peripheral vision is needed. Then ask them to pass and move in a small area.

Next, add more players so there are more passing options and more awareness is needed. Now introduce the Numbers Game, passing in sequence; this really starts to introduce the awareness concept, but with one touch only.

Communication: Good communication is a must, so have players talk to each other, passing messages on to help each other all of the time.

Also, have them do this without any verbal communication as they then have to rely on themselves alone and in games unfortunately as much as we try, this very often happens anyway.

Do this **WITH** communication and **WITHOUT** communication. Even compare the two, some may get so good at this they can work it out for themselves most of the time as their peripheral vision improves.

Practice one touch with your team, then play games / scrimmages with your team and insist on it being **ONE TOUCH ONLY**.

There will be times when 2 touches are needed but do not allow it. Force the error if need be by insisting on one touch only.

Example 1: A player does not get his feet ready to receive and as a result does not make correct contact with the ball and possession is lost. Everyone can see that his feet were the problem, especially the player involved, and this will register in his mind for the next time.

Example 2: The ball is passed too heavily and quickly (pace and timing of the pass is wrong) and the receiver needs a touch to control the pass initially and then make a 2nd touch pass to keep possession. That is the passer's fault, not the receiver's; and they will learn that from this single pass. It is likely that a one touch play at this moment will not work, which is fine, because this will help them learn why it didn't work for the next time.

Example 3: No teammates move to give the player receiving the ball an option to pass it one touch. This is the fault of the player or players off the ball and not the receiving player, but you must still insist it is passed one touch so they pass it into the space the player should have moved into. Again, this will probably result in giving the ball away, but they will learn from that.

The players will recognize if possession was lost because there was not enough support off the ball, the pass was too heavy, or if it was the fault of the player's first touch if there were options off the ball.

When you first do it, particularly in a competitive scrimmage situation whether within your own team training or against another team, you may find it is incredibly ugly play; the players will more than likely struggle with it (or maybe not, they may surprise you).

And it may be ugly for quite a while; but just let it go. Do not be disheartened and don't let your players get discouraged. And **do not coach**, just let them play and work it out for themselves. Tell them you expect it to go wrong more than go right to relax them about it...

They will find with practice that they need to adjust the weight of the pass to help the next player, so foot sensitivity in passing will improve.

They will learn this through their own trial and error, not necessarily just what you tell them.

So say nothing; let them **FEEL** it.
- They will find they can't make it work if they just focus and look at the ball all the time.
- They will find they can't make it work if their body shape is not right to receive the ball.
- They will find they can't make it work if their feet are not ready to receive the ball.
- They will find they can't make it work if their teammates off the ball are not alert.

- They will find they can make it work if they start to learn to look away from the ball before they get it; and scan their options in advance of it.
- They will find it will work if they get both their body shape and foot preparation right, and in advance of the ball.
- They will find it can work if the players off the ball offer early options of support.
- They will find they can make it work if their first touch is good (which is a passing touch)

If they only have one touch then it has to be a good one. There are no second chances. This will focus their mind and their body.

So what will this teach the players; without you even saying a word:
- Looking before receiving the ball:
- Looking away from the ball as well as at it:
- Knowing options in advance of receiving:
- Weighting the pass correctly to help the receiver:
- Getting their foot preparation right (how many play flat footed?? This won't let them if they want to be successful).
- Getting their body shape right, facing where the next pass is going; in advance of the ball:
- Getting into position quickly "Off the ball" to help the player receiving; and it has to be before the receiver gets the ball as they only have one touch to move it on again either to feet or to space:

They will recognize if the fault and failure to maintain possession was in the weight of the receiving pass, or in the next first touch pass by the receiver, or because of poor support off the ball. It is not difficult to identify which it is.

It will not be because of pressure or interceptions by defenders because in the early stages there will not be any defenders so the players can play without pressure.

It is easy to see for everyone why it works (or not) if they are honest with themselves and do not look for excuses for failure.

I would do this for 30 to 45 minutes without interruption and then play a non - conditioned game afterwards to see how it changes their play.

It may not happen in the first instance. In fact it may take several attempts to make it work, but it will work. They may not be able to string 3 passes together initially; do not give up on this. It will develop at a different pace depending on the age group and ability of the players, so some will take longer than others.

It is a **MENTAL GAME**; players need to work hard mentally as well as physically to make this work. If you have a friendly scrimmage against another team, do not worry about winning, do not worry about how ugly it looks, do not care about the score, and have them do it.

Do not care what the other coach thinks you are doing or not doing.

Do not try it only once and give up.

Finally; am I discouraging dribbling and turning and individual skills development? Absolutely not! But players need to be able to do it all, and this conditioned training will help them recognize in offense:
- When and where to dribble and keep the ball in their possession (when the conditioned game is not being played and they are allowed to be free)
- When and where to pass:
- When and where to receive and turn (when the conditioned game is not being played and they are allowed to be free):
- When and where to shoot one touch or take more touches:
- When and where to cross:

Yes, learning one and two touch play will also help them become better at dribbling and turning because it will help teach them when and where to do it, and each skill will need to be learned, one touch, two touch, dribbling and turning, for them to become better all round players.

I do see players who can dribble and beat players; and that is great. But I also see the same players doing it when the pass is a better option and they lose possession because they did not recognize the moment to release the ball. They were not aware of the options and thus ended up dribbling for the sake of dribbling, likely with their heads down so they couldn't see their support, to the detriment of the team.

This training will help them know when and where to choose the right skill.
In an indirect way, it helps their dribbling and turning decision making as well as their one and two touch decision making.

The next question from you will be: At what age do we start this?
I think you can do it with technically good players at 6 but as they get older it will of course get easier and the more you do it the easier it will get.

Remember, still do all the individual skills training, they absolutely need that! But most kids learn skills naturally just by playing with a ball on their own or in make up games with friends. Soccer Awareness using one and two touches is not so naturally or easily developed, which is the reason for this book.

There will be much more failure than success when initially implementing this one touch training, but players will be forced to think more quickly, move more quickly to support, get in position more quickly to receive, and focus on their first touch (pass). The coach will see who can do it, who needs work with it, and who is willing to work hard and get open to help a teammate on the ball.

Strength, speed and ball dribbling skill mean very little in one touch play. The lesser skilled players will learn very quickly how they can play a more useful role in the team, while the more highly skilled players, who often think "dribble" first, will be forced to develop anticipation and passing skills which will make them more complete players.

As I said before, it is no use being a great dribbler if you can't make it fit into the team concept. This type of training helps this aspect of team play develop. It is a win-win situation; "over time". It is a marathon, not a sprint we are talking about here; so persevere.

Think about the opposition, what does it do to them when you play one touch successfully? For one thing, they haven't time to close you down and win the ball as easily as they would if the receiving player took 3 or 4 touches, because as soon as they get tight to the player on the ball it has been passed on already, and they are out of the game, and our player is past them looking for the next phase of play. Also, the opponents have to work much harder off the ball to win it back, as the ball moves much more quickly passing it than with a player running and dribbling with it.

Ces Fabregas of Arsenal and France, Frank Lampard of Chelsea and England and Paul Scholes of Manchester United and England are wonderful examples of players adept at this type of play.

MANY OF THE SESSIONS IN THIS BOOK CAN BE DEVELOPED TO EVENTUALLY USE ONLY ONE TOUCH TO TEST THE ULTIMATE AWARENESS OF THE PLAYERS.

So what does one touch play help teach players? Not just one touch, that's for sure!

FOR THE INDIVIDUAL RECEIVING PLAYER IT TEACHES:

Quicker Thinking: The game is getting much faster so players need to think much more quickly to be able to cope with this increase in pace; which means they have less time to make decisions.

So...1-touch creates "quicker thinking players"

Body and Foot Preparation: One touch means getting the body / feet into appropriate position to receive.

So...1-touch develops body positional awareness (eg. may need to let ball "run across the body" to "save" the touch)

Quicker Play: The game is getting faster so players have less time on the ball so a natural progression to cope with this is to use fewer touches of it. This means using one touch more; and acting more quickly particularly in tight situations; hence observation BEFORE receiving the ball is a necessity. One touch play forces the player to do this if they want to be successful. This means "LOOKING BEFORE RECEIVING THE BALL, ASSESSING OPTIONS EARLY"

It requires a look over the shoulder, to the sides and behind the player; **BEFORE RECEIVING THE BALL**

Improves TECHNIQUE: One touch demands / promotes technical excellence when distributing passes (using 1-touch) received in the air (foot, thigh, chest, head) It also improves the first touch by lots of practice relying just on it

Improves and speeds up the **SKILL** Factor: This is "decision making" awareness "when and where" situational play. Skill is the end product of technique, the how, why, when and where of the technique.

Faster Ball Movement: The ball is moving faster too; as well as the players move faster which suggests quicker passing sequences.

So, faster ball movement, faster running of the players; quicker closing down by opponent's means everything is quicker; so thinking and decision making has to match this. Hence being very good and successful at one touch play is an essential part of a modern day player's makeup.

Limited Space Possession and Tight Situational Play: One touch teaches players how to maintain possession in tight spaces or when closely marked:

Ball Mastery: One touch requires players to demonstrate ball mastery when receiving (cushion pass to teammate in close support vs. hard pass to teammate supporting at a distance) So...1-touch teaches players how to correctly "weight" their passes

Fitness: More frequent and quicker movement off the ball means players have to work harder to support the player on the ball as they have little time with it and need instant help. If the ball is being passed consistently by one touch then the ball is travelling faster and more frequently so the players have to work just as quickly and frequently off the ball to cope with this and maintain possession of the ball; thus it improves specific football fitness.

Time Management: One touch play means thinking quickly identifying options early so this in many instances can give the player more time on the ball because they have already seen where the space is to play before they have received the ball. So, one touch play creates Time on the ball to allow for more touches; if needed; by identifying options earlier

Identification of Players and Space: One touch play offers the means to a faster identification of players positions; both teammates and opponents

Offers the means to a faster identification of when and where to pass to feet or to space and where the space or player is to pass to

On the Ground Patterns of Play: One touch play encourages passing on the ground to maintain possession so it is easier for the next player to control the ball.

FOR THE ATTACKING TEAM:

Movements OFF the Ball: Training with one touch means the player receiving the ball has to move it on quickly therefore players have to move OFF the ball more quickly to help support the player receiving it.

This is a VERY IMPORTANT aspect of one touch training as it involves all the other players off the ball and their positioning to help the player on the ball, preferably before they receive it so it can happen more quickly.

Style of Play: Encourages a fluid, attractive style of play and develops a good tempo / speed of play

Combination Play: Encourages combination play (wall-passes, set-up passes, third man runs). There is no better play than a give and go one touch pass combination to beat defenders so it is difficult to defend against, especially in and around the attacking third / penalty area when quick play is applied

<u>Aesthetic Effect</u>: Is "pleasing to the eye" (Arsenal / Barcelona / Manchester United)

<u>Counter Attacking Play</u>: Useful when teaching the counter-attack as fewer touches means the ball travels' faster

<u>Ultimately</u>: One touch play is designed to improve the player's first touch in the redirection of the ball, to help players identify their options before they receive the ball, and thus know which option next is best.

This next option may not be a one touch pass in the actual game situation but may be a dribble with many touches, a turn, a run with the ball, a cross; a pass or a shot.

By learning one touch passing; which to be successful needs the player to be able to identify options before receiving the ball; the players develop an awareness of many things including teammates positions, opponents positions, where the space to play to is etc.

One touch is challenging mentally, physically, technically and tactically.

Better players will thrive on "one touch sessions", and rise to the challenge of it

FOR THE DEFENDING TEAM:

<u>Defending Team Shape</u>: It may be compromised because of the speed of play. Defenders can't slide, drop; press etc in time to create defensive blocks. And this creates frustration because defenders always seem to be reacting to the ball's rapid movement often one step too late because of the speed of play. Thus, it offers less time for defenders to close you down.

It moves players around (because it is physically demanding thus it creates gaps to play in / through)

<u>Facts</u>: Statistics show that 1 touch play is a significant factor in the build up to scoring goals, for example; goals scored by Manchester United from one touch build up play was almost 50% last season. So now without Ronaldo; who was a great dribbler; and so had lots of touches on the ball when creating and scoring goals, and was the heart of the team having much possession of the ball, you could theorize that this percentage should rise, perhaps significantly; with the current players making one touch play even more significant in their development of play and also in your training.

<u>Scoring Goals</u>: 70% of all goals are one touch finishes which again emphasizes the importance of developing a great first touch.

A particularly good training session to use for this training is the "Numbers Game" and the "Three Team Game" (Coaching Clinic Session Plan 20). Using them both together is a good idea as a progression from easy to more difficult. Try two-touch first then one-touch when it is on to do so. I advise doing this for 15 minutes every training session, it can even be your warm up. The more you do this the better the players get and when you let them go free flay; observe their attention to the next pass; in advance of the ball; without the one-touch restriction (that conditions them to do so in order to be successful at it).

COACH PARTICIPATION

Coaches, do it yourself, play one touch with your players and feel what it is like, think what they think, and tell me; "what does it make you think about as the ball is coming to you"?? What do you have to do to make it work for you? It will help you understand how it works and why it is so important.

If you do this and come up with answers 99% of the time it will be what the players are thinking and learning from it too. So you will know, in a psychological sense, what your players are thinking; you will know, from a physical standpoint, what your players need to do with their bodies in terms of their positioning, body stance, first touch, and so on. This is to your advantage as a coach, don't you think?

TWO TOUCH PLAY

Follow the same format above for two touch play also and have practices and games where you use two touches only as a development from one touch conditioning play. One touch to control the ball and place it in the direction you need to go, the second to pass or cross or shoot.

Again coaches, try it with the players and feel what you have to do to make it work in terms of your peripheral vision and the need to look in advance of the ball to gain the most success. Knowing what they have to do to make this work, both physically and psychologically, can only enhance your coaching methodology and your understanding of how players learn.

THREE TOUCH PLAY

Three touch incorporates a first touch control, a second touch set up, and a third touch pass, shot, cross and so on. Work backwards from this starting with three touches in teaching the awareness training, then going to two touches and ultimately to one touch where the players' awareness has to be razor sharp to make it work.

The development of good soccer awareness involves knowing what to do with the ball before getting it, what to do with it when you get it and what you do after it has left you.

A PSYCHOLOGICAL APPROACH TO SOCCER

This system of coaching will begin to teach each player the psychological, physical, technical and tactical fundamentals of soccer and together these form the basis of the requirements needed to be able to play soccer. The degree of improvement a player attains using these aspects depends on his own commitment (in terms of repetition of practice and belief in the system) and level of ability. Don't expect results overnight. Players have to be patient in learning this new approach as it takes time and great concentration to develop.

The players must be both psychologically and physically prepared to meet the demands of the program. The process is ongoing throughout their playing career and will be further influenced by the experience gained from every coaching session and every game played over time. We are trying to establish the following:

Teaching players the Correct Technique in order to perform the task efficiently and effectively. The players must pay particular attention to the first touch of the ball.

Psychologically being able to develop composure on the ball, to relax under pressure, creating in the mind of the player Imagination / Insight in the Use of the ball; each pass is unique to that moment.

Tactical considerations will be covered teaching the ability to look Beyond the ball, having the capacity to Anticipate Situations, an Awareness of others' positions (own players, opponents and the ball), movements off the ball and an appreciation of Space.

Physical work will be a natural part of the program aiding relevant types of fitness.

The program is aimed to develop the above in all players to aid the **DECISION-MAKING PROCESS**.

THE DECISION MAKING THOUGHT PROCESS OF THE PLAYER ABOUT TO RECEIVE THE BALL AT ANY ONE MOMENT IS AS FOLLOWS:

1. OBSERVE WHERE THE BALL IS COMING FROM.

2. OBSERVE HOW THE BALL IS COMING (ON THE GROUND, IN THE AIR).

3. KNOW WHERE TEAMMATES ARE BEFORE RECEIVING THE BALL.

4. KNOW WHERE THE OPPOSITION PLAYERS ARE BEFORE RECEIVING THE BALL.

5. BEFORE THE BALL ARRIVES, GET BOTH FEET INTO THE CORRECT POSITION AND THE BODY IN THE CORRECT POSITION TO RECEIVE IT.
6. DECIDE "WHAT" TO DO WITH THE BALL. (TECHNIQUE / SKILL TO USE (EMPHASIS ON A GOOD FIRST TOUCH) - PASS, RUN, SHOOT, CROSS, DRIBBLE, DUMMY / LEAVE. (WHAT ARE THE OPTIONS?). NARROW THE LIST OF POSSIBLE OUTCOMES FROM ALL AVAILABLE OPTIONS.
7. OBSERVE "WHERE" THE BALL IS TO BE MOVED, PASSED OR PLAYED. CAN BE BASED ON WHERE YOU ARE ON THE FIELD OF PLAY. (ASSESS OPEN SPACES AND SUPPORTING OPTIONS ON THE FIELD).

8. DECIDE "WHEN" THE BALL GOES. (THE TIMING OF THE TECHNIQUE / SKILL USED)

9. DECIDE "HOW" THE BALL GOES. (THE SELECTION OF THE TECHNIQUE / SKILL USED)

10. DECIDE "WHY" THE BALL GOES. (COMPARE ALL OPTIONS WITH THE TEAM'S TACTICAL OBJECTIVES).

We as coaches are trying to coach players to assess their options **BEFORE** they receive the ball (Anticipation), **NOT** after. Decisions on which option to take can be determined depending on how much time on the ball the player has. If there is no time and the player is being closed down as he receives, he may have to also determine which option to choose before receiving the ball.

Otherwise, with time on the ball the player can wait for the right moment and determine the correct option to choose based on the positions of his or her teammates and opponents. The player identifies this time (or not) on the ball by looking at the options "before" receiving the pass.

Players off the ball have to be on the same wavelength as the player on the ball to make this happen. The movements of the players off the ball constantly create new situations on the field for the player on the ball to assess and respond to with the correct pass, dribble, and run, shot, cross and so on.

Let's be clear, this training system develops the speed of thought in a player, to help him make decisions based on the amount of time he has on the ball. It promotes quick one touch play but also promotes the ability to keep possession of the ball based on observations of positions of players on both teams before receiving it.

It allows players time when they have it and helps them to use that time to choose the correct option. It still may be a one touch pass but it may also require more touches on the ball until the correct option opens up; a dribble, a run, a turn, a shot, a cross, a pass.

The development of this system of coaching sets the foundations for the above process to be integrated into the players' make – up. It develops **QUICK DECISION MAKING** to allow them to work ahead of the opposition.

The sessions are designed to teach players to develop ability on the ball (developing a good first touch is the beginning) and ability to look beyond the ball (Awareness), i.e. **TECHNICAL** and **TACTICAL** ability.

The practices we use are **NO opposition** games to begin, **SHADOW PLAYS**, to allow a developmental program to take place without a loss of possession through pressurizing from defenders. Essentially there are no defenders, just other players who effectively simulate pressurizing situations by working in the same area. Using these methods of coaching we are giving the player a chance to develop **COMPOSURE** on the ball.
From the no-opposition games we will introduce opposition, initially using an overload situation. Ultimately the coaching will include full-scale practices to put players in the pressure situations they face on the field in regular team play.

This system of coaching is a long-term approach to improvement. Results don't happen overnight. We are creating a New Learning Environment for the player. The four aspects of work; psychological anticipation, Technical ability, Tactical awareness and Physical capacity are interlinked.

While a player has ten individual thought processes to consider, all these cannot be established in one go. Over a period of time the coach must try to increase the number of observations the player makes starting with number one: observing where the ball is coming from. This is the easiest because the player has to look anyway to see where the ball is before he can receive it.

The coach must try to build into the players each observation as it happens. Over time and with much practice the players learn to assimilate each observation more quickly until eventually they will all combine in the mind into one.

On reception of the ball and the ensuing success of a good first touch to control the ball the player deciding to pass the ball must think about the weight, accuracy and timing of the pass. The success or failure of this can be highlighted in most of the exercises used in this book and the coach can focus on this.

The use of regulation soccer balls is good for these exercises but you can also use smaller soccer balls to practice.

THE FUTSAL BALL AND THE AWARENESS COACHING METHOD

An Introduction: The use of a futsal ball is based around touch, control and passing. It can't be kicked long easily and it's difficult to get off the ground. It is geared around developing fast feet and soft touches on the ball.

(A) It is a Size Two / Three ball (regular balls are sizes 4 or 5). Due to its' smaller size, a greater degree of precision is needed to dribble and pass it but when the skills are mastered and you switch to a conventional ball these skills are easier to perform.

(B) Because it is less responsive, passes must be kicked firmly to ensure pace and accuracy.

(C) It is heavier than a regular ball so it doesn't bounce as much. This emphasizes passing on the ground. Paradoxically the weighted ball is easier to control and helps the receiver develop a better first touch (the most important touch on the ball in soccer). It is a specially designed ball. It differs from a conventional ball in a number of ways: it is smaller (size 2.5) than a conventional ball (size 5), much heavier and is filled with foam to reduce its bounce (10%). This means there is virtually no bounce so the ball stays on the ground and it doesn't bounce much above the ankle. This encourages the players to use their foot skills and to increase passing throughout a game and keep it on the ground (a ground pass is far easier to control than an air pass).

It demands a greater concentration and accuracy from the players and places the emphasis on the development of quick feet, close skilful dribbles, precision passing and immediate ball control. Because the ball is heavy it almost "sticks" at the foot of the receiving player, which gives him much more confidence in quickly controlling the ball.

(D) Players have many more touches during a small-sided game practice than with a conventional ball because the Futsal ball isn't spending so much time out of play or bouncing off players. Its heaviness ensures it isn't bouncing everywhere.

This is where we start to begin to link training with this ball and the Awareness Coaching Method. By allowing greater contact on the ball due to minimal rebound, players can control it more quickly and thus have more time to focus on the next pass or move. This can only help their thought processes, which will in turn help their decision making and quick passing, speeding it all up both in the mind and with the body.

Players tend to worry about and spend too much time thinking about their first touch when they should be thinking about what to do next. If they know, with the help of the futsal ball, that their first touch will be tighter; then they should be able to relax on the ball and it "should" move their focus more to the next stage; which ultimately can be the next touch to themselves, or the next pass, or whatever the particular situation asks for (it could be a dribble, cross or shot for example).

The Awareness Coaching Method thus focuses on increasing players' confidence and relaxation on the ball and improving their technical ability to control (first touch especially), dribble and pass the ball. Using this ball helps that development.

So our aims with this ball are to develop players who are confident and comfortable on the ball and able to relax with it. It will in addition develop a good first touch, which is the most important touch in the game. It has to be emphasized that players can never do too much training to help their development (with either the futsal ball or a conventional ball). It is no coincidence that the development of skills goes hand in hand with hours upon hours of practice.

COACHING PRINCIPLES CONSIDERED IN THIS PROGRAM

Most of these games are not drills but are free flowing game oriented workouts aiding peripheral vision development and improving work both on and off the ball. They are Non-Directional initially and later more Directional in their make up, which leads us up to actual game play.

TECHNICAL
1.   First Touch
2.   Passing – left / right, short / long
3.   Control
4.   Dribbling
5.   Receiving and Turning
6.   Combination Plays
7.   Switching Play
8.   Tempo
9.   Transitions

TACTICAL
1.   Positional Sense (supporting)
2.   Awareness
3.   Communication (verbal and non)
4.   Decision Making (when and where)
5.   Creating Space
6.   Understanding

PHYSICAL
1.   Speed
2.   Flexibility
3.   Strength
4.   Stamina
5.   Fitness
6.   Confidence

PSYCHOLOGICAL
1.   Composure
2.   Attitude
3.   Concentration
4.   Desire
5.   Easily Coached

The above principles are addressed at different levels of development depending on which particular level of progression you are working on, but they are addressed nonetheless. From a psychological sense **COMPOSURE** (relaxing) and **CONFIDENCE** on the ball are both extremely important qualities in a player. Along with a good first touch, these qualities help a player maintain possession of the ball instead of panicking and rushing a pass and ultimately giving possession away.

As players progress through this training you as a coach can assess when they are ready to move to the next progression and when they are ready to cope with opposition to test their composure development. Over time you must increase their exposure to pressurizing situations so they develop this ability gradually and consistently. Do not leap from a session with no opposition where they can relax on the ball to a full-scale player for player session where the pressure is intense. Use an overloaded practice next, for example 6 v 3, and gradually build up to the full-scale workout over time.

THE AWARENESS COACHING METHOD FOR SOCCER

KEY POINTS CHECKLIST AND BASIC SET UP:

1. Head Up (avoid looking down at the ball and consequently not observing what is around and where players are in relation to each other). This applies to all eventualities, be they dribbling with your head up (and seeing the field while you dribble), turning, passing, shooting, crossing and so on.

2. Looking Before Receiving – anticipating the next play before you receive the ball, thinking ahead, looking over your shoulder (eyes in the back of your head!).

3. Positioning of both feet to receive the ball – balanced footwork, up on the toes to receive the ball.

4. Body Stance Open, side on, half turned for greater peripheral vision plus moving off at an angle to receive (the angle and distance of support is crucial so you can see most if not all of your passing options).

5. First Touch - Move the ball on your first touch away from pressure (good first touch is crucial). Relax your body as you receive the ball.

6. Big First Touch – out of your feet into space away from the pressure on receiving. Player must recognize this space before receiving the ball.

7. One Touch – Two-Touch – Three Touch play, particularly one touch, looking for the support player to work an angle off the receiving player so the ball can be laid off one touch. In this we are working on the support player's position as well as the player on the ball i.e. thinking two moves ahead.

8. Changing Pace- Change pace on reception of the ball because the player may need to get away from a defender.

9. Changing Direction - Turning or moving off at angles on reception of the ball. This provides a basis to work from but using your imagination you can develop other ideas that can be applied in this session and be equally effective.

10. Determine Length of Pass – short or long, try to include variation. Deal with the weight, accuracy and timing of the pass.

11. Determine the Type of Work on the ball e.g. turns, dribbles, 1 – 2's, passes, one touch, two touches, three touches; crossovers, all after receiving etc.

12. Passing to Feet the receiver can move to the ball along the line of the pass, not just standing still (in a game standing still may invite an opponent to intercept the pass, but this will depend on the individual situation). For example, two players can be running forward against each other. The player whose team has possession may suddenly stop, while the opponent continues his run, thus creating space by standing still.

13. Passing to Space, forcing the movement of the receiver with a pass to space. It can be the passer dictating where he wants the receiver to go, or the receiver pointing to show the passer where he wants the ball to go. Both need to recognize where the space is. When passing to space, the passer must weight the pass correctly, be accurate with it and have correct timing.

14. Crossovers / Takeovers / Combination Plays – not passing, principles are: using inside foot to exchange, take / leave ball, use as a decoy, accelerate away, communication.

15. Playing the Give and Go – two teams, one team a ball each, one team without a ball each passing and playing 1- 2's. Emphasize one or two touch lay off and passing into space so the players don't need to break stride as they receive the return pass. To begin, have players without the ball and receiving it standing still, then as they improve have them moving to play 1-2's.

16. Verbal Communication – Use words during the practices (and in games to help the receiver). For example:
    a) "Man On" – to simulate a situation in a non-competitive practice so the player doesn't turn, but plays the way he is facing.
    b) "Turn", helps the player to turn and thus switch the point of attack and lets the ball run across the body. The passer must see there is space behind the receiver for the turn.
    c) "Time" so the players on the ball know they can take 2 or 3 touches if they need to.

17. No Communication – a test for players to make them think for themselves with no help from others i.e. no verbal or non verbal help (no calls of man on, turn or pointing).

18. Fitness – Pass the ball then run to the furthest line of the area you are working in (sprint work). Also it helps spread players out and move off the ball.

19. Switching Play – by letting the ball run across your body to change direction and switch play, saving a touch and not even using a touch, hence a no touch turn and change of direction, using the upper body to disguise your movement with a feint one way and the ball going the opposite to fool the opponent, using the pace of the pass to help you. You need to recognize where the space to move to is before you receive the pass.

20. Overall Passing – Concentrate on the weight, accuracy, angle and timing of the passes depending on: the distances the ball is being played, whether it is to feet or space, the positioning of the other team's players (simulating defensive organization), the positioning of your own teammates.

21. Support – Once you have made a pass, look to support others in possession to receive again (avoids standing admiring your pass and hence be out of the game), then we deal with angle and distance of support again. Look to move to support the next pass as the ball is traveling to a teammate. Move to the ball if receiving it to feet to save time and prevent opponents intercepting the pass. If you have time you may move away to open up more space in front of you and create a little more time on the ball. This will depend on where the opponents are, of course. The correct decision on which move to use is dictated by the given situation.

22. Awareness from "On the Ball" players with few touches (the basic concept of this book).

23. Awareness from "On the Ball" players when dribbling, turning and running with the ball – This is required from the player when he decides the best option is to run or dribble with the ball, maintaining possession of it and thus they need the ability (awareness) to see beyond the ball and what the next options may be while at the same time controlling and manipulating it.

24. Awareness from "Off the Ball" Players – Awareness training also looks to develop the awareness of players without the ball to help those "on the ball". If the "off the ball" players do not move to support the "on the ball" player, then their awareness of making the next best decision may be adversely affected.

GAME PROGRESSIONS:
Basic Set Up: Two Teams, one ball, passing to anyone. Then two balls passing to anyone. Two teams / two balls – one ball per team passing only to teammates, passing through the other team (half the number of passing choices compared to the last progression).

Develop
(A) Number of touches on the ball; fewer means the ball must be moved more quickly. Go all in to start, then three, two and eventually one touch passing (but have the restriction as a guide only). As the number of touches decreases, the ability needed to anticipate the next pass and where it should go increases. Insist that players only play one touch if it is on to do so as it isn't always the correct choice to make.
(B) Size of area, tighter means closer control needed.
(C) Number of balls per team up to 50 / 50 ratio. 1 ball to two players per team e.g. 12 players, 6 balls. Work on 1-2's, crossovers etc.
(D) Make it Competitive; have a time period over which each team must maintain possession of the ball or balls. If a ball runs out of the area (thus possession is lost) or bumps into another ball then the other team get a point. Start with the teams in different areas then as they improve have them play in the same area to increase the difficulty. Increase the difficulty by going two touches; if a player uses more than two touches the other team gets a point. Use your imagination to invent new scenarios for this.

Two teams / two balls, passing to opposite colors (other team). Here we have color discrimination, passing in sequence and vision. Increase to four balls; two per team. Four teams of 3 players / one ball each group: develop as follows:

(A) Go to free spaces to receive and pass the ball to another teammate of the same color. Three or two touch play. If the ball is passed to another color, this player must pass it back one / two touches to the same player they received it from.

(B) Coach signals, players sprint in four directions to corners of the grid and continue passing to each other. Do the same but different colors in each corner (three in each). Quick reflexes, color vision required.

(C) These sessions allow continuity regarding PASSING and SUPPORT and help players to develop CONFIDENCE and COMPOSURE on the ball. Development can be monitored, progression can be clearly judged and the coach can move the players on to the next level when they recognize the time is right. I have carefully developed the levels of progression of these sessions to ensure each level is addressed at the correct time.

COACHING METHODOLOGY AND THE PLANNING OF CLINICS

To be effective a coach should be able to change to different coaching methods to suit the moment. Every coach has his own style; some do it quietly, some are more demonstrative, and some are more vocal (but don't commentate). As long as they do it in a positive manner and create positive results in their players, all styles can be effective.

Coaching Style is based on personality, temperament, philosophies on how the game should be played and the ages and abilities of the players. There is no one universal style, every coach is different.

Coaching Method is different. The methods you use to coach are important in getting the best out of your players and you should be able to base your coaching around three different methods which can be implemented in various degrees at different times.

* The **coaching method** should be one of teaching / guiding / helping the players to think for themselves and be encouraged to make their own decisions from as young an age as possible; so the **question and answer** and **guided discovery** styles are best.
* The game is about **players, not coaches**, and games should be based on player decision making.
* Coaches set the team play framework. The players decide what do to within that framework.
* As coaches we are trying to make ourselves redundant to some extent, so players need us less and less as they improve their decision making.
* The coach has the great responsibility to develop this decision making aspect of learning with players as well as the technical and tactical skills they teach.

I tell coaches if they have to shout and give constant instruction to players during games it means they did not teach / guide them properly during their training sessions.

COMMAND, QUESTION AND ANSWER AND GUIDED DISCOVERY

1. COMMAND METHOD

In theory, the coach decides, the players listen and comply. But do they really listen? Do they learn? Or most importantly, DO THEY UNDERSTAND?

Using this method you can't be sure if the players truly understand what they are doing or why they are doing it, they just did what you told them.

Were you right in what you told them?

For example, you tell a player to move to a certain position on the field and he does it. Does he know why he needs to be there? Maybe, but you will not know if he does. In a game situation will he know where to go?

2. QUESTION AND ANSWER METHOD

The coach seeks to stimulate the player into a response to a direct singular question. For example:

"Where should you pass the ball in that situation?"

"What should you do in that situation?"

"Why did you do that in that situation?"

"When is the best time to do that?"

"What would be a better way to do that next time to gain more success?"

The player needs to think for himself, and you know if he understands or not by his response. Asking questions is a great forum for learning if done in non-threatening and positive ways with the correct tone of voice.

3. GUIDED DISCOVERY METHOD

The coach leads the players to make their own decisions. For example: "Show me where you should go to help the player on the ball". Again the players have to think for themselves and are more likely to remember and learn from their self determined action.

Soccer is a game of the moment and players, not coaches, need to decide at that moment what they should do on the field. The coach's job is to prepare them to be able to make that decision for themselves. What we have is a Command Method (autocratic / bossy) and a Co-Operative Method (democratic / guiding) but sometimes also a good coaching approach may involve saying nothing, letting them play / practice with no direction. Just watch. This is more important than many coaches realize.

WHY CO-OPERATIVE?

1. It helps players become thinkers and make their own decisions.
2. Fosters relations between coach and player by sharing the decision making process.
3. Players enjoy it more.
4. As well as having skills, players develop the ability to change situations, exhibit discipline and maintain concentration.

HOW DOES IT HELP THE COACH?

The coach needs more skill and knowledge, choices of solutions means they are seldom absolutely right or wrong but you need to have an answer. This improves you as a coach as you yourself need to think more deeply about your solutions to problems.

External factors can influence the method used. For example, a large group of unfamiliar players needs more of the Command Method whereas a smaller, familiar group of players needs more of a Co-Operative Method of coaching.

CONCLUSION

Based on the above discussion it is clear that soccer is a game of free flowing play that ultimately requires the players to be the decision makers much of the time. The coach needs to help them get there by encouraging them in training to work it out for themselves and when they can't, guide them to the right decision. Game situations are difficult in as much as you often don't have time to ask "where should you be now?", but over a period of time and with patience the players will take on more responsibility on and off the field and improve their performance because of it. A by- product of this which must not be overlooked is that the coach will improve his ability and knowledge.

HALF TIME TEAM TALKS

Team talks at half time are a perfect opportunity to embrace this idea, get away from the commentary (see CNN comments) and ask questions to stimulate the players into thinking about what happened in the first half, what was good, what needs work. You will be surprised (or maybe not) how astute the players are when responsibility is shared with them as to how we can improve the second half based on the evidence of the first half. If they miss something pertinent you can then advise them of that point. Focus on only two or three main points. Encourage them to be a part of the decision making process by involving them in the process.

OTHER COACHING METHODS

Self Check – The coach gives players key points to check when practicing alone. This is particularly effective for technique development. Give them challenges, tests or tasks, for example simply kicking a ball hard against a wall and working on first touch control, relaxing the controlling foot on contact with the ball, taking the pace out of the ball and keeping it close. . . Make sure they are learning to use both feet to control the ball.
The aim of this is to develop self-thinking players who practice away from the coach.

STAGES OF LEARNING

1. COGNITIVE PHASE (planning)
   The learner thinks about the task. Movements will not yet be fluid as the player is concentrating on what to do next and how to do it.
2. ASSOCIATE PHASE
   The learner knows what to do but still needs practice to be consistent and effective.
3. AUTONOMOUS PHASE
   The skill is learned and becomes automatic, fluid, and effortless.
   The coach needs to use this three- phase model to recognize the stage of development of each player.

COMMUNICATION SKILLS

Help you gain a greater understanding of how players learn.
Consider the communication aspect of your coaching.
1. How players learn – Coaching effectiveness should contribute to the players' learning.
   - Learners learn, coaches help this process.
2. Find out more about your players
   - Who are they – Age / Experience?
   - Why are they involved in soccer and your team?

3. Do they have the same objectives as you?
    a) Establish goals for each player.
    b) Offer feedback individually and collectively.
    c) Feedback to other significant people –Parents / Officials.
    d) Measure their commitment.
    e) Review the goals with them.
    f) Amend them where appropriate e.g. based on training and games.
    g) Develop long-term goals.
4. Is their learning part of a total learning environment?
    a) Learning from individual sessions.
    b) The whole club must be committed to learning and improving.
    c) The coach helps them to learn and improve performance.
    d) The coach needs to help players learn on their own.

COMMUNICATION IN COACHING

Organization of practices is a factor in communicating with the players in the most effective way.

TRADITIONAL METHOD (tried, tested and proven).

a) Warm Up.
b) Skill Practice.
c) Scrimmage.

OTHER FORMATS

1. Whole / Part / Whole Method

After a warm up, begin with a game. When a need arises to highlight a skill / technique / tactical development, concentrate then on small group work on the point you are covering before going back to the game.

2. Coaching Then Stepping Away

Example One

a) Work for 20 minutes on an aspect of play.
b) The players get better; the coach provides feedback to help.
c) Both coach and player are satisfied at the end.

Example Two

a) Work for 20 minutes on an aspect of play.
b) The coach helps for 10 minutes then encourages the players to practice for 10 minutes with little help.
c) Improvement at the end is not as much as in example 1.

One week later – The players in Example 1 have forgotten more than players in example 2. Reason – In example 2 there was less feedback so the players needed to pay more attention to feedback from the task itself than feedback from the coach. They had to work it out for themselves.

OCCASIONAL PRACTICE

Some things happen rarely in a game. For example a corner from the right or a free kick from a central position, so stop your session and throw in a single practice occasionally.
By using a structure you can increase the work time and decrease the talk time. Players arrive for training and know what to expect and can get straight into the warm up without prompting. More demonstration and less explanation works best. Showing is more effective than telling. If you aren't a player yourself, get one of your better players to demonstrate for

you. If you have time use the session planner (on the following pages) to record what you did and how it went and what you may change for next time to make it better. Build up your own record of what you did over a season and you can plan a program for yourself.

HOW TO ORGANIZE A COACHING CLINIC SESSION PLAN

1. ORGANIZE THE EQUIPMENT (BIBS, BALLS AND CONES)
2. COACH ONLY ONE TEAM AT A TIME TO AVOID CONFUSION
3. COACH (AFFECT THE ATTITUDE OF) EACH INDIVIDUAL PLAYER IN THAT TEAM
4. STAY ON THE SAME THEME
5. USE DESIGNATED START POSITIONS TO BEGIN EACH PRACTICE TO PAINT THE PICTURE YOU WANT TO CREATE
6. LIST THE KEY COACHING POINTS
7. THINK INDIVIDUAL / UNIT / TEAM – SIMPLE TO COMPLEX AND DEVELOP LOGICAL PROGRESSIONS INTO THE SESSION
8. SPECIFY THE SIZE OF AREA USED AND MAKE IT RELEVANT TO THE NUMBERS AND ABILITY OF PLAYERS USED
9. DIVIDE THE FIELD INTO THIRDS FOR EASIER POINTS OF REFERENCE IN SMALL - SIDED GAMES
10. USE TARGET GOALS, TARGET PLAYERS, OR LINES FOR OPPONENTS TO PLAY TO IN PHASE PLAYS AND FUNCTIONS
11. ISOLATE THE AREAS AND PLAYERS IN FUNCTIONAL PRACTICES TO KEEP IT SPECIFIC
12. USE OFFSIDE WHERE NECESSARY FOR REALISM
13. USE A QUESTIONING / GUIDING COACHING METHOD RATHER THAN COMMAND
14. FOR ATTACKING THEMES LIMIT THE NUMBER OF TOUCHES THE DEFENDING OPPONENTS HAVE IF THEY WIN THE BALL. WE WANT TO WORK WITH THE ATTACKING PLAYERS, NOT THE DEFENDING PLAYERS
15. FOR DEFENDING THEMES LIMIT THE NUMBER OF TOUCHES THE DEFENDING TEAM HAS WHEN THEY WIN THE BALL. THIS FORCES THE DEFENDERS TO TRY TO WIN THE BALL BACK.

A COACH'S CHECKLIST FOR A COACHING CLINIC SESSION PLAN

To help you understand how important it is to structure your plan to ensure it is as effective as possible, the following guidelines may help.

1. PREPARATION
2. MANNER
3. ORGANIZATION
4. TECHNICAL
5. OBSERVATION
6. COMMUNICATION

A)	Preparation	1. Produced a Coaching Clinic plan
		2. Organized facilities and equipment
		3. Outlined the theme to the players
B)	Manner	4. Encouraged two-way communication
		5. Demonstrated motivation / positive attitude
C)	Organization	6. Demonstrated effective time management
		7. Organized space and players
D)	Technical	8. Conducted warm up and cool down
		9. Produced technically sound information and appropriate practices
E)	Observation	10. Showed ability to analyze players
		11. Progressed to the needs of the players
		12. Adapted the practice as required
F)	Communication	13. Provided accurate demonstrations
		14. Used guiding question and answer coaching style
		15. Finished with positive feedback in the closing discussions

TRAINING STRUCTURE:
AN EXAMPLE OF A CLINIC PLAN FOR TRAINING

It would be useful if we all worked at structuring our clinics along the same lines to ensure we provide the correct coaching for all the players in all the teams. The following presentation is one way to set it up and it helps you manage your time for a session. This is how we want to do our training clinics for everyone. We have one hour 30 minutes per clinic, but you can change the amount of time spent on each phase depending on how long your clinic is.

1. WARM UP: Ball each and Awareness workout. Players must get lots of touches to get comfortable on the ball to begin the clinic.
2. CO-ORDINATION AND SPEED WORK: Balance / quick feet. Also, strength work for the older ages. This can be at the end.
3. THEME OF THE DAY
4. SCRIMMAGE: To practice when, where, and how to apply the theme.
5. COOL DOWN: Ball each and Awareness workout if time allows.
6. CONCLUDING DISCUSSION: What did they learn today?
   1) 10 minutes, 2) 35 minutes, 3) 30 minutes, 4) 10 minutes, 5) 5 minutes.
   TOTAL = ONE HOUR AND 30 MINUTES

EXAMPLE: A TYPICAL AWARENESS COACHING CLINIC SESSION PLAN

THIS IS A BREAKDOWN OF THE COACHING AND TRAINING THAT GOES WITH EACH CLINIC PLAN

1. COACHING CLINIC PLAN CHECKLIST
2. WARM UPS
3. FAST FOOTWORK AND CO -ORDINATION
4. INDIVIDUAL CLINIC PLAN THEME
5. SMALL SIDED SCRIMMAGE GAMES
6. COOL DOWN (SAME AS THE WARM UP THOUGH AT A SLOWER PACE)

As the coach you can do them in any order. You may want to change the small sided game to after the warm up but before the theme, or the fast footwork to the beginning when the players are fresh.

EFFECTIVE WARM UP FOR SOCCER

Can coaches please explain to their players why we do a warm up to reinforce the concept?

Main Objectives

1. To allow the ATP-CP (Alactacid) and the oxygen (lactacid) energy systems to produce energy to get up to speed in preparation for the work they will do.
2. To warm muscles and connective tissue (ligaments and tendons) and stretch them to their working lengths to reduce the chance of injury.
3. To allow us to mentally focus and get ready for the task at hand and practice some of the skills that may be required.

Elements of Warm Up

1. Activities to Raise the Heart Rate
   Gradual increase recommended, heat produced in the body warms up the muscles.
2. Game specific movements
   Slow pace – half pace – faster pace.
   Changes in direction – turning – striding out
   Passing – receiving and turning.
3. Stretching

ALL MOVEMENT ACTIVITIES CAN BEST BE PERFORMED WITH, RATHER THAN WITHOUT, SOCCER BALLS DURING WARM UP.

EFFECTIVE COOL DOWN FOR SOCCER

Can coaches please explain to their players why we need to cool down to reinforce the concept?

Main Objectives

1. Remove Waste Products of Exercise: Lactic acid is a by-product of exercise and causes muscular soreness and stiffness after a match or training. Light activity afterwards can accelerate the removal of such waste products and help the body to recover more quickly (up to three times more quickly than when players simply stop).
2. To Provide an Opportunity for Stretching Work : Some muscles after activity don't return to their normal length for up to two days , hence stretching immediately when they are still warm can help prevent this.

Elements of Cool Down
Game Specific Movements

1. Maintain blood flow and assist removal of waste products by low intensity work such as passing, turning, running, changing direction.
2. Longer Hold Stretching
3. Maintenance of muscle length.
4. Limb Shaking
5. Promotes the return of blood to the heart and feelings of relaxation e.g. players lying on the ground, raised legs with a partner gently shaking their legs.
6. Re-hydration particularly sports drinks.

AS WITH THE WARM UP, ALL MOVEMENT ACTIVITIES CAN BEST BE PERFORMED WITH, RATHER THAN WITHOUT, SOCCER BALLS DURING COOL DOWN.

WARM UP AND COOL DOWN FOR TRAINING AND MATCH SITUATIONS

Warm Up and Cool Down are both important parts of any coaching session or indeed any game situation and should be included at all times, particularly at a young age where doing so reinforces good habits. Due to the great need for players to have as much contact on the ball as possible to aid technical development, I recommend coaches get away from warming up and cooling down without the ball and introduce its use at every session, be it at a game or at practice. I will include some practices you can use as a reference.

Al Ain youth players in action.

1. Divide into two teams to start. A Ball each dribbling, turning, controlling the ball, practicing skills at a slower pace; if it's a warm up to build to full pace or slowing down if it's a cool down.
2. Include changes of pace in this, switching balls between players. Coach can provide passive pressure and can condition the content; the players decide when and where to implement it.

An example of effective use of a ball during warm up and cool down:
Five minute warm up = 3.5 minutes with the ball (1.5 minutes stretching). 1 touch per second means 210 extra touches.

Five minute cool down: as above = 210 extra touches. Total is 420 extra touches on the ball per player by just incorporating the use of the ball. Ten minutes either side of the clinic would provide 840 extra touches if you have the time, and help to reinforce the awareness concept.

A Ball Each

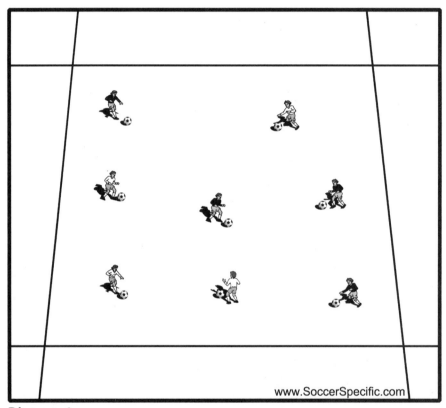

www.SoccerSpecific.com

Diagram 1

Players must keep their heads up and observe their surroundings, having an awareness of what to do with the ball while having possession of it.

A way to test if they are really looking around and behind is to ask them to stop, and then ask if they know who is immediately behind them.

AWARENESS CONCEPT INTRODUCTION

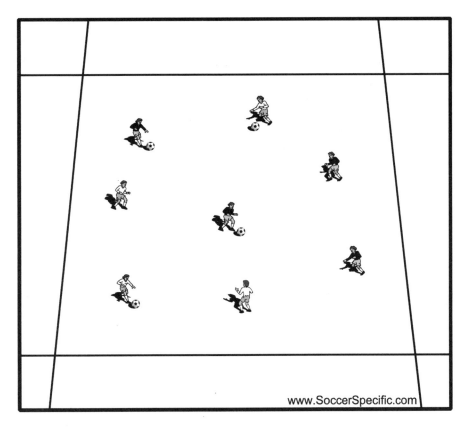

Diagram 2

1. Refer to the awareness information sheets to structure your warm ups and cool downs. Use one or two balls per team for passing and moving (or more). You can keep it interesting by changing the theme for each awareness clinic e.g. passing to feet or space, opposite colors, receiving and turning, one touch / two touch, 1-2's, crossovers etc.
2. This workout is game specific and should particularly be used before actual games.

AN EXAMPLE OF A THEME FOR THE CLINIC SESSION PLAN
AN INTRODUCTION TO AWARENESS TRAINING

This practice is designed to allow the players to be gently introduced to the fundamentals of the **AWARENESS COACHING METHOD,** enabling them to practice in a more dynamic way. They can move anywhere in the area now.

TWO TEAM SET UP

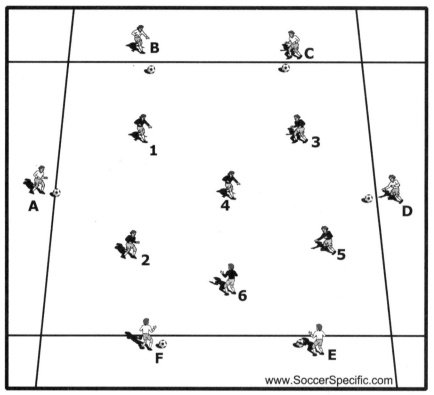

Diagram 3

1. **Coaching Points:**
   a) Head up (awareness of the area and the players in it)
   b) Looking before receiving to receive and turn; to see who is free, to see here other players are, to see where the space is to take the ball.
   c) Body position open to receive,
   d) Focus on the first touch and where to take the ball; decide BEFORE receiving the ball whether it is best to use the first touch for a pass or to set up the next touch.
   e) Concentrate on the quality of the pass to the outside receiver.
2. One team inside, one team outside. Each outside player has a ball to begin.
3. Pass to an inside player who receives and turns and finds another outside free player with a pass. Then look to receive from another outside player.
4. The outside player receives and moves the ball side to side until another inside player is free to receive a pass. This ensures all the players are working both inside and outside the grid.
5. **Competitive:** Have each player count the number of successful passes he makes in a given time and see who makes the most. Observe and comment on those who try to do it too quickly and lose control of the ball and lose the momentum of the session.

6. Change the practice to the balls starting with the inside players. These players now look to pass and receive a give and go from an outside player.
7. Rotate the players so both teams have the chance to play in the middle of the grid.
8. Move both teams to the middle; divide the grid into two with each team passing to their own team within their own grid area, keeping teams separate to begin.

AWARENESS CHANGEOVER SESSION

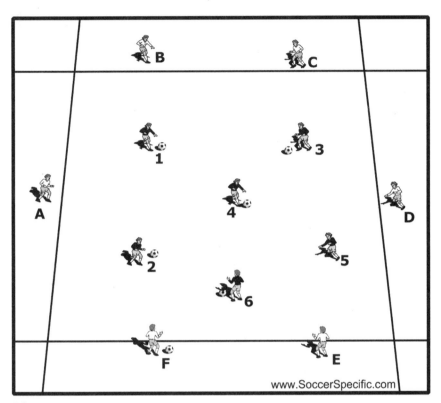

Diagram 4

1. Inside team has a ball each and looks to find a free outside team player to pass to. Outside player brings the ball back in, inside player moves outside the zone waiting to receive a pass from someone else.
2. Set up second touch with a good first touch. Awareness of the free teammate(s).
3. **Coaching Points:**
    a) Quality first touch of outside player.
    b) Decision making of inside player in terms of when, where and how to pass
4. The Coach can create conditions:
    a) Get a turn in or dribble before passing.
    b) Unlimited touches, then 3, then 2 touches.
    c) Play 1- 2 with inside player then go outside.
    d) Do a crossover with outside player rather than make a pass.
5. Inside player passes to outside player and closes down quickly, simulating a defensive movement. The receiver has to make a good first touch away from the pressure.
6. This is a good session because even though everyone is working hard, they get short intermittent rests, thus maintaining quality.
7. **Competitive:** Have each player count the number of successful passes he makes in a given time and see who makes the most.

A GAME SITUATION WITHIN THE THEME

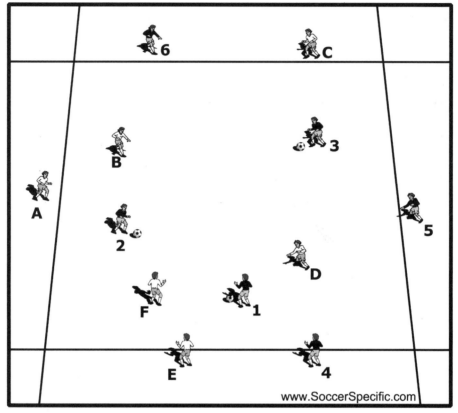

Diagram 5

1. Numbers team can only pass to numbered players on the outside. Likewise, letters team can only pass to lettered players on the outside.
2. **Develop:** Play 1v1s in the middle (same players against each other). Have it passive to begin, with the defending players just shadowing the attacking players as they receive and turn and move.
3. Make it competitive. A lot of receiving and turning under pressure can occur now in the playing area
4. **Develop:** Have a 3v3 small sided game in the middle.

SMALL SIDED GAME SCRIMMAGE

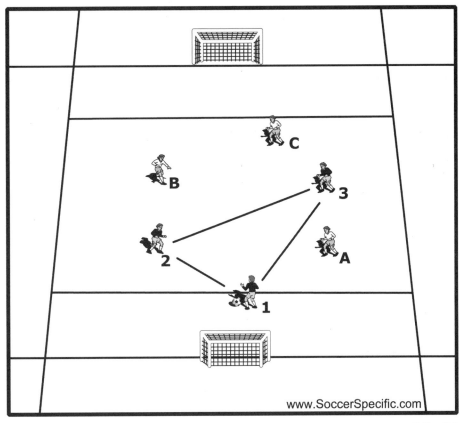

Diagram 6   **35 x 20**

1. Mini soccer in three's is a great way for young players to learn how to play the game and develop their awareness abilities. Coaches try to teach the game where players support in triangles and in a team of three a natural triangle forms.
2. It is especially important to play this at younger age groups but is actually important at ALL age groups.
3. It guarantees lots and lots of touches for each player and in the formative years especially it is vital for the players to work on their technical ability. There are many opportunities for each player to pass, dribble, shoot, turn and tackle. Only one ball between six players.
4. This is a great medium to start this development but also within a game situation.
5. When a player is on the ball he should always have two options of a pass plus the option to do something individual.
6. One player can be the goalkeeper and also the last defender and can pick up the ball anywhere within the 5 yard line. You must encourage this player to move up and out of this zone to support his two team mates during the game when they gain possession. Or just play without goal keepers.

COOL DOWN

This is the same as the warm up but reducing the pace of the play.

A Ball Each

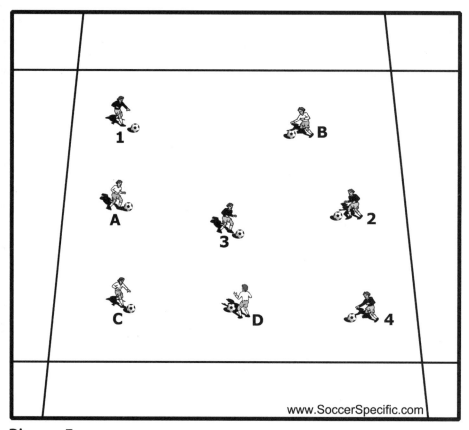

Diagram 7

Players dribble around with a ball each, making sure to look up and around, gaining an "Awareness" of their surroundings so as not to bump into each other.

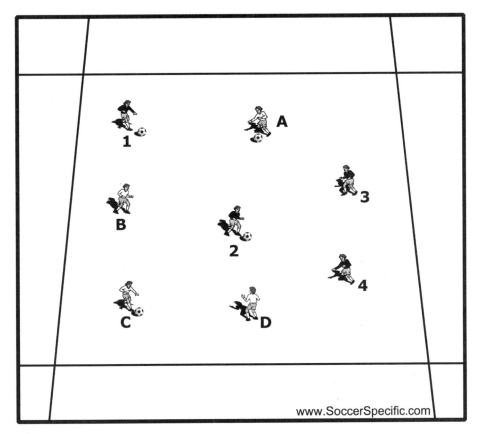

Diagram 8

1. Refer to the awareness information sheets to structure your warm ups and cool downs. Use one or two balls per team for passing and moving (or more).You can keep it interesting by changing the theme for each clinic e.g. passing to feet or space, opposite colors, receiving and turning, one touch / two touch, 1-2's, crossovers etc.
2. This workout is game specific and should particularly be used before actual games.

CONCLUDING DISCUSSION

CHAT WITH THE PLAYERS ON THE CLINIC AND WHAT THEY HAVE LEARNED

This concludes an example of a typical clinic plan that will cover about 90 minutes of training.

2

METHODS OF ASSESSING AWARENESS AND INTRODUCING CONTINUUMS OF DEVELOPMENT

AWARENESS AND WHAT IT MEANS

My first thought is to state categorically that without the required intrinsic **desire, application and dedication from the player** this training will **NOT** achieve this potential.

Awareness in soccer means stages of thought (psychological) processes combining with technical, tactical and physical aspects and their ensuing movements in play. I have devised a method of explaining how awareness can work that equates to these psychological, technical, tactical, and physical aspects of a player's make up.

Other coaches can look at this and no doubt interpret it in other ways and perhaps even take it in another direction, which is great. Remember this is not a black and white situation, as nothing in coaching is. It is just my "interpretation" of what awareness training is and how I like to teach it to players.

I cannot emphasize enough the importance of players making early decisions through this training. This is not just about making the right decision to play one or two touch, but also being able to identify early when to dribble and/ or turn with the ball, run with the ball and so on; using the full spectrum of skills.

The one and two touch aspect is really about teaching quick thinking and early decision making; and is a way to ensure it happens.

Once the quick thinking and early looking is established in the minds of the players; through playing one and two touch; they can start to incorporate it into the other skills such as when to turn, to dribble, beat a player 1 v 1; run with the ball; and so on and not just use it to play one or two touch.

They can then identify early "when and where" to hold onto the ball too, because any given situation may dictate that is the right thing to do at that moment...

So practice the one and two touch training, then let it go free; with as many touches as you like. Players then are free to identify and use all the options available in their repertoire. The one and two touch training is really a means to an end of the psychological side of the player's development. That is, thinking quickly in all situations, assessing the options, and using the best one available...

They may still play one and two touch (even when there is no restriction or condition on the number of touches allowed) if it is the best thing to do at that particular time, and they may also beat players 1 v 1if it is on to do so (and of course they assessed / identified that early due to the early **LOOK**).

In many cases doing this gives the player on the ball extra time and space to play because he already knows where the space is, if he has time to use it, and where the players are (opponents and teammates) before receiving the ball.

Using Opposite Runs as an example of the passing player holding onto the ball rather than passing it quickly.

For the uninitiated this means a player running one way; then checking and running the opposite way, but in the same running phase (to get free of a defender).

Opposite runs of strikers, for example, depend on this time and space factor. Because for a striker to make an opposite run, the player on the ball has to have time and space to wait until the first movement has taken place before the pass is made off the 2nd movement / run (and this may take more touches on the part of the passer). Both the passer and striker have to be able to identify that moment and use it accordingly.

Playing one and two touch is not the only way to play, though it is a major part of playing in my opinion. It needs to be supplemented by players developing their 1v1 technique and skills also. Players have to assimilate certain stages of thought and action in a logical order or continuum, as I have presented it here.

A player's success can be dependent on getting these phases in the correct order. This is presented in a way that is designed to help you identify certain aspects of the game and to evaluate how good each player is at each one. It can help identify their strengths and weaknesses and help you decide what they need to do in order to develop and improve.

I believe all players can be fitted into each and every continuum I have shown below at some time in their development, even in an individual game situation. But one continuum will feature as the strongest and most used; and from that you can identify each player's developmental needs. And as they develop as players it is interesting to watch as they move from one continuum to the next (a better one hopefully) as their ability in all these aspects improves.

WORD ASSOCIATION

Here I have attempted to form a link between a player's technical, tactical, psychological and physical attributes with the associated positive words of the continuums: "look", "communicate", "positioning", "control", "technique", "skill", "mobility", "transition", and the associated negative words: "don't look", "no communication", "poor positioning", "poor technique", "lose possession" and "standing still", in order to have a way of assessing their abilities in these aspects of play.

The technical, tactical, psychological and physical aspects of a player's makeup are interwoven and can overlap each other. For example, the player thinks (**psychological**) about the right decision to make, then must add the **technique** of the action to that. He then needs to **control** the ball and then act the next decision out (**tactical understanding**). All cover the same points, though one is a thought, the next an action, and the next an action (ultimately called a skill) that results in a decision made.

You can also include the physical aspect of this too, as the physical action of the body ensures that the resulting decision occurs.

Hence the associated words used here are designed to make the connection with the four aspects of player makeup. The continuums represent having and maintaining possession or losing possession and transition.

LOOK / OBSERVE:

Look is a psychological aspect (because it is in the thinking and identifying options phase of the continuum). It can also be a tactical aspect, but still in the mind, not the actual tactical decision. This phase helps the player determine the best tactical solution for the next phase of play by observing what is around him (own players, opponents and where the space is).

This represents the player looking for support before receiving the ball so a decision can be made "in advance" of receiving it, thus allowing defenders less time to close the player down and the player receiving the ball to see his options earlier.

CHOOSING OPTIONS:

The choice we are looking for is not necessarily the simplest or easiest one (nor the one we are encouraging for that matter), but potentially we are looking for the one that can hurt the opposition the most.

In a game situation it may be that a one touch pass into the striker is needed from the midfield player receiving a pass from someone else. If he takes two or more touches to get to the striker with the pass then the striker may by then be offside or have been closed down by the defender.

A simpler option may have been to keep possession with a pass to a more open player and with more time to do it (because a one touch pass is often the hardest to execute due to the lack of time).

The main point here is the quicker they see the options presented, the more options they see and likely the better chance they have of choosing the one that may hurt the opponents the most. The **Look** stage of the continuum plays a big part in this, especially as it is the first stage and is perhaps the most important part of the continuum to develop.

COMMUNICATE:

Communicate is a psychological aspect, the same as "look" in terms of the thinking and identifying options phase of the continuum. The passing player communicates with the receiver, the receiver has seen what he needs to do and communicates this to his teammates, and / or the teammates off the ball have seen what options there are, as the ball is travelling, and have communicated this to the player on the ball (communication from both parties).

Communication can be in the form of verbal communication, visual eye to eye contact or physical communication such as pointing to show where the ball should go (either by the receiver or the supporting player; or both). Communication can of course appear at any stage along each continuum; but the sooner in each the better the chance of helping and thus gaining success in the phase of play.

POSITIONING:

Positioning is a psychological aspect (knowing where and when to position) and a physical aspect (the actual body movement) of the continuum. It includes foot preparation, body position and moving into space to receive. Mind and body preparation plays a vital part here. If the mind and body position or angle of support (in space) and the foot preparation are wrong, the player's balance, technique and ultimately his control will surely suffer.

Foot preparation and body position:
This often can be the difference between good control and bad control and keeping possession or losing it, and so can affect the situation even before the ball is controlled. A good first touch needs to be away from defenders, perhaps towards the likely target player (though not always as in the case of an ensuing reverse pass) and into the space, and is aligned with technique; being the first touch to control.

Emphasize to players to not be flat footed when they receive the ball. They should be up on their toes and ready to receive.

CONTROL:
Control is a technical aspect (first touch control) and a physical aspect (using the body) of the continuum.

This is the first controlling touch by the receiver if the pass, the no touch turn, the cross, or the shot is not to be made with the first touch. It is essentially receiving and controlling the ball.

TECHNIQUE:
Technique is both a technical and a physical aspect of the continuum; and is the "how" to do it. The decision of "when and where" to make the technique work is in the next "skill" phase. As mentioned in control, mind preparation, body position and foot preparation can affect this one way or the other.

This is the end product of the technical part of this process. This can be a one or two touch pass (or more touches if the need is there), a dribble, perhaps a 1 v 1 confrontation, a turn, a cross, a shot or a run with the ball, depending on what is the best option at that moment in time (or combinations of any of these).

Technique is a term used to describe a basic action or movement. Techniques form the building blocks on which skills are developed, so that players who have a refined technical ability to produce a particular turn or dribble can deploy that technique in the right place at the right time.

SKILL:
Skill is a psychological, technical, physical and tactical aspect of the continuum: psychological through thinking about the best option available, preferably in advance of the ball; technical in terms of the technique of the player with the ball; physical in terms of the actual body involvement and tactical as in the end product, which is keeping possession by good decision making and picking one of the best options available.

Skill is choosing to use the right technique at the right time, the "when and where" of the process. The term skill refers to an ability to select and implement an appropriate and effective response from a range of possibilities. In other words, a skilled player knows "what to do" and "where to do it".

Where **SKILL** is mentioned in each continuum it "represents" the action being a successful one. The skill can represent a pass, a 1 v 1 dribble, a shot, a turn, a cross, or a "combination" of these by the individual player. For example, a dribble, a turn and then a cross or shot.

NO COMMUNICATION:

This is as simple as it states; where neither the player on the ball nor those off the ball have communicated with each other to aid the process of ball maintenance.

LOSING POSSESSION:

This means what it says also, and is representative of the skill used being unsuccessful, hence possession is lost in the skill phase of the continuum.

Reasons for this result can vary and should be considered by the coach on a subjective and individual player basis.

Was it because their technical level of play was poor? Was their understanding of the when and where (skill) to implement the technique (decision making) poor? Was it because the player was lazy and had a poor attitude in trying to maintain possession and thus gave the ball away cheaply (psychological)? Was it just a sloppy, thoughtless, lazy pass maybe (more common than we coaches would like)? Did fatigue play a part (physical)? Or was it simply a great defensive decision by the opponent?

What is the "norm" for this player?

A pattern will emerge for each player as to how and why they lose possession.
The cause can either be one or a combination of technical, tactical and psychological aspects. Technical and tactical as their technique and decision making may be poor, resulting in the loss of possession and physical in terms of perhaps not protecting the ball and keeping possession of it or, as stated before, fatigue and perhaps a lack of fitness?

Some players obviously lose the ball more than others, it is up to you to assess this and find the main reasons why. Therefore subjectivity is required and we are relying on the coach's knowledge of the game to identify those reasons why.

MOBILITY:

Mobility (movement) is certainly psychological (as players have to think about where they need to go next in the phase of play to be of best use to the team); but also physical, as it is a physical motion; and it can also be a tactical aspect as the player needs to know "where" to move to in a tactical sense.

After the ball has been technically received and the skill has been implemented, what does the player now do? Now we are considering the ensuing positioning of the player "off the ball".

Too often players stand still and admire their pass instead of moving to support, either directly (by receiving the ball back again) or indirectly (by perhaps taking a defender out of an area to create space for a teammate) or rejoining the play in a later phase.

So **mobility** in the continuum of events represents the fact that the player has immediately moved again to help his team, beyond the successful skill he used to keep possession in the first place. This can apply to teammates off the ball also.

TRANSITION:

Transition is primarily psychological. The player has to want to do it and think about where he needs to do it. It is also physical as it is a physical motion.

This is the mental and physical change in the player in order to try to win the ball back immediately once it has been lost. This is showing that the player has the capacity and attitude to become an instant defender and so shows good defensive qualities. When transition is mentioned in these continuums it is always in the "positive sense", meaning the player works hard to win the ball back after losing it. There will be levels of this that the coach has to identify with each player, as some players work harder than others in this particular facet of the game. This can apply to teammates off the ball also.

STANDING STILL:

Standing Still is a psychological aspect. The player wants to do it or he doesn't, so it can come down to an attitude of mind (lazy player); or even a lack of understanding of where to go next. This can apply to teammates off the ball also.

I have used this extreme term to highlight this situation in a game; and it is used in a negative context.

It is the opposite of **TRANSITION** in its meaning and highlights where the player did not transition and did not mentally switch on for the next phase of play.

So, after losing possession of the ball, a lack of transition (denoted by the term "Standing Still") to become an immediate defender and to try to win the ball back can often be due to an attitude problem rather than a lack of understanding and can be measured in a desire (psychological) to win it back (or not) as much as anything.

Therefore it could also be a physical problem (fatigue perhaps) or a psychological one. The coach has to identify which reason or reasons there are for each particular player.

In maintaining possession it can mean perhaps the player is standing still and admiring the fact he at least kept possession, without immediate thought as to what he can do next for his team. Contrary to this, standing still after keeping possession may be the best thing to do to get free from an opponent; for example if a defender runs past you assuming you will move and you stand still to get free. But again it is up to the coach to assess and observe the differences.

A pattern with the individual player for this term will clearly develop and likely standing still for the right reason will be obvious in its isolation; but for the vast majority of the time it will be a negative thing.

TEAMMATES "OFF" THE BALL:

To make all this work, the players "off the ball" must be in tune with what the player "on the ball" is trying to do and must move to help him and it must be done using both communication and field positioning.

If this does not happen then all the good work of the player on the ball may be wasted because there is no one open to play to in the next phase of play; or the player on the ball may be forced into making an individual move or play until a support opportunity from a teammate opens up.

You can equate the aspects of "mobility"; "transition", or "standing still" to "off the ball" players also.

CONTINUUMS OF DEVELOPMENT:

The following continuums show what can and does happen and ask the questions which are the best continuums to develop and use in order to achieve a likely success? You could conceivably have sub – continuums between these but I am trying to limit the number for clarity and ease of understanding. For example, Look and Communicate can flip flop for the same effect. Communicating then looking before receiving the ball can be as effective as looking and then communicating (communicating can be visual or verbal, can be by the receiver, the passer, or players off the ball as the ball travels with phrases such as "man on", "turn", "time" and so on).

1. LOOK / COMMUNICATE / POSITIONING / TECHNIQUE / SKILL / MOBILITY
   ### (this is one touch play)

This is potentially the best continuum because the player has looked and so knows what the options are in advance of receiving the ball, and the player will have communicated his intensions to teammates (or them to him, or even both); and assessed the best option is a one touch pass, a no touch turn, a one touch cross, or a one touch shot in a given situation.

As there is no control needed; the first touch is actually using one of these techniques (thus saving time in the play and therefore giving the defenders less time to close them down and thus prevent the move from being successful).

This **TECHNIQUE** then becomes a **SKILL** once the correct decision has been made and the required choice taken.

Once the skill is performed successfully the player then moves immediately "off the ball" (MOBILITY) to help the next phase of play.

These consecutive phases used in this continuum are the sign of a good player.

Also realize that there are many things that the player needs to process before they even touch the ball involved in this. The breakdown is:

a) Good Footwork to receive the ball; which in turn helps the first touch, so the feet are well prepared to receive the ball, the player is lively and on their toes and not flat footed; able to execute several options if necessary; as allowed by their foot preparation
b) Taking a look around for all options to increase their peripheral vision before receiving the ball
c) An open body stance to be able to change the direction of play if needed
d) Moving into space to receive, opening the angle up
e) Communication from the passing player and also from the player about to receive the ball; and from teammates to that same player to help him or her recognize the options available (verbal and visual)
f) Then the first touch occurs.

2. LOOK / COMMUNICATE / POSITION / CONTROL / TECHNIQUE / SKILL / MOBILITY
(This is a minimum of two touch play)

This is also a successful continuum because the player has assessed his or her options be-fore receiving the ball, got their feet, body in position and moved into space, communicated their intensions (or others have helped them by communicating to them; or both) and used a minimum of two touches to move the ball on (it can be many touches as long as they maintain possession of the ball in this continuum).

The first touch is to control the ball using good technique, thus allowing themselves time on the ball they otherwise may not have had if they had waited to control first and then look. The player has decided that a pass, a 1 v 1 dribbling confrontation, a turn, a run with the ball, a cross or a shot is the right decision to make (or combinations thereof); and has done so (SKILL), and once this successful skill is performed the player is on the move immediately "off the ball" and getting into a better position on the field to help his or her team in the next stage of de-velopment of the phase of play.

3. POSITION / CONTROL / TECHNIQUE / LOOK / COMMUNICATE / SKILL / MOBILITY

Here the player positioned correctly, and controlled the ball first with more than one touch, and then looked at the options, but did well enough to make it work using the "when and where" of the skill, and then made good movement "off the ball" to support the next phase of play.

Not as good nor consistently successful as Looking before controlling, receiving and having good technique because this means the player does not see options before they get the ball, and thus give themselves more time on the ball to make the right decisions.

But the player can still make it work with good control and technique; though perhaps under more pressure than the other way of doing it, where the player has better awareness and has an earlier look to assess all options available and have time to pick the best one.

More technically skilful players will be able to make this work much more than less technically skilled ones because their technical skills will help them get out of trouble but having a look first and giving themselves more time will allow them to play without getting in trouble in the first place. This is a common one amongst players and was where I was as a player much of the time.

4. POSITION / CONTROL / TECHNIQUE / LOOK / COMMUNICATE / SKILL / STAND STILL

The player manages to keep possession and make the right decisions up to the point of their thought processes and movements off the ball; where he or she is then not join-ing in the attack due to standing still, and therefore is out of the game in the next phase. So, the player is successful in control, technique and skill but lacking in understanding of where to go "off the ball" to support future plays (or is lazy or tired, you the coach have to rec-ognize which it is and act accordingly).

5. POSITION / CONTROL / TECHNIQUE / LOOK / NO COMMUNICATION / LOSE POSSESSION / TRANSITION

Looking too late, assessing options too late, because positioning control and technique came before look, but despite the fact the player has lost possession he or she immediately switches into a defensive mentality to try to win the ball back, this shows a great attitude on the part of the player but the when and where decision making factor (skill) needs improvement and changing the control / look around so look is first would help this too..

6. POSITION / CONTROL / TECHNIQUE / LOOK / NO COMMUNICATION / LOSE POSSESSION / STAND STILL

This is likely to be unsuccessful too, because the player positions then controls the ball first (and may even lose it in this part of the continuum), then assesses his or her options next (which may be too late and they get closed down by an opponent and lose the ball), does not communicate nor is communicated to by teammates; or then passes (or perhaps dribbles under pressure because that is the only option left) the ball (but it may be rushed so unsuccessful) and then stands still, therefore not being involved in the next stage of the movement.
If losing possession of the ball and then standing still and therefore not immediately transitioning into defending mentality from an attacking mentality, then this player is totally out of the game and no use at that moment in time to the team.

This type of player needs a LOT of help to improve as most facets of the continuum are poorly developed and it is a knock on effect starting by not assessing the next options early enough and never really catching up.

So to be successful a player must link the thought processes to the more obvious physical processes involved in playing the game and these different continuum's describe the differences and the potentially different outcomes, due to which order the words or actions are used and performed (successful or unsuccessful).

7. POOR POSITIONING / POOR CONTROL / POOR TECHNIQUE / DON'T LOOK / NO COMMUNICATION / LOSE POSSESSION / STAND STILL

This last one is the ultimate where the player gets "everything" wrong, yes it is the absolute extreme but I put it in just to show all the things that can go wrong and the many different areas of play you may need to work with a player to improve their game.
A poor 1st touch control leads to poor technique (ensuing more touches on the ball), they didn't look to view options and perhaps give themselves time on the ball by doing so, and so may be closed down quickly and put under immediate pressure, no team mate suggested "man on", or "pressure" to help them either in communication, which all then forces them to make a bad decision and give possession away, and rather than chase to win it back they give up.

ASSESSMENT: Look at all your players closely; which continuums do each of them generally fit into?

Obviously at times they will do all of these to some extent, but certain continuums will outweigh others in the amount of times each player does them in a game situation, and this can determine which players are the most successful on the field; based on which continuums dominate in their game make up.

We would like those players with the "LOOK" first in the continuum, to be the ones they are most aligned with; so they are giving themselves the most time to assess each situation; and then having the most options to choose from, options being any of the following: dribbling and beating players 1 v 1 and beyond, quick passing, running with the ball, crossing or shooting, turning with the ball and maintaining possession; or even combinations of these.

I believe you will easily be able to identify which players belong to which continuum and hence work out their strengths and weaknesses from this and thus be able to help them to improve same.

So we have in the positive with combinations of thought and execution on and off the ball:

1. LOOK
2. COMMUNICATE (can be a two way positive, the players themselves on the ball, their teammates off the ball)
3. POSITION
4. CONTROL
5. TECHNIQUE
6. SKILL
7. MOBILITY
8. TRANSITION

In the negative:

1. LOOK TOO LATE (OR NOT AT ALL)
2. NO COMMUNICATION (from either the player on the ball or their teammates off the ball)
3. POOR POSITIONING
4. POOR TECHNIQUE
5. LOSE POSSESSION
6. STANDING STILL

Each continuum can have both positive and negative elements at certain points; the more positive elements players have, the greater the chance of success.

To be successful the players need to:

1. Be good at thinking ahead of the ball; looking and observing options (hence have a sharp soccer mind),
2. Have good communication skills;
3. Have good technique to use the ball once they get it in order to be able to maintain possession of it;
4. Have a tactical understanding (skill set) in order to make the right decisions amongst the various options they have at any one time (where the technique becomes a skill) including an understanding of where to move to "off the ball" to provide support.
5. "Off the ball" players need to be tuned in to what the "on the ball" player is trying to achieve even the most positive continuum may be unsuccessful if the player on the ball has no options due to poor support by his or her teammates.
6. Have the physical and mental capacity to bring it all together by knowing where and when to move to "off the ball".

MEASURING / ASSESSING PERFORMANCE:
When training; as a method of self assessment or measurement (or as close as one can get without an entirely objective process); I like to ask players to count; just for themselves; how many times they each give the ball away in a given timed period.

I ask them to add them up to a final number and then think about what happened in each situation and if there was a certain aspect of their play that was causing them to give the ball away.

Hence whilst they are working on playing as a team player they are also at the same time focusing on themselves as individual players and assessing their own efficiency.

Therefore they had to think about what the reasons were for giving possession of the ball away and if one stood out then that would be the most likely skill they needed to work on to become a better player, and thus not give possession way to the same extent, as they develop more as a player.

Examples could be:

1. Poor footwork, the feet are not ready to receive the ball (a very common one, perhaps the most common one), so they are getting it wrong even before they touch the ball and this leads on to a poor first touch. Players often get too flat footed and are not light on their feet.

2. Poor body position (closed stance); so their directional options for the next decision are limited (they may still maintain possession by going back to the player whom they face but they will miss out on better options if they opened their stance up and looked).

3. Poor or no movement into space to open an angle up to receive.

4. Next perhaps then a poor first touch (that perhaps was caused by the poor footwork, poor body position or lack of movement into space to receive in the first place), or ;

5. Not looking before receiving and knowing options in advance of the ball and thus getting caught in possession unnecessarily (this is in the mind, not thinking quickly enough), because they did not see the defender coming in to close them down or did not see their next options quickly enough, or;

6. For players off the ball not moving to help the player receiving the pass; and it also needs good communication from them (but I told the player receiving to not expect this often and that they needed to rely on their own awareness by looking for themselves, this is a fact of life with soccer and communication because players do not talk enough to help each other).

So a three way support mechanism; the player passing with accuracy and touch to help the receiver, the player receiving scans the options themselves, as the ball is arriving; players off the ball move to; create several options for the player receiving for his or her next pass or phase of play.

REWARD SYSTEM
Having done this I then encourage their quick thinking using one touch play by asking them to add up the number of times they made a successful one touch pass and deduct any mistakes or giveaways from their score.

This meant they were successful with the first and perhaps most effective continuum identified previously. I call this "lose a life and gain a life", as they continuously add up their score in their heads as they paractice.

It is important that players not get obsessed with passing one touch just to get one life (or point) back, as not every situation warrants or needs a one touch pass.

Of course this is not an entirely objective measurement but it can be an indicator of the things they are good at and the things they need to improve upon.

If players mentally focus and use this idea they can identify for themselves their strengths and weaknesses and therefore have a somewhat objective idea of what they need to work on to improve. You can apply this method of self assessment to many game set ups and situations in training.

AGE RELATED
For younger players, meaning 6 to 9 year olds, it is best to introduce these ideas in a non pressurized situation, where they are likely to give up the ball at times without pressure anyway; and you can analyze this with them.

Without pressure means the focus could be on footwork as much as anything, which is the best place to start to help them. No pressure narrows the field of possibility for error.

CHOOSING OPTIONS:
Guard against them just passing the easy pass for the sake of, challenge them to really look to see all the options and try to choose the one that hurts the opponents' the most, there may be a simple 4 yard pass that won't affect the defenders, but there may be a one touch switching play pass to the other side of the field that will hurt them more, as we have a free player there and the change in play will be more effective than the easy pass.

You can observe players and see those who attempt to take the right choices (those choices that, if successful, cause the most damage to the opponents). You may get a player who takes every easy option and gets a good score in the drill, but never takes chances. This is ok for maintaining possession of the ball, but won't unlock the door for the team like a telling but perhaps risky decision might. This is where your observation will come into the equation. It can be a balancing act between making the right choice (perhaps a more difficult one), making the easy choice; and mixing them up, as sometimes only the easy pass is on anyway.

This is why it is not a totally objective process. It can't be in such a dynamic game as soccer. The subjectivity of the coach's experience comes into play when assessing players with this system in mind.

PLAYING PERCENTAGES AND PERFORMING IN SAFETY AND RISK AREAS
You can also apply logic to the decision made by players when you look at the safety and risk areas that players are in. For example, you would encourage the easy option in the defending third of the field, where a risky play could result in a goal by the opponent.

Conversely, you would encourage the more risky but potentially damaging option against the opponents in the attacking third of the field because if possession is lost there we can still recover the ball quickly and not be too open to a damaging attack against us.

Yes it would be a higher percentage chance of keeping possession with the easy option, but the rewards are greater using the lower percentage option.

Example: In the attacking third we have two options; an easy pass that has a 90% chance of success but doesn't penetrate the opponent's defense, or a difficult pass between defenders that penetrates and puts the striker in a position to score but has maybe a 30% chance of being successful because of the limited space to pass it into and the number of defenders between the passing player and the striker receiving the pass. Which does the player take? Fear of failure would suggest the easy one. Taking the chance would be the difficult one, but it may result in a goal. The player has to decide: was the difficult option the best one to take? Maybe it was the best option at that moment even though its percentage of success was low.

Hence the higher percentage option with the most chance of maintaining possession is not necessarily the best option to take. It can depend on the individual situation at any given moment and also on which part of the field it is happening.

The better the player, the more often he will make the right decision, using both the easy and more difficult options that present themselves in the game.

CONDITIONING GAMES IN TRAINING:

FREE PLAY, TWO TOUCHES AND ONE TOUCH PLAY:

Conditioning the game situation in training can help identify what players are good at in these continuums.

Playing a game with each player able to have an unlimited number of touches allows them to "get out of jail", meaning get out of trouble and keep possession, even if their decision was not the best option to take at that particular moment.

As an example, perhaps the player did not look early to scan his options as the ball was coming (as in the best continuums) so he missed the opportunity for the one touch pass (which at that moment was the best option available) but his dribbling skills allowed him to still maintain possession of the ball.

Making the game a two touch maximum starts to focus their minds in quick thinking and quick decisions and does not allow them to get out of trouble (get out of jail should their decision making be poor) with lots of touches.

Rotating between games of two touches and free play (as many touches as they like), but including the one touch successful pass option in both, is a good way to focus their minds on the job at hand and understand the options they have available to be successful.

Scoring in the game goes as follows: Players add one point to their score when they give the ball away and take one point away when they perform the reward theme successfully.

A few Examples of good games to play for this:

THREE TEAM AWARENESS GAME

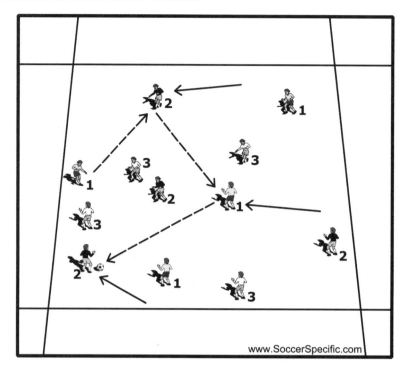

www.SoccerSpecific.com

1. Working with three teams (numbers depends on how many players you have, e.g. it can be 4 v 4 + 4 or 5 v 5 + 5 etc). Teams (1) and (2) work together to keep the ball from team (3). If team (3) regains possession the team who gave it away becomes the defenders. The defenders reward is they keep the ball and link with the other team.
2. Rules: Once possession is gained, to establish who gave the ball away the player who gave the ball away calls the color of his team and then everyone knows they are now defending and the game continues without a stoppage.

With younger players it may be best to do this (because the ball may be given away a lot more for one thing); whoever won the ball puts his or her foot on the ball to stop play and the coach can call out the team who gave it away. Play begins again working on transitions.

3. **Develop:** Increase difficulty for attackers by:
   a) Reducing the zone size.
   b) Decreasing the number of touches on the ball of each player.
   c) Conditioning the passing to be only to the other attacking team's players e.g. (1) only passes to (2) and vice versa, therefore only half the numbers of passes are available per player.
   d) Using two balls so that as they pass one ball they are now increasing their awareness and vision by looking for the other ball coming.
   e) Asking players to take off their pinnies so they really have to look and can't rely on color identification.
   f) No talking or pointing, so players have to rely on their own vision.
   g) Prohibiting verbal communication
   h) ULTIMATELY PLAY ONE TOUCH

THREE TEAM POSSESSION GAME

Three teams, two teams work together, one defends, creates an overload situation in attack, for example 15 players, three teams of 5, a 10 v 5 OVERLOAD game.

Possession changes as one of the players gives the ball away to the defending team. They then become the next defending team. This is a good transition game from attack to defense and defense to attack. This game can be in an area of 40 x 40 yards and the challenge to the players can also be to move inside to outside (outside being just inside the touchline) and outside to inside to ensure they avoid standing in one area. Plus, it takes greater vision or awareness inside the area; where they need to look around and open their stance up to potentially change the direction of play; than on the outside where they can see everything easily.

Encourage players who play centrally on the team to get in the middle of the area and dictate the play, be the pivot for the team, the player who transfers the ball from one side to the other, the link player. This can be one, two or even three players at a time.
Equal numbered teams in a possession keep away game; this would be the next progression from the overload game being a more difficult challenge of the players. Same principles and ideas as above apply.

Transition games: In two halves, creating overloads in each half as each team gains possession. Team A have to get the ball in one half and play a 7 v 3 for example, team B have to win it back with the 3 defenders and get it back to the other half and have a 7 v 3 in their favor, and so on.

3. Equal numbered teams in a possession keep away game; this would be the next progression from the overload game being a more difficult challenge of the players. Same principles and ideas as above apply.

4. Transition games: in two halves, creating overloads in each half as each team gains possession. Numbers Team have to get the ball in one half and play a 6 v 3 for example, the letters team have to win it back with the 3 defenders and get it back to the other half and have a 6 v 3 in their favor, and so on. Change the overload to suit the level of the players harder for better players; easier for less skilled players (maybe a 6 v 2 in one half with 4 waiting for possession to be gained and transferred).

THE ULTIMATE: PLAYING ONE TOUCH IN A COMPETITIVE OVERLOAD
GAME SITUATION (see Clinic 51)

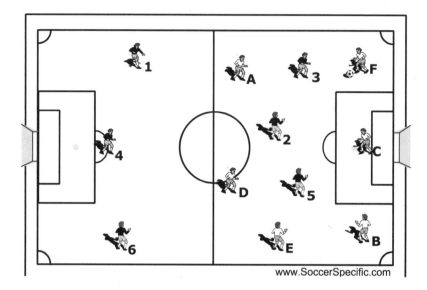

www.SoccerSpecific.com

1. Here we have 3 target players to pass to and a 6v3 over-load which makes it easier for the attacking team to maintain possession of the ball so we now play 1 touch only. Obviously this will mean the players are really tested in their awareness.
2. The target player receiving the pass initially has two touches because it is a long pass and likely with pace, but as they get good at it insist on a one touch transfer which means the other two target players need to be ready to help.
3. **Coaching Points:**
   a) Awareness of all players positions before receiving the ball (own players and opponents) plus where the spaces are to pass to.
   b) Correct foot preparation to receive the ball, having then to make a one touch pass
   c) Correct body position, open stance in the way you are going to make the pass, unless you are using a fake then pass to fool the defender. But a body position as such that it helps you make a successful next pass.
   d) Correct pace / weight of the pass to help the next player when receiving it, that player having to move it on one touch too.
   e) Movement off the ball by all the other players to help the player on the ball, but do it before the player receives the pass not after.
   f) Asking players to position between defenders and into spaces to help the player about to receive the ball to move it on one touch.
   g) Finally, when you think the players are ready have them play a 6 v 6 and one touch only game in a scrimmage.
   h) Test them in a proper scrimmage game against opponents now; you can play 2 touches only in the first half and one touch only in the 2nd half.

Or; play one touch in the first half and free play the second and see its overall effect. Do they start to identify one touch passing opportunities in the 2nd half that were better than perhaps dribbling or running with the ball, because the ball moves faster than the player and passing it quickly gives the opponent less time to adjust and counter. Prepare for ugly play initially when playing one touch only.

THEMES OF PLAY

You can work on different THEMES in these possession games based on how you reward the players. For example each of the following situations constitutes a different reward mechanism to adhere to:

Quick thinking / Quick Passing: One touch successful passing; this improves quick thinking, early identification of options, in advance of the ball, quick passing.

Switching the Play or point of attack: Playing in thirds and being able to pass from one outside third to the other outside third successfully across the middle third can create a switching the play reward.

Defending 1v1: For a defending team, the individual winning possession and keeping it can be a reward, so they get a life / point for that.

Gaining success in a 1v1 dribbling situation; through beating a player with a dribble and therefore maintaining possession: You can use this in free play all in games where players have unlimited touches each time they receive the ball.

Several themes in one can also be used; just playing the game or scrimmage you can incorporate all of these into the equation and ask the players to process in their minds all the ideas as to where they go right and where they need to improve.

While interpretation is involved in identifying certain situations, I believe these continuums can provide important information for coaches in the development of their players and it certainly helps them identify the area in need of improvement in individual situations.

The Evaluation of Individual Player Awareness
Using the Continuums Development Model

Player:

Team:

Coach:

Date:

Scale 1 - 6 : **1**- Needs to work very hard to improve, **2**- Needs improvement, **3**- Average, **4**- Good, **5**- A strength, **6**- Excellent

WORD ASSOCIATION: COMBINING THOUGHT AND ACTION

Continuum	Score
LOOK / OBSERVE: (BEFORE RECEIVING THE BALL; ASSESSING OPTIONS)	
COMMUNICATION: (THE PLAYER RECEIVING)	
POSITION (FEET PREPARATION AND BODY STANCE BEFORE RECEIVING)	
CONTROL (1ST TOUCH IN ISOLATION)	
TECHNIQUE (1ST TOUCH AND BEYOND)	
SKILL (WHEN AND WHERE / DECISION MAKING FOR THE TECHNIQUE)	
MOBILITY (MOVEMENT OFF THE BALL ONCE IT HAS BEEN PLAYED)	
TRANSITION (POSSESSION CHANGES AND HOW THE PLAYER REACTS)	

This is my latest thought on how to evaluate Awareness through the Word Association Continuums of Development Model so it is not only applicable "Theoretically" but also in a "Practical" sense and the two can be interlinked.

In the training sessions I have done I was able to show and explain at every point of the continuum where a player was in terms of their ability as a player as a whole; by my observation of that player with regards to each word. Thus I will be able to identify over a period of time at which point or points the player has weaknesses; and at which point or points he has strengths.

I want coaches to learn this method of evaluation and use it. It is a new way to think and assess players. It focuses the coach's mind to break down a player's ability into "specific areas" and it specifically forces them to look in a certain way at a player; and therefore it is easier to assess him rather than just looking him and trying to make a judgment "as a whole".

Is the whole (player) more important than the "sum of the parts" (the word associations of the breakdown of the player's makeup) then? Is the solution to value the different parts of the player's makeup separately; and then to add the values of the different parts of the whole together to make the final player?

So; while the whole (the player) is very good, improving "one part" (it could be the "skill" part, or maybe the "look" part) can be the difference between a good player and a great player. How many times have you looked at a player and said he is a good player, but he just lacks something, and you can't put your finger on what it is? This continuum can help in this. And this method of evaluation through "Word Association" helps us to indentify that particular part that perhaps we can't identify by just looking at the player "as a whole". It is not an exact science but it is a useful method to look at and assess individual player development.

Valdivia of Al Ain Football Club

DEVELOPING THE LINK BETWEEN FOOT AND BODY POSITIONING AND THE AWARENESS OF OPTIONS

THE IMPORTANCE OF CORRECT PREPARATION OF BOTH THE FEET AND THE BODY TO RECEIVE THE BALL

Fast footwork helps players develop the necessary footwork to help them in their awareness training.

Prepare the body (and especially the feet) to receive, to be in a balanced position, and to know what to do with the ball before receiving it (thought processes). These are all important components the players have to master, and it is all **BEFORE** they even touch the ball.
We work on what they do when they have it at their feet, but we need to sort out **FIRST** of all what they do **BEFORE** they get the ball at their feet.

I see so many players in a flat footed, closed body stance, with their head down when they are about to receive the ball. Is it a surprise when they have a poor first touch and more often than not give the ball away?

They need to be light on their feet, up on their toes and ready to receive. They should have an open body stance so they have directional options and know their decision making options in advance of the ball. Being thus prepared will allow them to both choose and execute the move quickly and efficiently.

An example in a game: a player is closed down quickly by an opponent and needs to have the correct foot preparation, thought awareness, and body positioning to get out of trouble with the right pass, run or dribble.

Awareness training and fast footwork and coordination training go hand in hand. It is the link between the body and the mind. We need to get the players to the stage where they **INSTINCTIVELY** " prepare their feet", move and open up their bodies. We need them to see what to do before they receive the ball, where their first touch has an added purpose; not just simply to control the ball, but to control the ball to enable them to make their "next movement successfully", whether that be a one touch pass, a one touch into space or towards a teammate then a pass, or to run with it, to dribble with it, to cross it, to receive and turn with it, or to shoot with it. These are all about making the right decisions at the right time regarding body and mind.

To receive and pass the ball quickly and effectively requires excellent footwork to decrease the time and the number of touches it takes to control the ball and maintain possession of it. The awareness method of training is the psychological aspect; the footwork is the transference and connection to this, initially without the ball, but ultimately with it.

All training is game specific. The AWARENESS COACHING METHOD work is based upon developing a balance between ball handling and functional running and sprinting in combination with jumping, stopping and turning.

Exercises requiring quick feet and change of stride length will be particularly important. Repetition of the exercises is important throughout the season on a several times a week basis to develop the correct habits regarding co-ordination, comfort in running, awareness of the efficient use of arms and legs in running and the synchronization of limbs. We are intending to develop a 6th sense in teaching the players to use the right techniques at the right times.

The application of body co-ordination and speed work is particularly important in the 6 to 12 age groups and will go hand in hand with an increased amount of technical skills training that leads into the awareness training method of development.

The 13 to 19 age groups will need more strength and endurance training as well. General observations on running indicate the need to be able to adjust the stride length with ease to suit the situation and to be able to adjust and vary the length of stride as the particular match situation dictates.

When running, long strides mean less contact with the ground so the player is more easily knocked off the ball and unbalanced. Better to adjust the way you run with shorter quicker strides so there is more contact with the ground, less chance to be knocked off balance, and a greater chance that the feet are in the correct position when and where they need to be.

Far too many players play flat footed. They do not get their feet in place early enough (or at all) to run or change direction or to receive the ball and be able to control it with comfort and effectiveness. This training is designed to cure this problem. It is about improving balance, foot co-ordination and speed.

Five to ten minutes of every session should be devoted to practicing this footwork at pace, without the ball, but then incorporating the ball as skills improve.

Quick feet are essential for a player to be successful at soccer and learning to use a shorter stride length on starting means the player gets away more quickly.

The routines in the first clinic plan are examples of simple circuits of cones that can be laid out to help the players develop this talent.

COACHING CLINIC SESSION PLAN 1

(For age 6 years and older)
OBJECTIVE: IMPROVING FAST FOOTWORK AND COORDINATION

The first order of business in implementing the Awareness Coaching Method is addressing the positioning of the players' feet BEFORE they have their first touch of it.

Hence our first clinic plan is focused on fast footwork. As with all the clinic plans the clinic will finish with a small sided scrimmage to ensure the players get to play with the ball, but the focus for this session is work without the ball and before they receive it with their first touch.

Basic foot movement in and out of the cones is the best beginning as it is easy to have success and it gives the players an idea of what you are trying to teach them.

Below are different set ups designed to achieve this end.

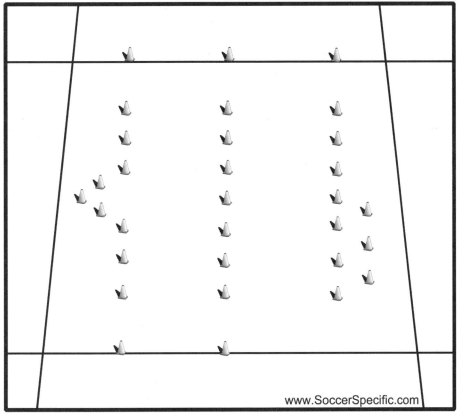

www.SoccerSpecific.com

Diagram 9   **30 x 30**

1. Players check inside and outside the cones, moving side to side and keeping on their toes for fast feet. Finish over the final 5 yards with a sprint.
2. Players go one at a time, one sufficiently behind the other so as not to put the player ahead under too much pressure and have them do it fairly slowly to get the rhythm. If they do it quickly they may miss cones and that would defeat the object of following the circuit and getting each step right.

3. **Develop:** As they improve you can have two lanes of the same circuit set up and have a competitive race between two players. They must make sure they do all the foot movements correctly and do not miss any out.
4. Add new circuits to the session plan. Below are several different ideas you can use to keep the players focused during the session.
5. It is about improving balance, co-ordination and speed. Players must do a 5 yard sprint at the end of each circuit. Do 2 circuits side by side so it is a race. Design your own circuits as long as the stride lengths and angles of movement are different to force the players to change their feet.
6. Five to ten minutes of every clinic should be devoted to practicing this footwork at pace, without the ball, but then incorporating the ball as the players' skills improve.

These routines are examples of circuits of cones that can be laid out to help the players develop this talent.

Coaching points:
a) Good balance through using initial shorter strides
b) Concentration on foot placement and movements
c) Fast feet
d) Changing pace with a sprint finish (again focus on stride length)

Side to Side: Checking side to side between the cones with fast feet then a sprint finish. Practice forwards and backwards running (defending movement).
High Frequency: Long and short strides, changing the stride length as happens in a game, adjusting the feet. Players are stepping between the cones.
Checking and Dummying: Bouncing side to side in one movement, with feet wider apart and as fast as possible, throwing a dummy with the upper body. This is good for dribbling movement, dropping the shoulder on one side and moving to the other side (Matthews dribble for example).

CO-ORDINATION WITH AND WITHOUT THE BALL

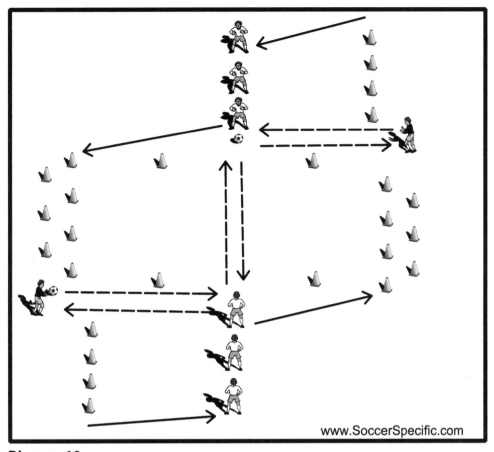

Diagram 10

Each change interrupts the motion of the player, forcing him to change his feet and thus help him develop and improve his movement and foot coordination.

DEVELOPING FAST FOOTWORK:

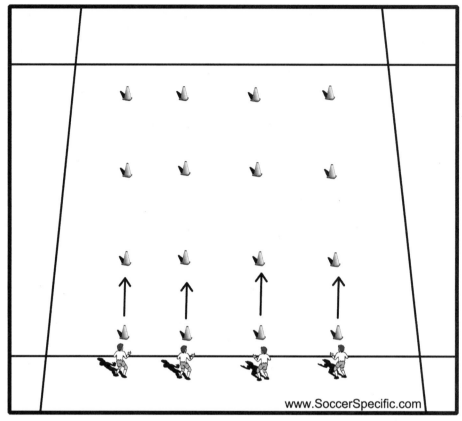

Diagram 11   **30 x 30**

EMPHASIZING THE IMPORTANCE OF THE FIRST STEP

1. Lots of quick standing starts, emphasizing the importance of the first stride (emphasize also a short step). This is the most important stride as it is the explosive one. In this routine the players practice many of these.
   The theme is a quick start and sprint and a quick stop. There must be a pronounced stop between runs as we are working on that explosive start. Players all sprint forward one cone on command from the coach and stop quickly, then turn and sprint back together on command. Always run the way you are facing. The first group should just sprint and stop.
2. Sprint forward one cone and stop but face the same way. The next command is to turn quickly and sprint back.
3. Sprint to the side (turning at 45 degrees and sprinting).
4. Jog backwards then turn at pace and sprint.
5. Sprint to any cone, it can be a diagonal run now. Who is the last player to find a cone? This is good for spatial awareness too. Where is the free cone?
6. Sprint to two cones and stop at the second, sprint to three cones and stop at the third. There is a change of direction now but make sure the players stop at each cone for a fraction of a second so their next first stride is from a standing start.

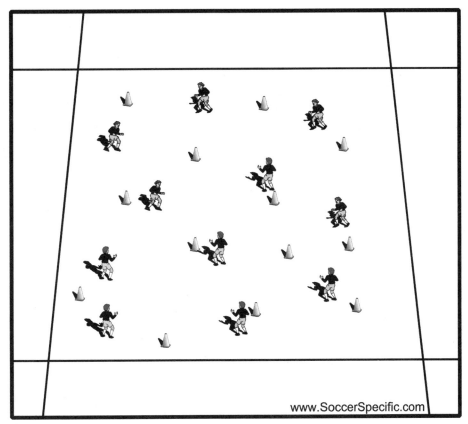

Diagram 12

1. Let it go free now. Players can move anywhere. This now involves them using anticipation, decision making, reaction and perception as well as co-ordination and fast feet to find space to move into without bumping into other players.
2. Peripheral vision development is starting to be introduced without the ball.
3. Coach commands can be "start" and "stop" so they are practicing acceleration, deceleration and lateral movement all in the one exercise.
4. You can also use the commands "turn", "jump" (for a header), "check", "sit down" and so on for which they have to do a short sprint after the command then stop on the call stop. All are movements specific to the game.

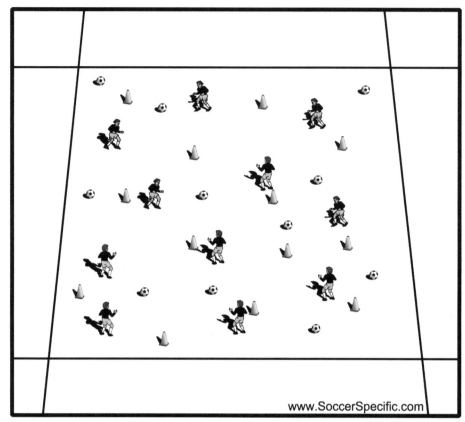

Diagram 13

1. Introduce balls and cones to the area.
2. Players jog in and out of them until the coach commands a sequence of events. Players have to sprint and touch the cones or balls with their hands. Once the sequence is completed they continue jogging.
3. Variations -
    a) Ball only once (as above)
    b) Cone only once
    c) Ball then cone once each
    d) Ball then cone then ball
    e) Ball then dribble it 2 yards and stop it then touch a cone
    f) Jump to head an imaginary ball then touch a cone
    g) Sit down then up and touch 2 balls
    And so on.

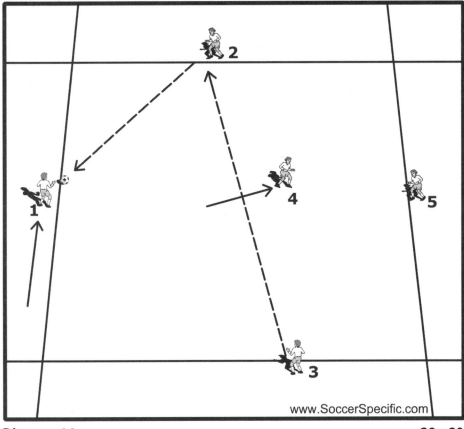

Diagram 14   **20 x 20**

1. Up to 5 players in a group with one of the players in the middle (could be three on the outside in a triangle for example). Outside players need to pass the ball to another player but at the same time try to hit the player in the middle with the ball below the knees.

2. This forces the middle player to move his feet quickly and be well balanced and mobile. It is just a fun warm up game for players to get them moving and focusing on fast feet and coordination.

3. (3) tries to hit (4) in the middle and (4) moves quickly out of the way. (2) moves on the outside also to get possession of the ball. (2) can try again to hit (4) or, as in this example, pass the ball to (1) for (1) to try, passing to (5) as a consequence of trying to hit (4).

4. The area can be as big or small as you like. Smaller means the player in the middle has less time to get out of the way. Maybe start at 10x10 yards then reduce it to 5x5 yards as the players get better at it.

5. Encourage players to pass quickly and accurately, making it hard work for the middle player. Rotate the players.

AN INTRODUCTION TO AWARENESS AND INDIVIDUAL TECHNICAL SKILLS TRAINING

It is vitally important that players develop their individual technical skills to a good level before they embark on learning the concepts of the AWARENESS COACHING METHOD.

When dribbling and turning and having lots of touches on the ball, players also need awareness of when and where to use these skills. One of the main problems players have when dribbling is their peripheral vision; what are they looking at? Often they are looking down at the ball as they dribble and do not see the possibilities around them beyond the dribble and often end up dribbling too much against too many players and ultimately lose the ball.

So the first awareness concepts we look to teach are those of dribbling with the ball and keeping the head up, looking away from the ball for the options the dribble has created.

THIS IS AWARENESS "ON THE BALL" WITH LOTS OF TOUCHES.

I have included and introduced in the book some simple ideas on dribbling skills, turning with the ball, receiving and turning with the ball, and running with the ball. While the awareness concept deals with quick thinking AHEAD of the ball and in many instances the right decision is a quick one or two touch play, there are many times when the right decision is to run with the ball, dribble with it or turn with it.

To be able to use all the tactical skills that go hand in hand with the Awareness Method of training, the players need to develop these individual skills also.

Hence, the first part of these session plans is designed to teach and help the players develop these individual skills. This is just a small introduction to technical skill training but it is designed to give you a flavor of what is required.

My main focus will ultimately be on Awareness Training with quick passing and movement using fewer touches on the ball, but these individual skill clinics serve as an introduction, with a few very basic ideas, to the Awareness Method of Coaching.

The Awareness Coaching Method is not trying to exclude the importance of being skilful in 1v1 confrontations, as it is incredibly important that players learn these skills, but it is trying to help players become great at all aspects of play and enabling them to learn to identify when and where it is appropriate to dribble and turn; when and where it is appropriate to pass, cross, turn, shoot and so on.

To reiterate: The following coaching clinic session plans cover the "main theme" we want to work on.

In addition to the main theme, each session should include the following:
1. The warm up
2. Coordination and Fast Footwork with and without the ball
3. A scrimmage to work on the ideas practiced in the theme (where you are able to)
4. The cool down
5. A discussion at the end on what they have learned from the overall clinic

COACHING CLINIC SESSION PLAN 2

(For age 6 years and older)

OBJECTIVE: IMPROVING TOUCH ON THE BALL

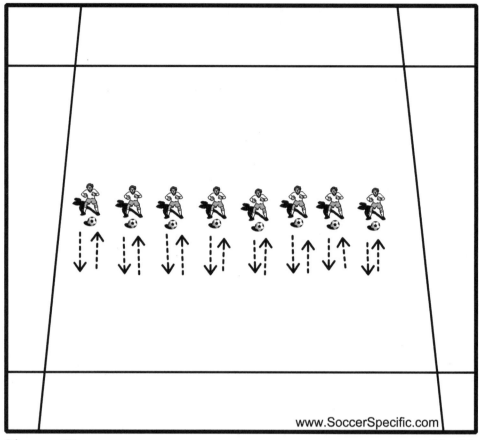

Diagram 15   **30 x 30**

1. Players are standing in the same position and have to use one foot to "pull" the ball back with the "sole" of the foot and "push" the ball forward with the "laces" of the same foot.
2. These are simple repetitions to repeat constantly to get a feel for the ball and to improve ball control, first touch and also co-ordination.
3. Younger players doing it for the first time need to do this at walking pace. Drag back with the sole, push forward with the laces. Then we do the same routine with the other foot.
4. Then focus on the foot without the ball. The players will be flat footed so they need to be bouncing on the other foot as they do the exercise. Demonstrate the difference between receiving a pass flat footed and on their toes and lively.
5. Now they need to do the movement with their heads up, looking around to develop awareness. Ask questions of the players as to why they need to do this.
6. Same idea but drag back with the sole and push forward with the side of the foot instead of the laces.

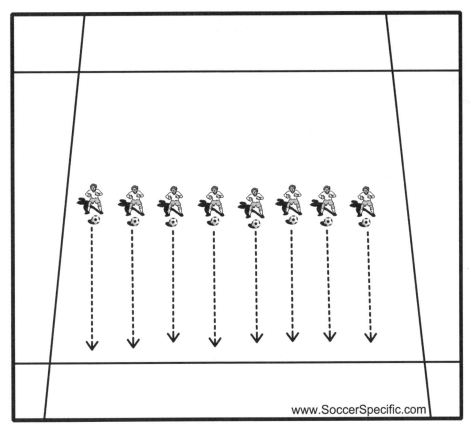

Diagram 16

1. **Coaching Points:**
   a) Good balance
   b) High Concentration on the technique
   c) On your toes, not flat footed
   d) Head Up while performing the task for Peripheral Awareness
2. Do it in a circle facing North, South, East and West on the call of the coach or have for example ten pulls with the sole and pushes with the laces at each direction. Quarter turns on each call going around in a circle.
3. **Competitive:** between the players to see who can do them the quickest but under total control and with correct technique.
4. On the coach's signal they now move up and down the field tapping the ball from foot to foot. After four taps they pull the ball back with the sole and push it out with the laces and move up field.
5. Once they get to the other end they turn back and repeat the exercise. This gives them lots of good touches on the ball to improve their control.
6. Progressions can be:
   a) Up and down the field with the right foot,
   b) Same with the left foot,
   c) Alternate feet up and down,
   d) Do the same routine but with the side of the foot instead of the laces.
7. Build some combinations into these routines, introducing turns and moves.

8. Move forward doing 20 push / pulls then do a step over turn and repeat with 20 back to where you started.
9. Do different turns with this routine so the players are getting lots of touches for control but also practice doing turns.
10. **Competitive:** Players must do four sets of 20 touches then three turns. Which player can do it the fastest and with good control?
11. Involve the awareness theme as they get good at this so they begin to look **AWAY FROM THE BALL** as they do the movements.
12. They must be able to do them correctly first before they attempt to look away from the ball at the same time.

INDIVIDUAL BALL SKILLS

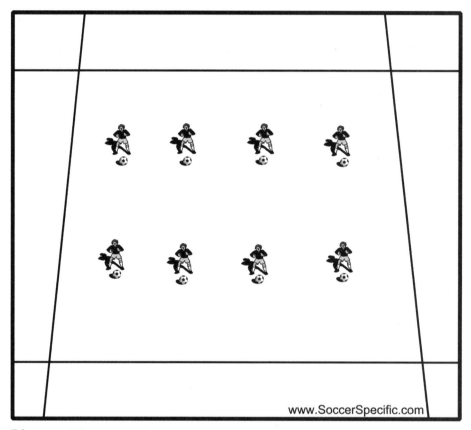

www.SoccerSpecific.com

Diagram 17

1. Using different techniques to control the ball.
   a) Simple juggling of the ball to improve foot control. How many times can they keep it up with **BOTH** feet? Make it a competition between the players.
   b) Using the inside and the outside of the feet and moving side to side. Move the ball with the inside of the foot then the outside to bring it back but with the same foot. Use a cutting motion.
   c) Inside and outside of the foot, roll the ball to the outside, cut it back with the inside and roll the ball to the inside and cut it back with the outside of the foot.
2. Moving a yard or so from side to side, maintaining control of the ball. This is great for acquiring a good touch on the ball and improving co-ordination.

3. Remind the players to keep their heads up. You can even walk around the area holding up a number of fingers and the players have to call the number out as they work.

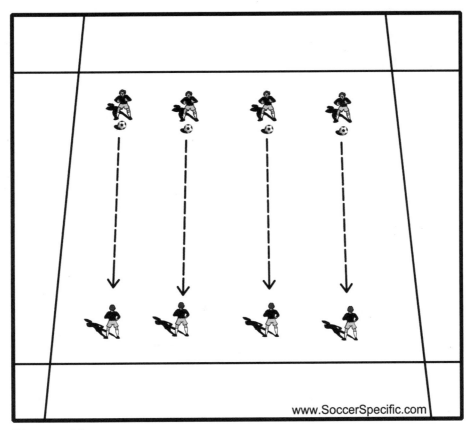

Diagram 18

1. Simple passing in two's back and forth. First two touches, then one touch where possible. Coach can dictate the distance between players.
2. Ask the players to look into "each others eyes" as they pass and NOT at the ball to see if they can keep possession.
3. This will be difficult at first but it helps to teach them to look up and not down at the ball during games, improving their "Awareness".
4. Players should be able to see their ball in the "peripheral vision".
5. Players should use both feet to pass the ball.
6. **Competitive:** Pairs try to make the most successful passes between them in a given time.

CONTROLLING TECHNIQUES IN TWO'S

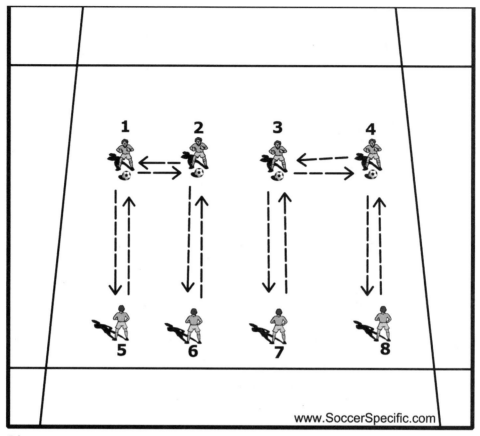

Diagram 19

1. Working in pairs. Once the task has been performed, the end players switch with each other. For example, (1) and (2) switch.
2. Servers stay in the same position and do 10 each then change.
3. **Techniques to practice:**
   a) Throw to feet to control with one touch and pass back (right and left)
   b) Throw to chest to chest down and pass back one touch on the half volley
   c) Throw to thigh to control and pass back one touch on the half volley
   d) Throw to head to head straight back (defensive or attacking headers)
   e) Throw to head to cushion down and pass back on the half volley one touch
   f) Throw to both feet alternatively so they have to control and pass with both feet.
   g) Throw and control with various parts of the body and volley the ball back.
   h) Combinations: chest, thigh, then pass one touch on the half volley.
   i) Throw to the ground, one bounce to the player who half volleys it back on the next bounce into their teammate's hands, softly and under control.
4. Use your imagination to practice other techniques, vary the distances between the players and so on.

COACHING CLINIC SESSION 3
(For age 6 years and older)
OBJECTIVE: IMPROVING BASIC DRIBBLING AND AWARENESS IN POSSESSION OF THE BALL

Warm up with some awareness work.

Principles of Dribbling:
1. Initial Movement: In a straight line at a slower speed.
2. Deception: Unbalance the opponent.
3. Accelerate: Into space using change of pace
4. Space behind opponent: pass the ball past defender and run.
5. Restricted space behind: dribble past defender (in slow, out quick).

Coaching Points:
a) Tight, close control.
b) Skill to use body to dummy and feint.
c) Skill in changing direction and pace.
d) A positive attitude.
e) Use of own or established dribbling techniques.
f) Looking around with your head up to have an awareness of where the other players are and where the immediate space is to move into.
g) This is more looking for yourself and when you are ON the ball.

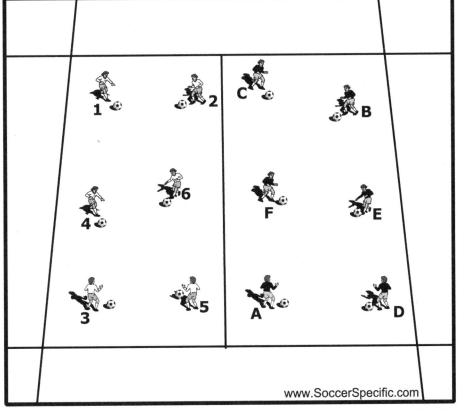

www.SoccerSpecific.com

Diagram 20   **30 x 30**

A way to test if they are really looking around and behind is to ask them to stop, and then ask them, without them looking again, who is immediately behind them. If they were looking they will know.

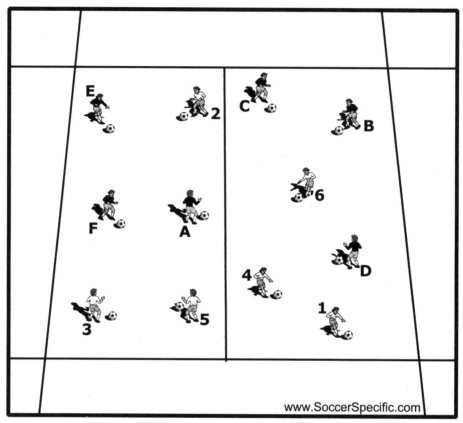

Diagram 21

1. **Coaching Points:**
   a) Awareness of where other players are while maintaining possession of the ball, ensuring players are looking around, away from their own ball.
   b) Dribbling and Turning
   c) Shielding
   d) Anaerobic Fitness work.
2. Moving around with the ball, staying in space with your own team to begin then mixing in with each other. Stop and check positions. Check how spread out players are. Discuss the implications of being in possession of the ball in a game and making it hard for the opposition to mark you by using as much width and length as possible. Therefore the players must use the spaces as effectively as possible.
3. Continue with dribbling and turning but emphasize keeping the head up, looking around, in front, and side to side and behind (for younger players equate it to a bird on a fence just looking around). The players can see the ball in their peripheral vision without looking at it directly.
4. Emphasize awareness of where other players are who are working in the same area by looking around; in front, to the side, and behind. Set the rule that when a player meets another player he must move to get away from that player as if he is beating a defender in a game situation.

5. Each player dribbling and turning in a tight area avoiding other players. Coach can dictate techniques practiced. Work on improving ball control with quickening movement.

6. Keep emphasizing looking away from the ball and not down at it so they get an awareness of player positions and where space is to play in. This is the basic beginning of awareness training.

7. Have players running INTO traffic, testing their ability to control the ball and observe others in the same spaces, again increasing the awareness concept.

8. **Commands:**

   a) Turn (checking that no one is behind them first of all with a look over the shoulder then a turn if the space behind is free) Doing different turns they are good at.

   b) Out (they run outside the nearest line and check back in, always looking over the shoulder to see where other players are so they do not run into them).

   c) Switch (changing balls and continuing dribbling)

   d) Dribble (using a dribbling skill they are good at in a tight area)

   e) Right foot only (inside and out) This is more difficult so they will tend to look at the ball, but remind them to look up when and where they can.

   f) Left foot only (as above)

   g) Quick (change pace and move more quickly for a few seconds but with the ball under control)

   h) Number (coach will hold his hand up with a number of fingers indicated, the players have to shout the number immediately by looking up and observing but also keeping control of the ball).

9. Finish with small sided games focusing on individual dribbling skills and a cool down.

COACHING CLINIC SESSION 4

(For age 6 years and older)

OBJECTIVE: DEVELOPING AWARENESS IN POSSESSION OF THE BALL WITH LOTS OF TOUCHES THROUGH A FUN KICK OUT GAME WITH A BALL EACH

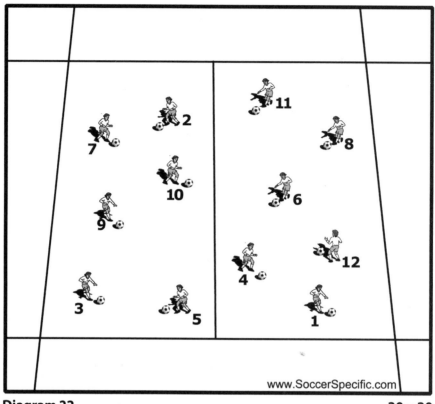

Diagram 22   **30 x 30**

Warm up with some awareness work.

1. Each of the 12 players has a ball to play with. They must protect their own ball but at the same time try to kick someone else's ball out the area. When your ball is kicked out you cannot kick anyone else's ball out. You can vary the game by allowing set number of chances before they are ultimately out of the game. When they are out have them juggle the ball to keep practicing skills.
2. Play until the last player is left with his own ball. This player is the winner.
3. A variation can be to have three areas of play. Players start in one area and if they are kicked out they go to the next and so on. This way you can have two winners in each group with an overall winner at the end. Another variation is to simply decrease the area to make it harder as there is less space to work in.
4. **Coaching Points:**
    a) Awareness of where other players are while maintaining possession of the ball, ensuring players are looking around, away from their own ball
    b) Dribbling and Turning,
    c) Shielding,
    d) Tackling,
    e) Anaerobic Fitness work.

KICK OUT GAME WORKING ON AWARENESS

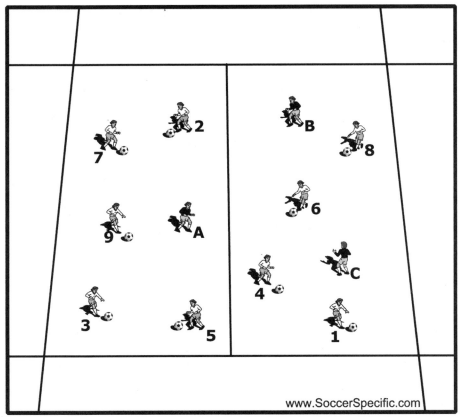

Diagram 23

1. There are 12 players in this exercise, 9 with a ball, 3 without. The 3 players without a ball try to win a ball off a player with a ball and kick it out the area. If a player has his ball kicked out he joins in with the other players, helping them keep possession through passing and support play.
2. To make this competitive, rotate the players so different groups of 3 work together and time each group to see who finishes in the quickest time.
3. **Progression:** Instead of simply kicking the balls out of the area, the defenders, after winning the ball, must try to pass it to the coach (who is constantly moving around outside the area). This represents winning the ball and keeping possession in a game rather than kicking it out of play and losing possession.
4. The session develops from an individual 1v1 attacking / defending workout to a passing and support situation. You can work on the defenders by encouraging them to work as a team, maybe in 2's for instance to have a better chance of winning the ball. The defenders can pass the ball around until one can find the coach with a pass. Attackers during this time can try to win it back before it goes out of the area and keep possession.

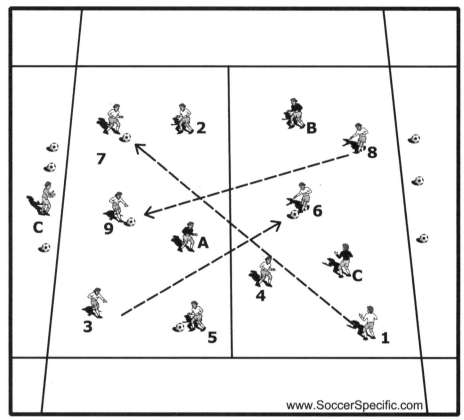

Diagram 24

1. This is showing the progression of the session where the defenders have won 6 balls and passed 3 to the coach, thus maintaining possession if it were likened to a game.
2. Coaches can move around so the players have to look to find his position to pass to him. Attacking players who have possession of the ball can also use the coach to play wall passes, so the coach is a target for the attacking players and the defending players.
3. **Coaching Points:**
   Attackers with the ball –
   a) Dribbling and turning practice,
   b) Shielding the ball,
   c) Moving and support play,
   d) Quality of passing, players keep possession by passing between each other once one or more lose their ball.
   e) Awareness of positions of both sets of players and where the spaces are.
   Defenders without the ball –
   a) Practicing defensive pressurizing skills,
   b) Teamwork (in 2's or more) to win the ball using supporting defensive skills –
      Angle / Distance / Communication,
   c) Maintaining possession after winning the ball,
   d) Awareness of the open player (the coach or a teammate to get it to the coach),
   e) Quality of the pass once they win the ball.
4. This game is fun and competitive for the players but it also provides a situation where they are learning important skills.

5. **Progression One:** Every ball won by a defender must be passed to the coach. This presents a bigger challenge and teaches the importance of not just dispossessing the opponent, but also maintaining possession after winning it. If the defending player passes the ball to the coach and it is not accurate and does not get to the coach's feet then the attacker who had the ball gets it back to continue in possession. This ensures quality of passing from the defender who has won back the ball in the first place.

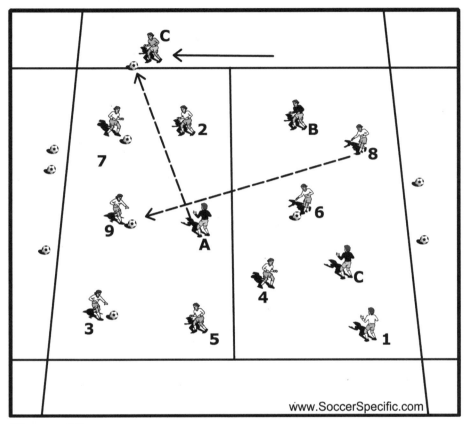

Diagram 25

6. **Progression Two:** Make it a two team game: one defends, one attacks. Time each team as to how long it takes for them to win possession of each ball and make a successful pass to the coach. The clock stops when all 6 balls have been passed successfully to the coach.
7. Now defenders need to have awareness too. When they win the ball they need to know quickly where the coach is to pass the ball. So, while they are defending trying to win the ball they are also watching the coach in their peripheral vision to see where he is.
8. Finish with small sided games and a cool down.

COACHING CLINIC SESSION 5

(For age 6 years and older)

OBJECTIVE: IMPROVING AWARENESS IN POSSESSION OF THE BALL AND DEVELOPING DRIBBLING SKILLS AT THE SAME TIME

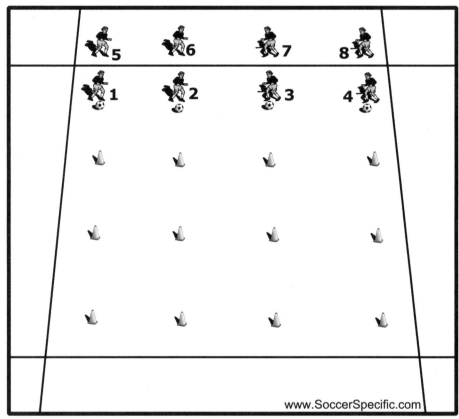

Diagram 26   **30 x 30**

Warm up with some awareness work

1. Players dribble in and out of the cones to the end, turn, then dribble back to the beginning and give the ball to the next player. They should dribble in various ways: inside and outside of the same foot, or inside and inside of both feet.
2. Variations can be dribbling to the end then passing back, dribbling to the end then running straight back with the ball, dribbling one way only and having players at each end to take the ball back.
3. Start with a non competitive situation with players just dribbling through the cones to get practice with no pressure. Ask them to LOOK AROUND when they dribble and not down at the ball.
4. **Going Competitive:** Have a race between groups after players get the feel for the drill. Lots of touches on the ball and dribbling practice under pressure here.
5. Include various ways to do this: dribbling through all the cones and back, or dribbling through the cones to the third one, then back through them to the start then back through them all again (so it includes more turns). You can mix it up in any way, but be sure to include looking around and behind before they turn as examples of awareness.

6. **Coaching Points:**
   a) Dribbling skills with the ball at pace
   b) Practicing various techniques as determined by the coach (inside of the foot, outside of the foot and so on)
   c) Ensure the players get the balance between going quickly but keeping good control of the ball
   d) Awareness principles practiced by always looking around as they dribble and before they turn.

WORKING ON SPECIFIC DRIBBLING MOVES: THE TECHNICAL DEVELOPMENT OF DRIBBLING – THE MATTHEWS, RIVELINO, DOUBLE TOUCH AND THE SCISSORS

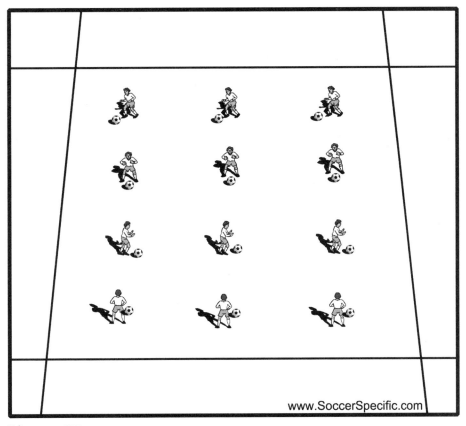

www.SoccerSpecific.com

Diagram 27

1. You can use any moves that you like, but I have included some here as examples. When players receive the ball and are aware in advance that there is no option to pass and they may need to dribble to get out of trouble or to beat a player to get a shot at goal, then we need players who have the ability to do so. This is again building up to the awareness concept being part of the player's makeup. We are trying to teach the players some basic dribbles and tricks on the ball that they can use once they have determined that the best option is to dribble with the ball.

2. **Coaching Points:**
   a) Technical dribbling skills but focusing on one at a time to master it. The skill is broken down in phases for ease of teaching.
   b) Non competitive dribbling initially so players are able to relax when practicing
   c) **Observation:** Constant reminders to look around and not just down at the ball (awareness in possession of the ball).
3. The above set up is an example of the progressive movement of one group of players. You can have 4 groups set up this way.
4. Practicing a dribble from bottom to top. This is the routine of working around the ball four times on the call of the coach, each time facing another 45 degrees around the ball. Do the moves then stop and wait for the next call. All players work in unison.
5. This is the total movement of one line of players but work with two lines opposite each other.
6. Move around the ball both ways so players work on both sides with both feet. You get four dribbles / moves per rotation. Do it slowly to begin, break down the technique. If you are not competent to do the technique/trick then have a player demonstrate it for you.

Diagram 28

1. On the coach's command the players do a Matthews, Rivelino or Scissors to the left. They then stand still until the next command, then do it to the right and so on. Doing it slowly gives the players a chance to work on and perfect the move. As they get competent the coach can get them to speed up the movement, working up and down the field, right to left and left to right. This ensures they do it with both feet.

2. **The Matthews** – Big toe/little toe technique. Lean one way, and check to the other. Bring the foot behind the ball to move it (for example, plant the left foot outside the ball to the left and bring the right inside the ball and move it away to the right with the right foot).
   The Rivelino – Fake to kick the ball, step over the ball outside to inside then move the ball to the outside with the same foot (for example step over the ball with the right foot from right to left then take the ball away to the right with the right foot and accelerate away).
   The Scissors – Step over the ball inside to outside then move the ball away with the other foot (for example, right foot inside to outside then move the ball to the left with the left foot).
3. You can also just fake them out with this by pretending to touch it the first time then touching it forward after the fake.
4. Emphasize body position with this move. Players need to have their bodies facing to the side they are pretending to move the ball.
5. All techniques look to fake the opponent one way then move the ball the other way. On each dribble the player must drop his shoulder one way to move the other way.

THE DOUBLE TOUCH

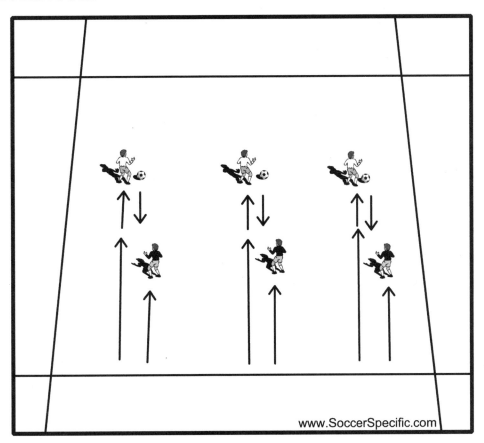

Diagram 29

Double Touch - Running forward, bring the ball back with one touch then pass it forward to yourself with the second touch, all the time keeping it in control at your feet. The first touch back is to fake out the defender who is running alongside you, so he thinks you are stopping the ball or changing direction and he'll check his forward run to react to this, but you continue to run forward by making the second touch forward and get away from him.

DRIBBLING AND FEINTING
Developing dribbling and turning in different directions and at different angles

DIAGONALS   DIAGONAL / SQUARE / FORWARD

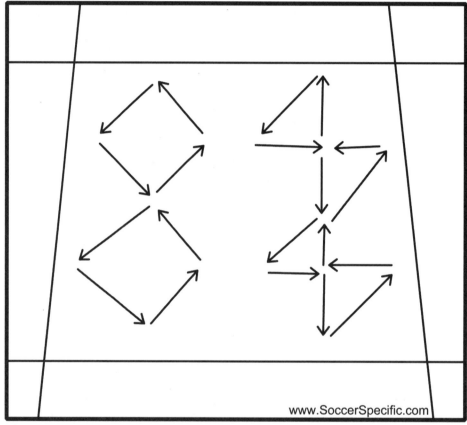

Diagram 30   **30 x 30**

1. The circuits are designed to make sure the players use both feet.
   At each cone they have to "cut" the ball back in the new direction. Talk about defenders and cutting away from them to attack at various angles.
2. Players meet in the middle so they must have their heads up to see where others are positioned.

You can use these circuits for sprinting purposes also without the ball. Use two start positions for continuous movement. Doubling the circuit means four start positions can be used. Players play at their own pace until they are comfortable with each technique. Pace is good but control is paramount. Lots of touches between the feet as you go, toe tapping the ball. Turning angles are different.

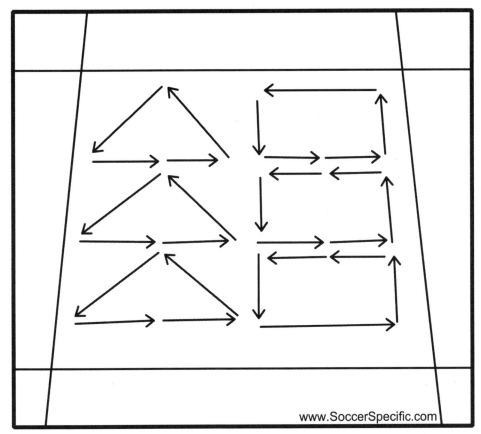

Diagram 31

Forward / backward movement intensity for when an opponent attacks from the side.

1. Types of Movement
    a) Using the inside of the foot only (with both feet).
    b) Using outside of the foot only (with both feet).
    c) Using the inside and outside of the foot on either side (one foot only).
    d) Step over / outside take (Scissors).
    e) Dummy step – foot beyond the ball then take it the opposite direction with the outside of the other foot (Matthews).
    f) Do a full turn away from pressure using the outside and the inside of the foot (Twist off)
    g) Drag back and turn – the ball moves behind the other foot.

COACHING CLINIC SESSION PLAN 6

(For age 7 years and older)
OBJECTIVE: IMPROVING DRIBBLING SKILLS: INITIALLY THROUGH PASSIVE NON – COMPETITIVE DRIBBLING PRACTICES

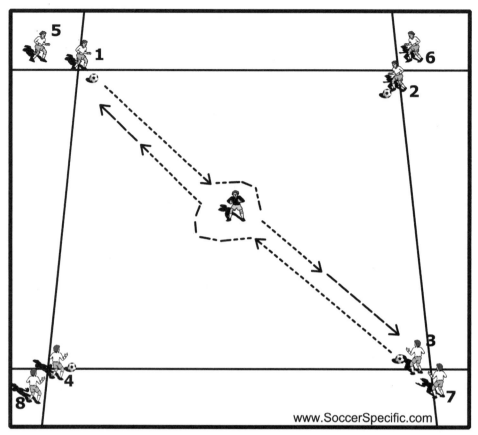

Diagram 32　　　　　　　　　　　　　　　　　　　　　　**30 x 30**

Warm up with some awareness dribbling work. Use the techniques practiced previously to improve them.

1. Alternatively have a cone in the middle, have two diagonally opposite players go at the same time, and they always have to go right on their dribble or left on their dribble so they go the opposite way and do not run into the other player. This is a good no pressure set up to begin.
2. Move from no pressure to passive pressure from the coach.
3. (1) starts slightly ahead of (3) and dribbles at the coach who offers passive pressure. Coach turns and offers the same to player (3) coming the diagonally opposite way.
3. Player (2) then starts to dribble at the coach followed by player (4).
4. Continuous circuit from these players, you may have 8 players doing this.
5. Players must perform a dribbling movement to beat the coach and go to the other side and start again.
6. This produces lots of opportunities to perform practiced dribbling skills, (already performed with success under no pressure) under passive pressure, getting ready to go to a session providing full pressure.

7. **Develop:** Players run with the ball from 4 sides at the same time, running through each other in the middle.
8. This is great Awareness training as the emphasis is of course on good ball control, but also knowing where the other players are in and around your space. Players must keep their heads up and observe players, space and also the ball.

DRIBBLING / RUNNING WITH THE BALL IN TWO'S

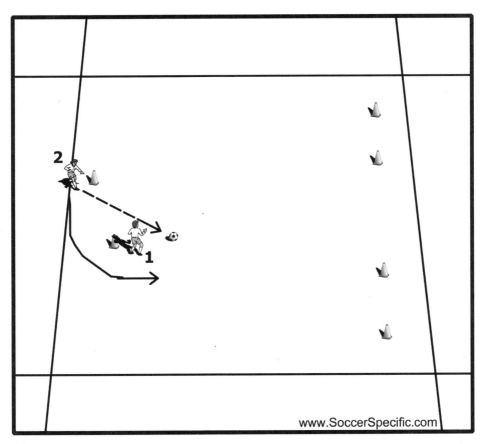

Diagram 33

1. This is a very simple exercise but it gets players running and dribbling with the ball with a little bit of pressure added.
2. Defender (2) passes to attacker (1) then does an overlap run around (1) and chases him down to try to beat him to the other side of the grid area. Attacker (1) has two goals to choose from to score in by running the ball through them under total control.
3. The defender (2) should not try to tackle or win the ball, just pressure the attacking player (1) by his presence. The defender (2)'s goal is to get to the line first through one of the goals to be the winner. Move into competitive defending when you think the time is right for your players.
4. Have several groups of four doing this, so as one pair works the other pair rests. Rotate the players so both get the chance to attack and defend. Have each player count the number of times he wins.

5. **Coaching Points:**
   a) Observation / Awareness: Playing with their heads up (awareness of options in possession of the ball)
   b) **Decision:** Which goal to attack
   c) Good first touch out of the feet to get into their stride pattern
   d) Running with the ball and dribbling technique quality

PASSING SEQUENCES IN THREES WITH AN OVERLAP AGAINST A DEFENDER

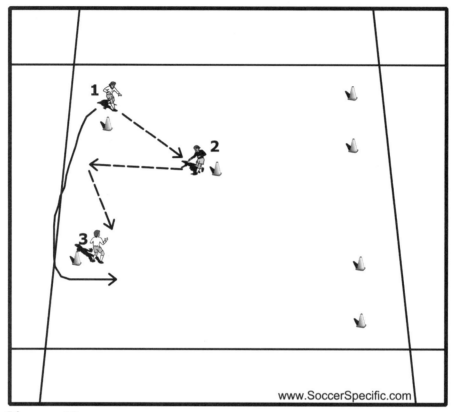

www.SoccerSpecific.com

Diagram 34

1. A 2v1 situation attacking the goal. Rotate the players to make this work so everyone has a chance to do all positions.
2. Attacker (1) passes to defender (2), plays a wall pass with him, all one touch passing, then plays a one touch pass to the other attacker (3) and makes an overlap run, creating a 2v1 situation. Defender (2) tries to stop them scoring.
3. If there is no keeper then use the cones to show small areas in the two corners of a goal so they have to shoot for the corners to score. If you want to have them work in fours then have a keeper also.
4. **Coaching Points:**
   a) Observation / Awareness: Play with heads up
   b) Quality one touch passing (weight, accuracy, timing)
   c) Angle and timing of overlap run to receive or act as a decoy
   d) Dribbling technique: Run straight at the defender
   e) Decision: Do I beat the player 1 v 1 or use the overload and play the overlapping player in?
   f) Quality of shot.

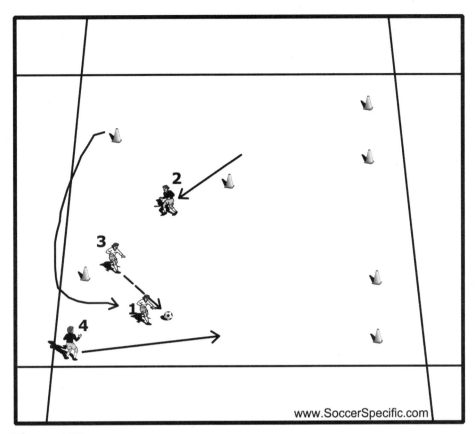

Diagram 35

1. Here we have the resulting 2v1 after (1) has made the overlap run around (3).
2. Encourage (3) to run directly at defender (2) to commit him to help create the 2v1 advantage. If (3) runs to either side at an angle away from the goal and away from the defender then the defender can hold both players up by staying between them and the advantage is less or even lost.
3. Rotate the players through the three positions.
4. **Progression:** Introduce a recovering defender (4) who can move when the attacker (3) first touches the ball. Player on the ball must have an awareness of where the defender is coming from.
5. The next progression would be to bring in another defender facing the two attackers so it is a genuine 2v2.

COACHING CLINIC SESSION PLAN 7

(For age 7 years and older)

OBJECTIVE: IMPROVING DRIBBLING SKILLS THROUGH SEMI COMPETITIVE DRIBBLING PRACTICES LEADING TO COMPETITIVE SITUATIONS

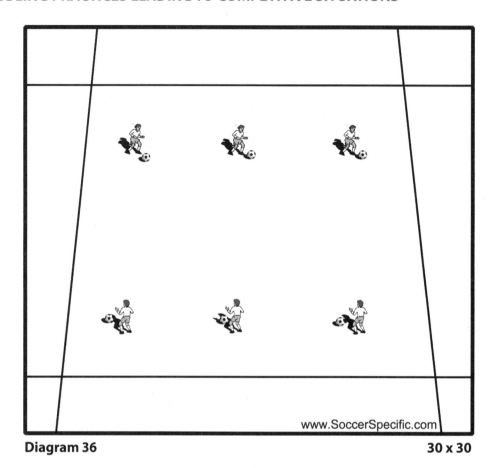

www.SoccerSpecific.com

Diagram 36   **30 x 30**

Warm up with some awareness dribbling work.

Progression –

1. SEMI COMPETITIVE: Have each group stand opposite one another 10 to 20 yards apart with a ball each. They must move towards each other on a call (everyone in unison) and always to the same side as they get close to each other. Do it slowly to begin and build up the pace as they become competent.

2. Have them get the timing right where they get about a stride apart, just out of tackling distance but close enough to commit a defender in a game.

3. Once they get past each other they stop and turn and go again on the next call. Do several repetitions with this to have them practice in this semi-passive way.

4. This is a good way to get many players working on the same skill in a small area with lots of work on the ball. Focus on one skill at a time and spend time on it to keep improving the technique of each player.

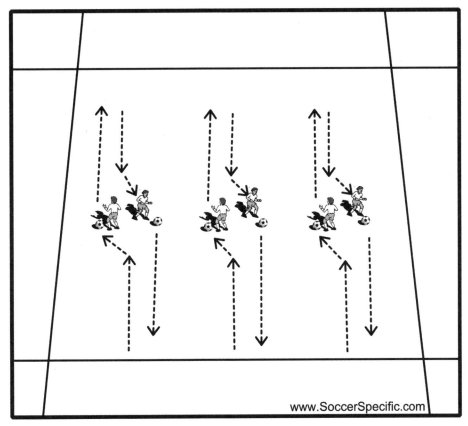

Diagram 37

1. Groups play in 1v1 situations as above moving up and down the area practicing their moves.
2. Moves to work on here are:
   a) The Matthews
   b) The Rivelino
   c) The Scissors
3. Practicing only three dribbles with the limited time we have gives each player a better chance to improve. It is better to get good at a few skills than to practice many different ones and be good at none of them. I believe having up to three dribbles is enough for each player to use if they get very good at them.

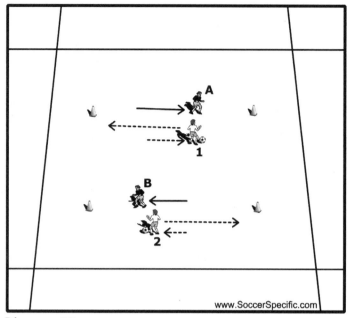

Diagram 38

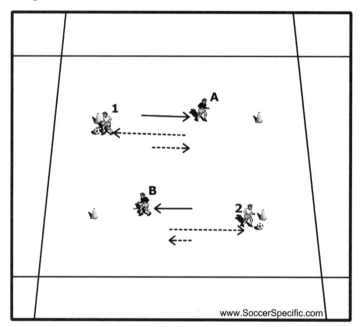

Diagram 39

1. Attacker (1) tries to fake out defender (A) by checking side to side. The game is not live until the attacker touches the ball.
2. Defender (A) has to stay behind an imaginary line between the cones and move off the movement of the attacker (1). The defender wins this confrontation by being first to the cone that the attacker is running to.
3. Attacker tries to get there first with the ball to win.
4. Lots of opportunity for the players to practice moves here and it helps develop their upper body movement to fake defenders out.
5. Players take turns to start with the ball as the attacker.

6. **Competitive:** If you have several pairs doing this, have the winners and the losers of each pair play each other.
7. Progression: Players have a ball each and either player can start the movement, throwing fakes until one touch on the ball and then it starts.
8. **Coaching Points:**
   a) Using the upper body to throw a feint
   b) Off-balancing the opponent
   c) Good first touch on the ball when moving it one way
   d) Pace with the ball to beat the opponent to the cone
   e) Good control of the ball at the end to win the race (tests the players' ability to stop quickly and keep possession of the ball)

1v1 ATTACKING PLAY SITUATIONS

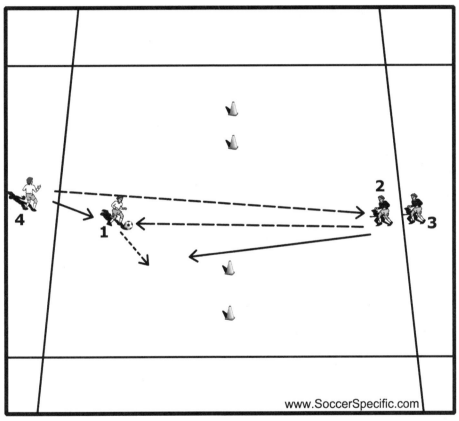

Diagram 40

1. 1v1 situations. Attacker (1) passes to defender (2) who passes back and the play begins (both one touch passes if possible).
2. As soon as the passes have been exchanged, defender (2) closes down attacker (1) quickly and play begins.
3. Two goals to attack and score through: one in front, one in behind.
4. Make it passive defense to begin to get some success. Attacking players need to dribble when they attack the first goal and dribble and turn back on the second goal to score through it.
5. Rotate the players so everyone gets the chance to attack and defend.

6. Players move forward to meet the ball so they are in motion right away.
7. **Coaching Points:**
    a) Observation / Awareness: Play with heads up
    b) Attack the space quickly
    c) Dribbling and turning techniques practiced
    d) Quality of Shot to score.

COACHING CLINIC SESSION PLAN 8
(For age 7 years and older)
OBJECTIVE: DEVELOPING COMPETITIVE 1 v 1, 2 v 2, 3 v 3 ATTACKING PLAY AND PERIPHERAL VISION

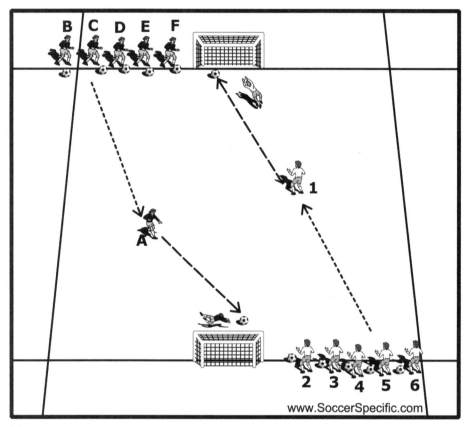

Diagram 41   **30 x 30**

1. Players run with the ball from both sides and shoot at goal.
2. When one has finished the next one goes.
3. Continuous shooting clinic.
4. **Develop:** Have the shooter receive a pass from a teammate behind, turn and shoot. The passer then goes onto the field and becomes the receiver.
5. **Coaching Points:**
    a) Quick attack
    b) Quality finishing
    c) Instant transition from attacking to defending

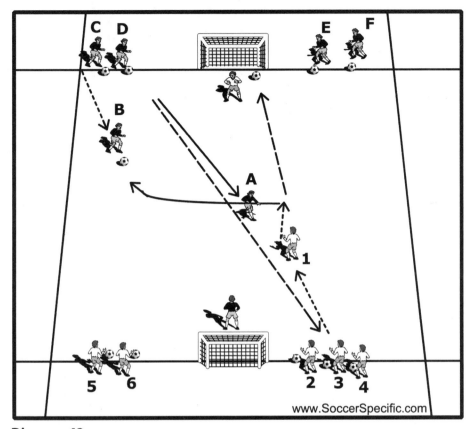

Diagram 42

1. (A) passes to (1) and (1) has to score as quickly as possible.
2. (1) then becomes the defender for the next attack from another lettered player. (B) now attacks (1) and tries to score.
3. Players will forget to defend, so it is 5 push ups when they forget.
4. Keep the score of the game to keep it competitive.

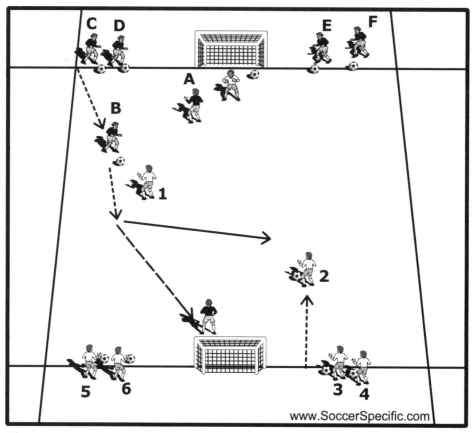

Diagram 43

1. (B) has the choice of shooting early from distance before defender (1) can close him down or dribbling around (1) and shooting at goal as above.
2. As soon as the 1v1 is over, (2) makes a run to attack and tries to score quickly. (B) must recover back quickly to try to stop him.
3. Keep the tempo up and encourage the players to attack with pace and a positive attitude to get a shot in on goal.
4. **Develop:** we have 2v1's; 2v2's and 3v3's and so on. As the numbers increase the emphasis is still on taking players on 1v1 but also to have the peripheral vision and awareness to see where teammates and opponents are at the same time.

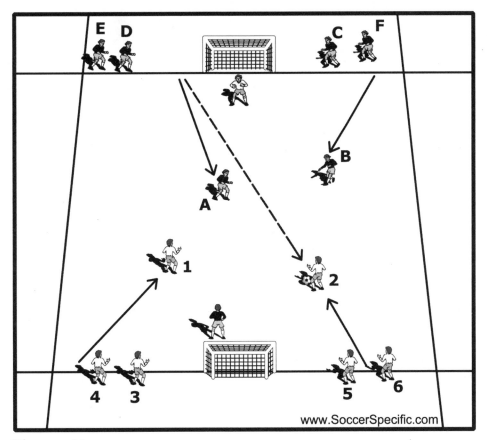

Diagram 44

QUICK TRANSITION 2v2 GAME

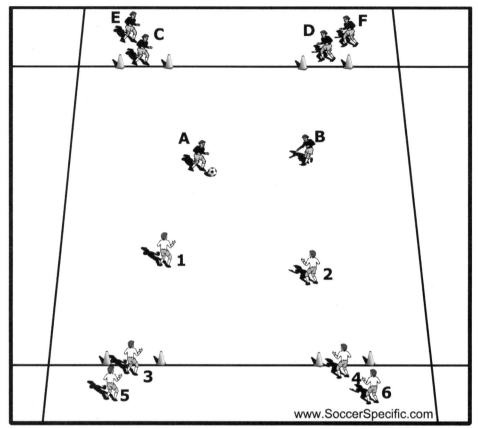

Diagram 45

1. A 2v2 game going to 4 goals. The team who scores stays on and must quickly defend the 2 new players coming in (one from each goal that the opposition defends).
2. Instant transition with the same ball that the opponents scored with. Here (3) and (4) are positioned to immediately bring the ball out to attack in transition. The other two players (1) and (2) must get off the field ASAP.
3. The first thought of the player on the ball has to be "Can I score?"
4. The first thought of the 1st defender is "Can I stop him from scoring, win possession immediately, and score myself?".
5. First team to 10 goals wins, keeping the competitive element.
6. If the ball goes out of play the coach can provide another one to keep things moving.

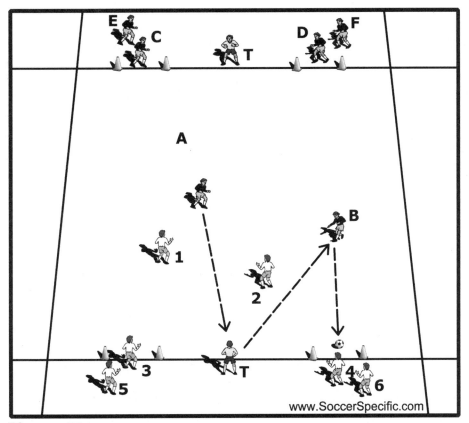

Diagram 46

1. Introduce a target player (can be a coach or a player). Now it can be a 3v2 effectively. Players can use the target to play give and goes with each other or with their immediate teammates.
2. Here B scores and (4) stops the ball and brings it out to form a new attack with (3). (1) and (2) get off the field quickly. (4)'s first thought as the ball is traveling to him is "where are the opponents weakest, where are we strongest?" This will dictate which direction the first touch of the ball is taken. Look to create give and go situations.
3. (A) and (B) stay on and defend, trying to win the ball back and score again.
4. Can be played as a 3v3 depending on numbers and using three goals each side.
5. Liken passing into the goal to a midfielder passing into a striker so they get the ball in there as quickly as possible.
6. Players must get between opponents and open up passing lanes into the goal.
7. This works on the fast break offensively and quick pressing defensively after scoring (liken to regaining possession in the attacking third).
8. Also with the wide goals we are looking to change the play and switch direction, which fits in with the theme of changing direction with the first touch.

Coaching Points - Attacking:
a) Fast Break and counter attack
b) Switching the point of attack if another goal is more open
c) Quick one and two touch passing
d) Positioning to open up passing lanes and getting between defenders to pass the ball in early
e) Creating 2v1 situations from a 2v2 set up and setting up a give and go.

Coaching Points - Defending:
a) Instant pressure as possession changes (transition after scoring from attacker to defender)
b) Regaining possession at the front with a scoring reward
c) Getting in front of the passing lanes to prevent the quick pass into the goal.
d) Working together with pressure and support. The support player supports the first defender, steps across to cover the passing lane to the second goal and also keeps an eye on the 2nd attacker.

Transition Coaching Point:
a) The team that has been in possession of the ball and has scored must immediately switch on mentally to being defenders and high pressuring the new attacking team to try to win the ball back and score again.

Develop:
1. Allow back passes to the players in their own goal so they can support the two (or three) attacking players on the ball.
2. Allow them only one touch so they have to make a quick decision and players receiving all need to get open to help them.
3. Vary the number of touches on the ball depending on the age and level of the players.

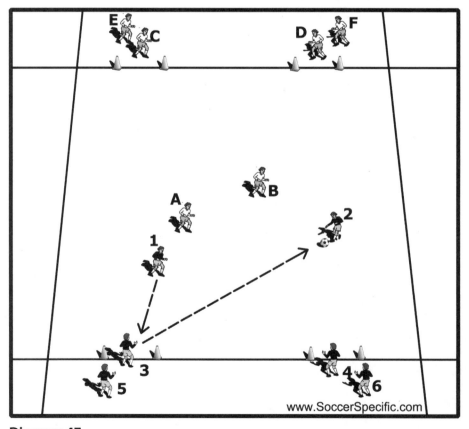

Diagram 47

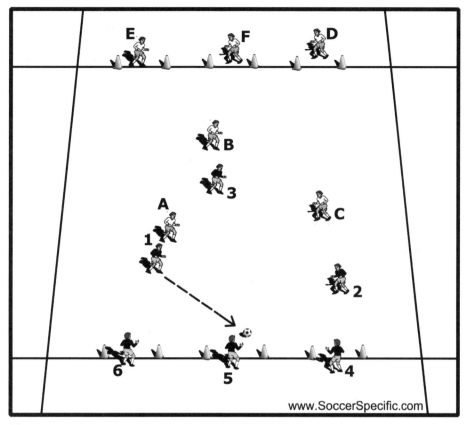

Diagram 48

Do the same set up but with three goals either side of the field and 3v3 games.
This offers more passing options and starts to get the players thinking about triangular support or diamond support if the ball is with a supporting player off the field.

COACHING CLINIC SESSION PLAN 9

(For age 7 years and older)
OBJECTIVE: IMPROVING ATTACKING 1 v 1 AND 2 v 2 CONFRONTATIONS

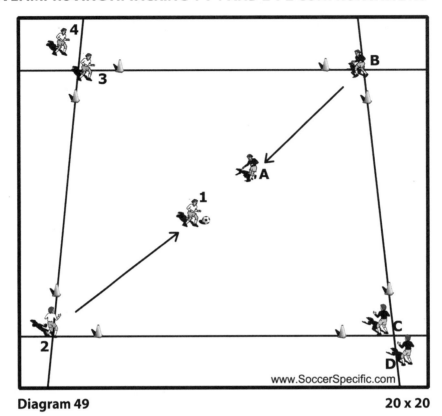

Diagram 49   **20 x 20**

Warm up with some awareness dribbling work.

1. Attacker (1) passes the ball to the defender (A) and gets a pass back and play begins. Do one pair at a time to begin.
2. Attacker (1) tries to score through defender (A)'s goal. If the defender wins it he has to try to score through the attacker's goal (reward for winning the ball). All players get the chance to attack in a 1v1.
3. Encourage the players to use dribbles, turns and tricks they have learned.
4. **Progression:** Have two pairs going at the same time so they need to be aware of the positions of the other pair playing in the same area. This develops awareness of their surroundings in regards to player positions and space availability.
5. This is now an intensive session with players working once and resting once at a ratio of 1:1.
6. Correct the faults! Step in and demonstrate to show the players what to do if required. Demonstration is better than explanation.
7. **Coaching Points:**
    a) Good control and first touch to set up the attack
    b) Running in a straight line at the defender so you can go either way
    c) Running at pace with the ball
    d) Using tricks and dribbles to beat the opponent
    e) Beating the opponent and scoring a goal
    f) For the defenders: Winning possession and scoring a goal.

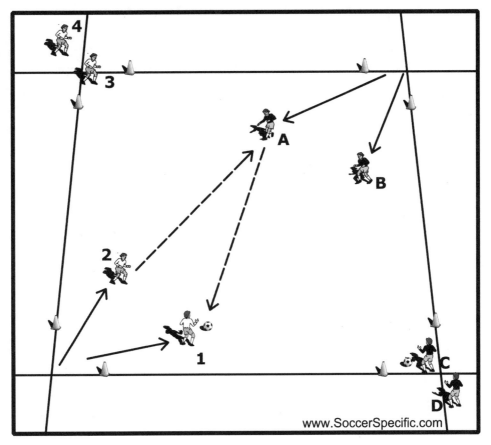

Diagram 50

1. Attacker (2) passes the ball to defender (A) who passes to attacker (1) and play begins.
2. Combination plays should be tried here; wall passes, takeovers, overlaps and so on.
3. **Coaching Point:**
   a) As above for the 1v1 situations but including combination plays, give and go's, takeovers, overlaps and pass or decoy and so on.
4. **Progression:** Two games of 2v2 in the same area developing awareness of player positions and space availability, getting players to look up.

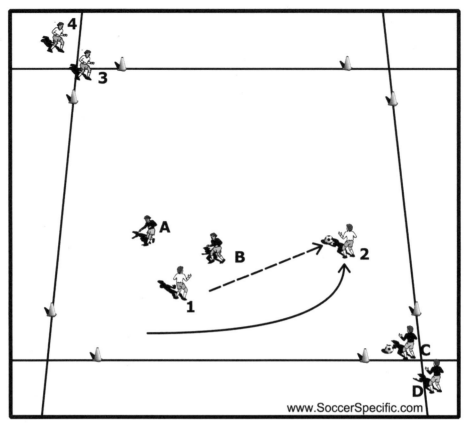

Diagram 51

1. Attackers (1) and (2) perform an overlap move. (2) passes to (1) then makes the overlap run to receive the pass back.
2. They are trying to isolate defender (B) and create a 2 v 1 in their favor, at the same time getting away from defender (A).
   If player (A) tracks player (2), player (1) can use the overlap as a decoy and attack player (B) in a 1v1 situation.
3. **Coaching Points in an Overlap:**
   a) Create Space – Receiver brings the ball inside to create space outside for the overlapping player, particularly in a wide area of the field.
   b) Communication – Overlapping player calls "HOLD".
   c) Timing of the run – When the receiving player is faced forward.
   d) Angle of the run – Wide, away from the defender.
   e) Timing of the pass – Into the path in front of the overlapping player with correct weight so the overlapping player does not have to break stride.
   f) Decoy or pass – Instead of passing, use the run to take a defender away from the space inside and come inside with the ball.

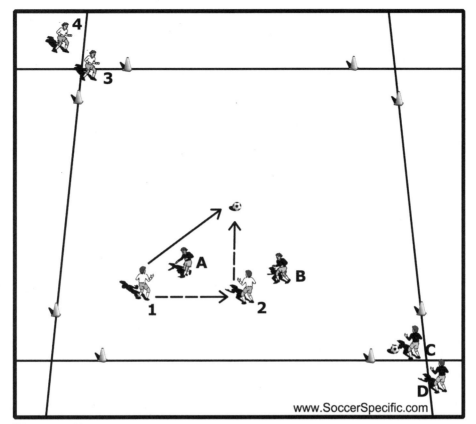

Diagram 52

1. Creating and executing a wall pass in a 2v2 attacking situation.
2. Here attacker (1) draws defender (A) close to create space behind. Attacker (2) supports at an angle to offer the chance of a pass and makes a one touch wall pass in behind (A). (1) makes the overlap run around (A) at pace.
3. (2) must make the pass before (B) has a chance to intercept it.
4. **Coaching Points of a Wall Pass:**
   a) Run straight at the defender
   b) Use outside of the front foot to pass for deception
   c) Quality of the pass (especially the timing, not too far away so a defender could drop off and cover the run or too close so a defender can intercept)
   d) Quality of one-touch layoff by supporting player (outside opposite foot is best to open up the angle of the pass)
   e) Quality of first touch reception and ensuing pass.

ATTACKING 1 v 1 CONFRONTATIONS

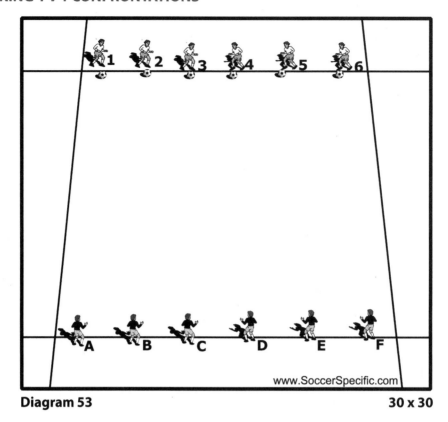

Diagram 53   **30 x 30**

Warm up with some awareness dribbling work.

1. This set up creates lots of opportunities of 1 v 1 confrontations with different players against each other. Begin with players passing and defending passively so the player on the ball dribbles past the defender successfully.

2. Numbered players have a ball each and can pass to any lettered player. They call the name of the player, pass the ball and close down quickly and the lettered player tries to score a goal by stopping the ball anywhere along the line where the numbered players begin. If a numbered player wins back the ball he scores by stopping the ball on the lettered player's line.

3. This is a big area to be able to score on which improves the chances of success. Have at least three 1v1's going at any one time. Players dictate when and where they do this depending on how many others are live in their 1v1's.

4. Players need to be AWARE of the positions of the other 1v1 confrontations so they do not clash with them. Ensure all players have the opportunity to be the attacking player in the 1v1.

5. **Competitive:** Each player counts the number of goals he scores. There will be a winning team and a winning overall player.

6. **Coaching Points:**
   a) Accurate passing to start the move off.
   b) Player receiving attacks the space quickly with a good first touch out of the feet to get going
   c) Observation and awareness of other players in the area so players do not run into each other (hence the player on the ball is looking around and not just at his immediate opponent and the ball)
   d) 1v1 tricks and dribbles to beat the opponent
   e) Ability to stop the ball on the line at pace to score a goal

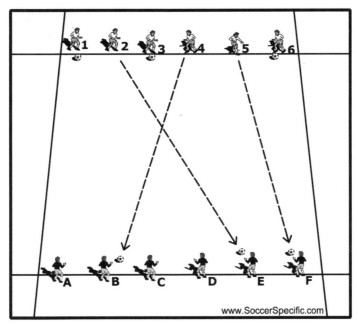

Diagram 54

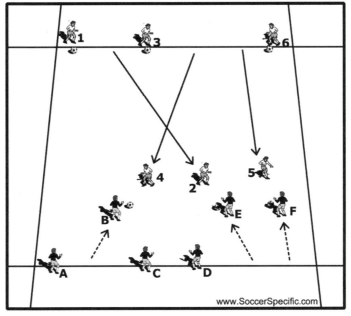

Diagram 55

A GAME SITUATION FOR 1v1'S

Divide the teams up into two 3v3 games with teams attacking the lines to score a goal. Play with one ball then two balls so there are some 1v1's and also some support play.

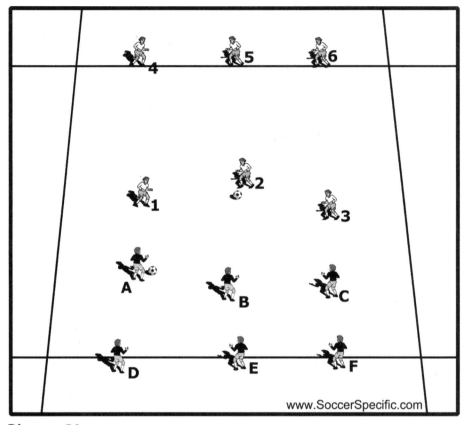

Diagram 56

Eventually have two 3v3 games with one ball each game, focusing on creating 1v1 confrontations and having players develop their awareness in possession, knowing their teammates' positions, their opponents' positions and where the space is to run, dribble or pass while at the same time keeping possession of the ball until the moment arrives to do any of those options.

FIRST AND SECOND TOUCH TRAINING DEVELOPING BOTH FEET
PROGRESSIONAL PLAN

1. This is mainly one and two touch passing. Practice using BOTH feet.
2. Side of foot passing, getting a rhythm going one touch to control then a second touch to pass back. Then passing and moving in to meet the ball and pass, and then out after passing the ball. Get a rhythm moving in and out, don't stand still.
3. One touch side of foot passing, moving in to meet the ball, one touch pass and then back again. Weight and accuracy MUST be good now to allow the teammate to pass back with one touch.
4. Decision Making: Passing player points his arm to one side, the receiving player has to pass to the other side.
5. Two footed Control and Pass - Inside and Inside: receive the ball with the inside of the right foot, move the ball first touch and inside and off line to yourself, then a second pass with the inside of the left foot. Do left foot first touch also.
6. Two footed Control and Pass: Inside and outside: Inside of the right foot first touch and pass with the outside of the left foot on the second touch and visa versa.
7. One footed Control and Pass - Inside and Outside of the same foot.: Move the ball inside and off line with the inside of the right foot and pass with the outside of the right foot. Repeat with the left foot.
8. One footed Control and Pass - Outside and inside of the same foot: Move the ball outside and off line with the outside of the right foot and pass with the inside of the right foot. Repeat with the left foot.
9. Feinting and Receiving - Fake to kick the ball one way and go the other: Perform this action with the various moves discussed previously.
10. Receiving and controlling the ball - Three touches: First movement is forward to receive the pass, first touch on the ball is forward again, second touch is to the side, and then the third touch is the forward pass back to the teammate. This is especially good for fast foot coordination.
11. Pointing: Introduce pointing again, passer points one way, receiver fakes that way and passes to himself the other way then passes to his teammate.
12. Competition and Pressure: Count the number of passes in a given time and see which pair does the best. Look for a balance between control and speed of passing. Do this for all the different progressions as a finishing point for each one so players need to do it under pressure.

WHEN PLAYERS ARE PASSING TO EACH OTHER, HAVE THEM LOOK INTO EACH OTHER'S EYES TO ENSURE THEY KEEP THEIR HEADS UP. THEY MUST NOT LOOK DOWN AND JUST FOCUS ON THE BALL.

THIS IS THE BEGINNING OF DEVELOPING AWARENESS OF OTHER PLAYERS AND THE SURROUNDING SPACE.

HAVE THE PLAYERS ALSO LOOK AROUND, TO THE SIDE, BEHIND, AS THE BALL IS TRAVELING, TO AGAIN EMPHASIZE THE NEED TO OBSERVE THEIR SURROUNDINGS AND NOT HAVE ALL THEIR ATTENTION FOCUSED ON THE BALL.

This information is designed to touch on the topic and to ensure the understanding of its importance. Technical training of this kind goes hand in hand with the awareness training we are covering in this book. This is great foot coordination practice to prepare the players for awareness training. Very simple and basic footwork is where to start. We are starting to get the players' minds trained and their bodies prepared to pass the ball one and two touch quickly and with quality. It is an easy introduction though, as the players are not moving around.

A great emphasis on all this ball work in two's has to be placed on the players developing an **AWARENESS** of other players' positions. This requires that they play with their heads up before, during and after possession. Have them look into each others eyes all the time so they have to look away from the ball and get their heads up. This means their **PERIPHERAL VISION** has to be developed and even in these simple exercises this process can begin to be worked upon.

COACHING CLINIC SESSION PLAN 10

(For age 7 years and older)

OBJECTIVE: IMPROVING ONE AND TWO TOUCH PASSING MAINTAINING AN AWARENESS OF WHAT IS "BEYOND THE BALL"

Another very simple way to get players to look around as they play is for the coach to hold his hand up periodically with a certain number of fingers showing for the players to see and call out. Developing this awareness off the ball is essential and this is a very simple way of aiding this development.

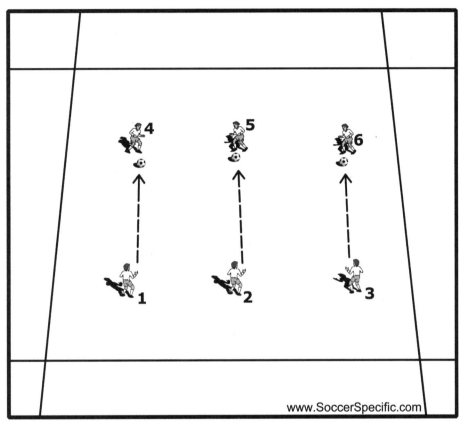

Diagram 57   **20 x 20**

1. Simple passing in two's back and forth, first two touches, then one touch where possible. Coach can dictate the distance between them.
2. Ask the players to look into "each other's eyes" as they pass and NOT at the ball to see if they can keep possession.
3. They should be able to see their ball in the "peripheral vision".
4. Using both feet to pass the ball.
5. **Competitive:** Count how many passes they can make in a given time.
6. **Coaching Points:**
   a) Head Up (looking into the other player's eyes)
   b) Ability to look at the player AND see the ball also in their peripheral vision
   c) Good first touch to set up the second touch / pass
   d) Technique of Passing

AWARENESS; FIRST AND SECOND TOUCH TRAINING
1ST AND 2ND TOUCHES ON THE BALL IN TEAMS OF TWO

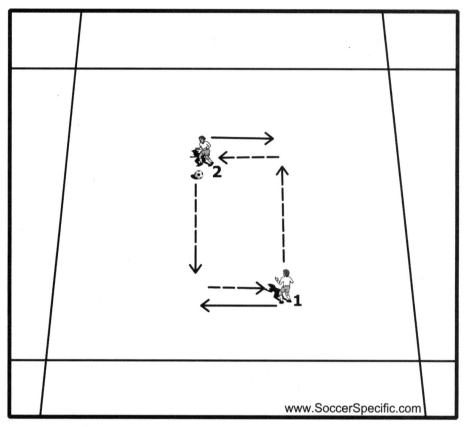

Diagram 58   **20 x 20**

Coaching Points:
a) Technique; Quality of pass (timing, accuracy, weight)
b) Decision and Observation; When and where to pass (head up)
c) Technique; Quality of first touch on reception (angle, distance, pace), and second touch to pass

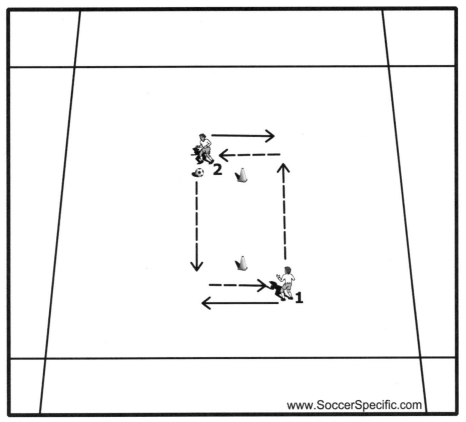

Diagram 59

1. Place a cone in front of each player as a target object to play around. This also helps the receiving player judge his first touch and how far it needs to go across the field before passing the ball with the second touch.
2. Player (1) passes the ball to one side of the cone to player (2) who must move the ball laterally on his first touch to the other side of the cone, then pass the ball back with his second touch. Player (1) then repeats the process.
3. Try to make the first touch a short, tight distance with the ball under control. Keep these continuous rhythms going but the coach can dictate which part of the foot to use: inside to outside, outside to inside, inside to inside and transferring feet and so on.
4. Work the ball also from left to right so players practice moving the ball both ways.
5. **Competitive:** How many successful passes can the pairs of players make in a given time using the required techniques?

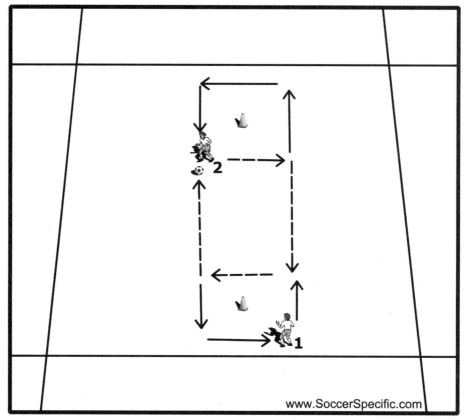

Diagram 60

1. Now use the cone as a target to get in front of. As the ball is passed the player receiving must get in front of the cone to receive the pass, pass back then move back behind the cone again.
2. This forces the player to move towards the ball as he receives it. This is an important movement because players often wait for the ball to come to them in a game and an opponent steps in front of them to steal it.
3. The movements are continuously back and forward: in front of the cone, receive the pass, move across with one touch, pass again with a second touch then behind the cone moving backwards and back across to receive again. Have the players develop a rhythm to get the best out of this practice.
4. Increase the distance between the players so they do not get too close to each other when both have moved in front of the cones to both pass the ball and receive the ball.
5. **Going Competitive:** How many successful passes can the pairs of players make in a given time using the required techniques?

DROPPING OFF TO RECEIVE A PASS TO CREATE MORE SPACE

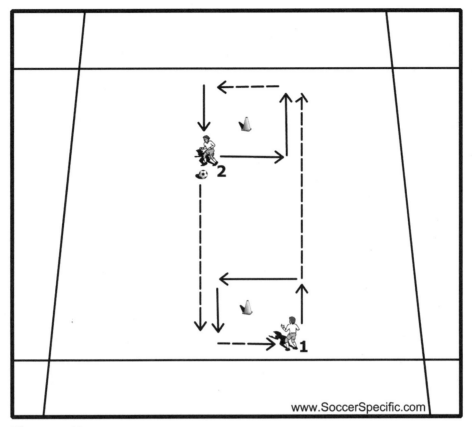

Diagram 61

1. It is not always the right movement to go towards the ball to receive a pass. Sometimes the correct movement is away from the ball to create more space to receive the pass.
2. Dropping off to receive provides "time on the ball" to make this movement. It may also be done to get away from an opponent attacking you from the direction the ball came from.
3. Here the player drops off to receive the pass, moves the ball to the side and passes back to the other player. Get them passing and receiving both ways, taking the ball with the first touch with both the right foot and the left.
4. You can do the same movement resulting with a diagonal pass across and between the cones as in the next two diagrams.

COACHING CLINIC SESSION PLAN 11

(For age 7 years and older)

OBJECTIVE: AWARENESS; FIRST AND SECOND TOUCH TRAINING: FIRST TOUCH ACROSS THE BODY AND A DIAGONAL PASS RETURN

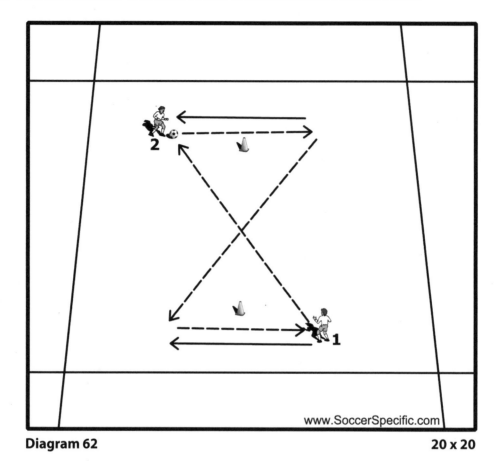

Diagram 62　　　　　　　　　　　　　　　　　　**20 x 20**

1. **Progression:** As above, the players now make a first touch pass to themselves to the side then a diagonal second touch pass back across the field to their teammate.
2. Two touch if possible.
3. **Coaching Points:**
    a) Technique; Quality of pass (timing, accuracy, weight)
    b) Decision and Observation; When and where to pass (head up)
    c) Technique; Quality of first touch on reception (angle, distance, pace), and second touch to pass

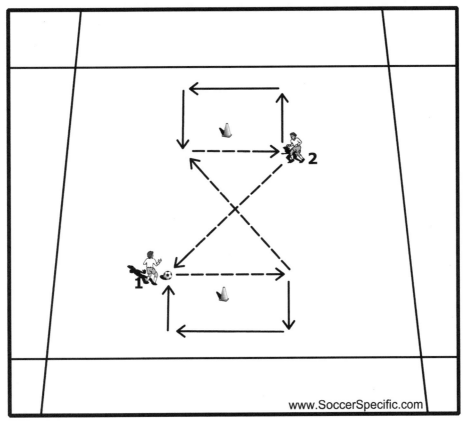

Diagram 63

1. Now the players come in front of the cone to receive the pass. (1) passes the ball from in front of the cone, then drops back, moves across to receive the diagonal pass back and moves forward again to receive and so on.

THREE TOUCHES FOR FAST FEET COORDINATION

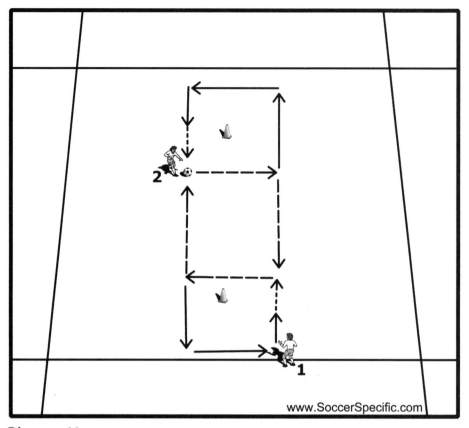

Diagram 64

1. Receiving and controlling the ball: Three touches on the ball. First movement is forward to receive the pass, first touch on the ball is forward again, second touch is to the side, and then the third touch is the forward pass back to the teammate.

2. This is good for fast foot coordination. You can condition the players to use either or both feet on this one. An example would be forward with the right foot on the first touch, across with the inside of the right foot on the second touch and forward with the outside of the right foot with the third touch. Or using both feet: forward with the right foot with the first touch, across to the left with the outside of the left foot on the second touch and forward with the inside of the left foot on the third touch.

3. Have players determine which feet they want to use and whether it is with the inside or outside of the foot.

MOVING FORWARD TO RECEIVE WITH A FIRST TOUCH ACROSS THE BODY, SECOND TOUCH FORWARD AND THIRD TOUCH PASS

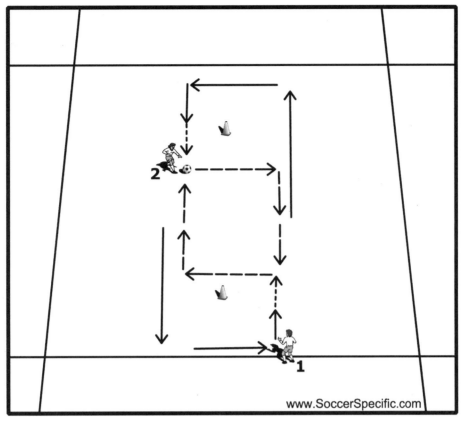

Diagram 65

1. Different routines can be established here with the coach testing the players to see if they can do the correct touch in the correct direction and be successful.
2. Here the first touch is across the body, second touch is forward and third touch is a forward pass.
3. Liken this to an opponent attacking the receiving player from the side so the first touch is across the body away from this player, and then forward, then a pass.

FIRST TOUCH ACROSS THE BODY, SECOND FORWARD AND A FORWARD DIAGONAL PASS

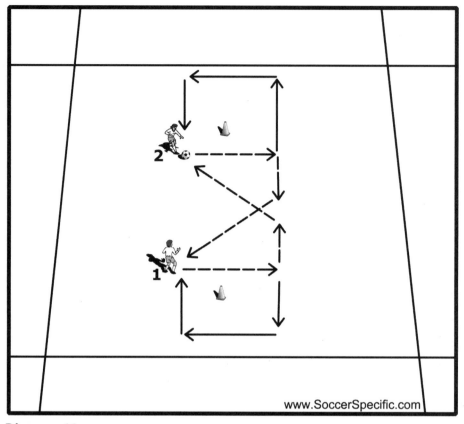

Diagram 66

1. Continuing the three touch drill, we now add a diagonal pass into the movement.
2. Here it is the 1st touch across the body, 2nd touch forward and 3rd touch a diagonal pass.

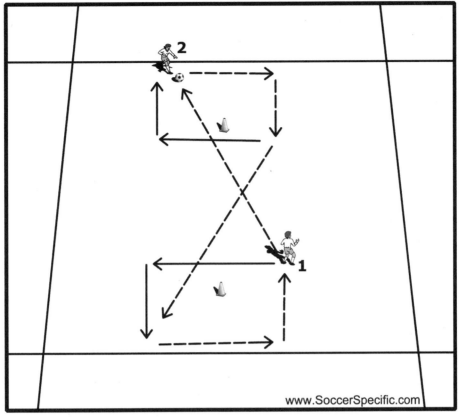

Diagram 67

1. Three touch movements. Again, drop off to create space in front but this time play a diagonal pass right foot to right foot or left foot to left foot. So here it is across the body 1st touch, forward with the 2nd touch and diagonal pass with the 3rd touch.

2. All these practices are designed to get the players to work on their first, second and in some cases their third touches on the ball. The set ups are designed also to make these touches and passes in different directions and are a good test. Touch on the ball, accuracy and weight of the touch and pass are important elements to master in these practices. This is all designed to get the players' technical skills strong enough to move them into the Awareness Training.

5

THE THOUGHT PROCESSES AND PHYSICAL
ACTIONS INVOLVED IN AWARENESS TRAINING
AND COACHING CLINICS TO PRACTICE THEM

COACHING CLINIC SESSION PLAN 12

(For age 8 years and older)
OBJECTIVE: IMPROVING SPATIAL AWARENESS

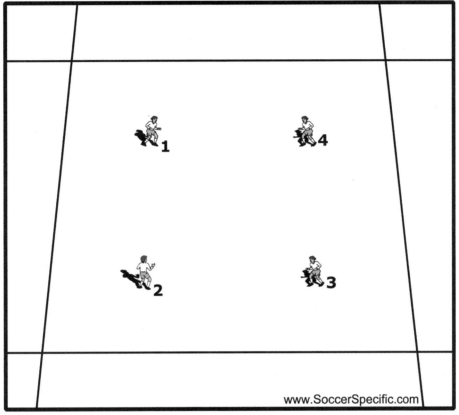

Diagram 68   **20 x 20**

1. This is designed to be an easy introduction for players to get used to the idea of how to find space without the ball.
2. As they practice this and get good at it they are introduced to using a ball.
   To begin you must build up the session slowly, one team only, without a ball.
3. The coach can call out different shapes and the players have to form them quickly, thus learning the important use of space.
4. Above is a rectangle, below is a diamond and so on.

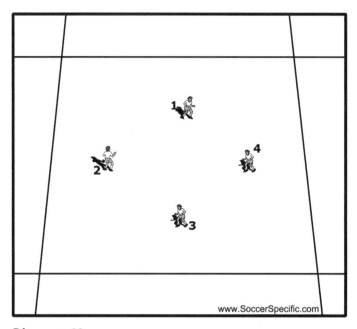

Diagram 69

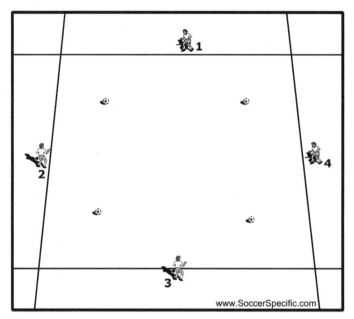

Diagram 70

1. We are now looking at a more **DYNAMIC** way of training with a greater freedom of movement.
   Players move around the zone finding space. Coach calls stop, the players stop, then check positions. They shouldn't be too near each other, showing they recognize how to use the spaces in the zone.
2. Add a ball each and do the above two exercises but on calling stop, or getting them into a shape and stopping ask the players to run out of the area and check where the balls are in terms of spatial awareness or team shape (e.g. a square).

3. Add another team and continue the process e.g.
   a) You can practice passing with hands to work support positions.
   b) Two teams, one with a ball each, the other without balls. On a call have the team with a ball each pass to the other team and then continue the movement.
   c) Two teams, a ball each team, passing and moving.
4. **Coaching Points:**
   a) Finding space off the ball
   b) Creating team shapes in those spaces (team work)
   c) Finding space with a ball
5. Ask players to move again and call a shape they need to form, e.g. a diamond, a square, a straight line. This indicates how quickly they can form a team shape. They are looking to maintain fairly equal distances between each other depending on the shape.

GROUP RHYTHM AND MOVEMENT (IN FIVES)

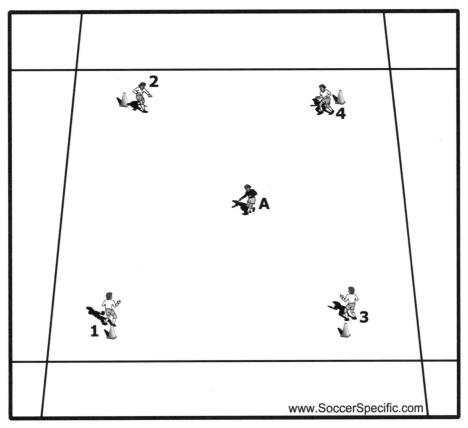

www.SoccerSpecific.com

Diagram 71

1. Lay four cones down for reference.
2. Exchange corners, player in the middle must beat someone to a corner.
3. Introduce a ball for each player to dribble.

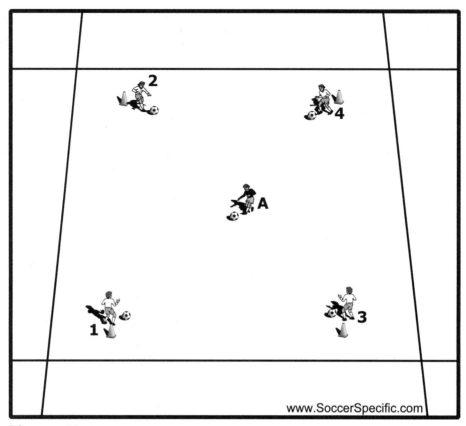

Diagram 72

Finish with small sided games and then a cool down.

COACHING CLINIC SESSION PLAN 13
(For age 9 years and older)
OBJECTIVE: DEVELOPING BASIC THEN PROGRESSED AWARENESS TRAINING IN THREES

This is a very simple idea with players in three's passing the ball back and forth, focusing on good passing but also starting to train the middle player to look over his shoulder before receiving the pass to see where his next pass should go. So he looks away from the ball as it is traveling to him or as the passer is about to pass the ball, all in a split second. The conditions added ensure the middle player does actually look to see where the next pass is going before he receives the initial pass, otherwise he will get caught making the wrong decision.

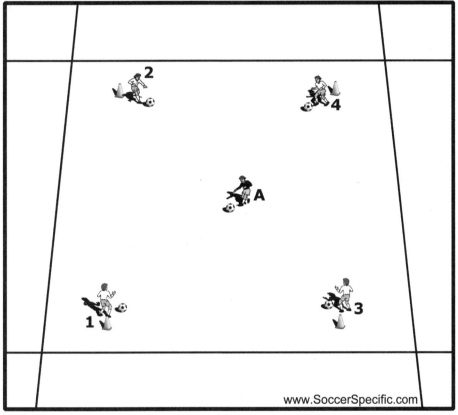

Diagram 73   **20 x 20**

1. **Coaching Points:**
    a) Look over shoulder "before receiving".
    b) Body Stance – half turned (can see behind).
    c) Support at an angle.
    d) Save a touch – let weight of ball determine this- let it run across the body and move one touch.
    e) Always looking around developing your Awareness of other players' positioning before, during and after receiving the pass
2. **Progression and Conditions:** Opposite player stays or closes the middle player down.
3. If closed down by the outside opposite player, the middle player passes back to the same player.

4. If not closed down, the middle player turns and passes to the opposite player.
5. This identifies if the middle player has looked to see where the player behind is before receiving the ball.
6. If (3) closes down on (2) as (2) receives the ball, and (3) then determines to turn and to pass the ball to (2), this shows that (3) has not looked to see where (2) is because (3) has turned to pass which is the wrong decision. If (3) had looked first, the correct decision would be to pass back to (1).
7. Try it one touch, particularly with the end players.

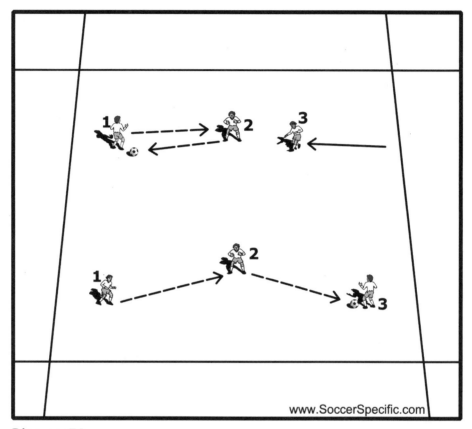

Diagram 74

PROGRESSED AWARENESS SESSION IN THREES

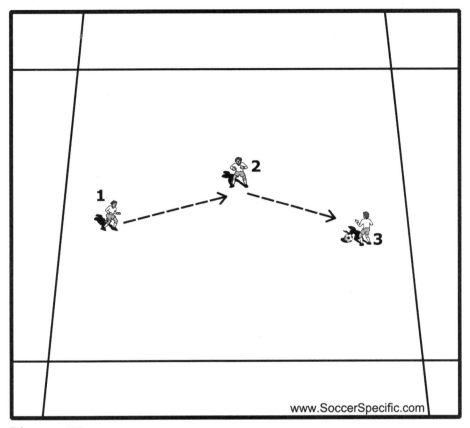

Diagram 75

Go through each progression in the order it is presented here. Do one at a time and have each player practice in the middle at every stage.

1. Begin by passing the ball from (1) to (2) to (3) and back. (2) receives and turns and passes. Passing must be sharp and accurate, one or two touch.

2. You can receive with the furthest foot away from the passer and pass it with the nearest foot, or save a touch and move it one touch with the inside of the nearest foot or the outside of the furthest foot. Let the weight of the pass determine this. Let it run across your body and move it one touch.

3. The player in the middle must open his body stance by going side on so he can see what is behind him. This makes it easier to receive and pass the ball on.

4. Look over the shoulder to see what's behind. Do this before receiving the ball, not after.

5. Position in the middle at an angle to receive. This makes a triangular support position and opens up the field of vision. Once the ball has been passed, the middle player moves to the other side at an angle again (can use cones to run to both sides). This forces the players to receive and pass with both feet.

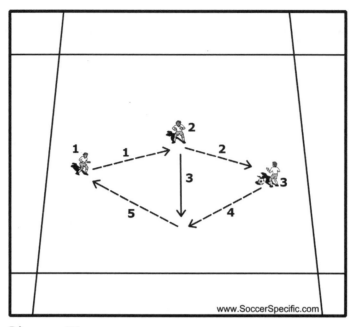

Diagram 76

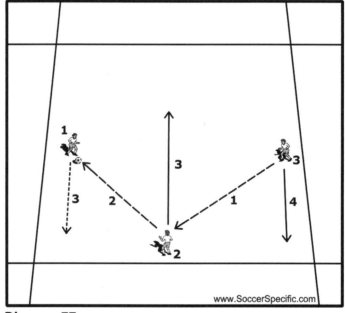

Diagram 77

6. Now working on the movement of the outside player to create a bigger angle to pass and receive the ball. Above, player (2) passes to (1) who moves the ball into space with a good first touch in order to pass the ball back with a second touch. The movement is shown below. Likewise (3) receives and moves the ball off at an angle and the cycle continues.

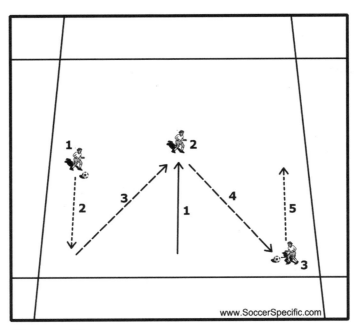

Diagram 78

7. Working on the middle player again. If he is marked in a game, he should look to come short to receive the pass to get away from the defender.

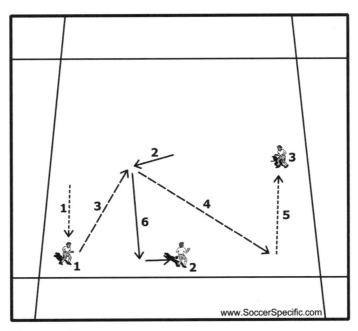

Diagram 79

8. Moving short to receive the pass helps to get away from the defender to receive in space with time on the ball. Keep the angle wide so you can still receive the pass side on. If you move short but more central you will receive the ball more with your back to the play with less room to work the ball in.

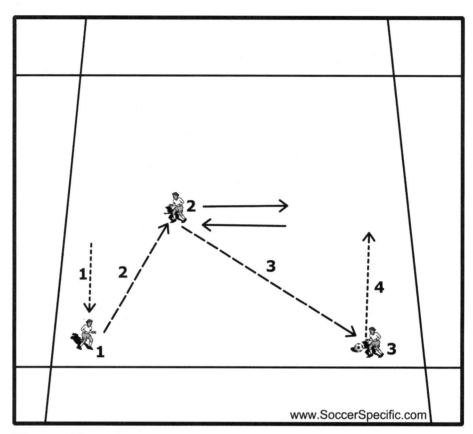

Diagram 80

9. Progress by the middle player moving away from the ball to take a defender away from the space and then checking back to receive the pass in time and space.

10. With these movements the passer must be aware of the receiver's movements to get the timing of the pass right. The receiver must be aware of how quickly the passer gets control and is ready to pass it to get the timing of the run right (therefore always looking).

11. These movements in a game are dictated by how much time on the ball the passer has. If no time then he comes short to receive the first pass, if time on the ball then the receiver can run a defender off the check and receive to feet.

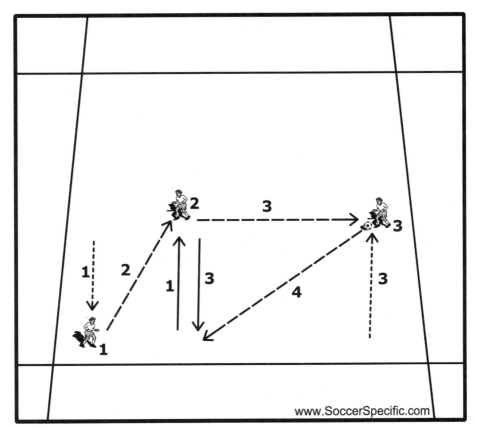

Diagram 81

12. The middle player receives the ball and passes into space to move the outside player. Previously it was a pass to feet and the outside player moved the ball.

13. The opposite outside player from the ball can decide to close down the middle player or stay away. If he closes down then the middle player must pass the ball back to the player who passed it to him. If he stays in position then the middle player passes the ball to him. This highlights if the player has looked to see where the other player is before receiving the pass. Put a passive defender in with the middle player to show how using a check-back can free up space.

COACHING CLINIC SESSION PLAN 14
(For age 8 years and older)
OBJECTIVE: IDENTIFYING LEVELS OF AWARENESS

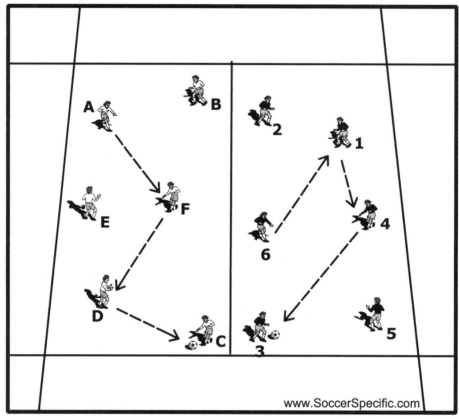

Diagram 82

1. **Coaching Points:**
   a) Looking around even if you do not receive the pass (always be aware of others' positions, just in case)
   b) Looking before receiving the pass, knowing what to do next
   c) Decision: When and where to pass
   d) Quality of Pass (especially the pace of the pass in one touch passing)
   e) Good support positions of players off the ball
2. Start with two teams but separate in their own grid as above to simplify the process Then mix the two teams later in the same area once they are starting to master the idea.
3. Have the players stand still and pass the ball around the group. They must look before they receive the ball to see where they are passing to. Make it 3 then 2 then 1 touch. This is particularly good for the younger end of the player spectrum where it often takes a few touches to just control the ball. Start with that; just passing it and not moving, then get them to look and then pass and so on and develop the idea this way.
4. To ensure they are looking, have the players call the name of the players they are passing to before they pass the ball. When they don't call the name you know they haven't looked ahead of the ball.
5. Observe which players can't do this and allow them more touches and more time and look to see how they improve with practice.

6. This is THE most basic introduction to the awareness coaching method and you only do it with THE most basic of young players starting to learn the game.

7. Progression –Now have two teams in the same area and have them pass to opposite colors so the choices are halved. Have the two teams play through each other but not against each other.

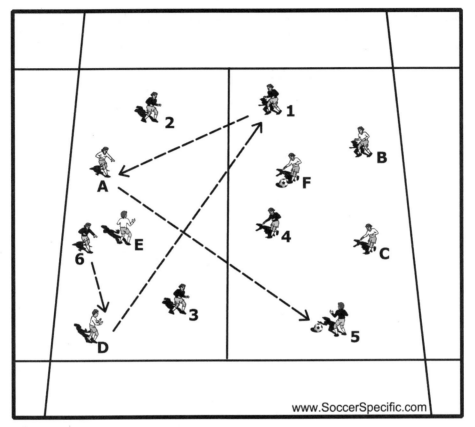

Diagram 83

1. Introduce 2 balls to the session then 3 and so on, but start with players standing still and not moving to keep it simple and to get initial success.

2. Have them begin to move around the area slowly like before but now with 2 or 3 balls to make the decision making more difficult as free players are harder to find.

DEVELOPMENT

1. Here we have all the players moving freely, passing and moving within their own team. Begin with one ball being passed around a team and as they become proficient introduce another ball to increase their awareness.

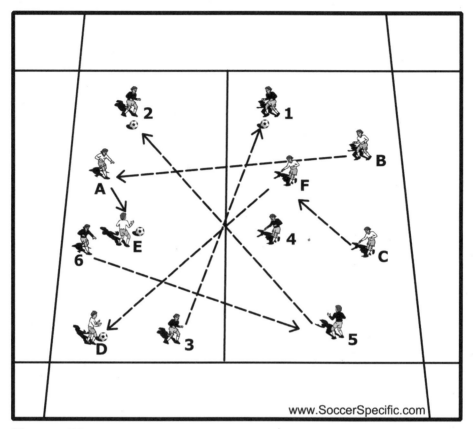

Diagram 74

2. Have the teams play throughout both grids to spread the play out and get the players comfortable and composed. As they improve you can change it to all players from both teams playing in one grid only so there is less room to work in and things happen more quickly. This is a test of their Awareness ability.
3. The Technical / Tactical Design within the framework of the clinic is described below and this information will get you started.
4. As players get proficient you can introduce new situations for them to deal with, all of which will be covered later. You may need to spend time repeating this basic set up before you move on to the other situational work. Be patient and ensure they get the basics right first.
5. **Progression:** Have 4 teams playing through each other, players passing to their own teammates. Then move to passing by the colors. For example: red passes to blue, blue to green, green to yellow, and yellow to red. This increases their awareness of where teammates are positioned.

TWO TEAMS PLAYING THROUGH EACH OTHER

The following information forms the basis of what we are trying to achieve with this clinic.

Coaching Points: Technical / Tactical Design

a) The players must play with their heads up (so they see what is around them).

b) Look over the shoulder before receiving the ball.

c) Body stance is open to receive the ball.

d) Awareness of teammates' positions on the field before receiving the pass.

e) Awareness of opponents' positions on the field before receiving the pass.

f) Move the ball on the first touch away from pressure into space (or 1 touch transfer). Receiver moves the ball away at an angle off his first touch.

g) Passing to space to move players into a better position on the field.

h) Passing to the player's feet.

i) Turns / dribbles / 1 touch / 2 touch / free play etc.

j) Communication (verbal, physical or through eye contact).

k) Angles / distances of support.

1. To increase competitive edge - Passer pressures receiver by closing him down after the pass.

2. Don't try to develop all the key coaching points all in one session, it may be you have to spend several sessions on just establishing the first key point of getting the players to play with their heads up.

3. Only when you are getting success with this should you move to working on the second point in your next practices.

4. This process of learning is the same as in the introduction where there are several things the player must think about even before receiving the ball, beginning with seeing where the ball is coming from and so on up to the selection of the pass.

5. Competitive: Have each player count the number of successful passes in a given time and see who makes the most. It is always good to give players a target to achieve to keep them focused on the task at hand.

PASSING IN TWO'S AND THREE'S

1. Two teams e.g. 6 per team. A ball between two, pass to the same person each time, moving around the zone.

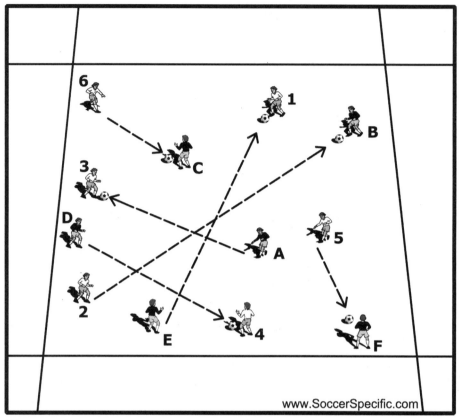

Diagram 85

2. Working opposites, the coach calls "time" on the ball and the players know they receive the ball when they check back (play off the second run).
3. Coach calls "no time" on the ball and players know they will get an early pass into their path (play off the first run).
4. This is particularly good for forwards to work on. Recognizing when there is time on the ball or not helps determine their movement off the ball.
5. To simulate turning and receiving to feet, (1) for example passes to his teammate then moves away to an outside line to check back to receive. Think about the angle and distance to receive and the body position (link this to coaching point number 1). When they receive the ball they do some work on it until their teammate is ready to receive again after checking and turning from the line. The check away to come back is likened to when a forward runs a defender off to create space to come back into to give them time on the ball.
6. Change to a ball between three, passing and moving off each other. Then have teams of four and two balls per team passing to any player in that team.

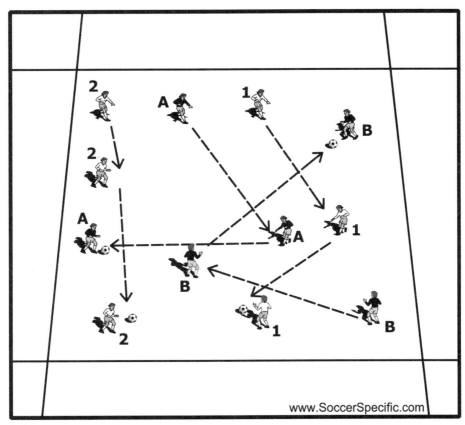

Diagram 86

COACHING CLINIC SESSION PLAN 15

(For age 8 years and older)

OBJECTIVE: TEACHING THE FUNDAMENTALS OF THE AWARENESS COACHING METHOD

This practice is designed to allow the players to be gently introduced to the fundamentals of the Awareness method, enabling them to practice in a more dynamic way. The above clinic and this one can flip flop or even be combined.

TWO TEAM SET UP

Diagram 87   **30 x 30**

1. Each target player has a ball and must pass to an inside player and the players play through each other to get the ball to the opposite side.
2. **Progression 1:** Players can rotate in and out as they make and receive a pass.
3. Constant passing and moving inside the playing area to receive and turn and pass.
4. Have a rhythm going between the two players on each team; one bad pass or control can spoil the movement.
5. **Progression 2:** Use only a couple of balls so there are lots of choices for all the players to make it a little easier and insist on only two touches inside and outside. Add a ball as they get better, thus reducing options and sharpening up their awareness even more.
6. **Progression 3:** Coaches can come inside the grid and act as support players, playing give and go's with the inside players. An inside player receiving a pass from an outside player calls to the coach early to support as the ball is traveling to him. This promotes good communication.

7. **Coaching Points:**
   a) Head up (awareness of the area and the players in it).
   b) Looking before receiving to receive and turn; to see who is free, to see where other players in the area are, to see where the space is to take the ball.
   c) Body position open to receive,
   d) Focus on the first touch and where to take the ball, for more touches or maybe a one touch pass if it is available.
   e) Concentrate on the quality of the pass to the outside receiver.

More Ideas:
1. One team inside, one team outside. Each outside player has a ball to begin.
2. Pass to an inside player who receives and turns and finds another outside free player with a pass. Then look to receive from another outside player.
3. The outside player receives and moves the ball side to side until another inside player is free to receive a pass. This ensures all the players are working both inside the grid and outside it.
4. **Competitive:** Have players count the number of successful passes they make in a given time and see who makes the most. Observe and comment on those who try to do it too quickly and lose control of the ball and lose the momentum of the session (for example they rush the pass, it is not accurate and the receiver ends up running away retrieving the ball, which wastes precious time).
5. Change the practice to all balls starting with the inside players. These players now look to pass and receive a give and go from an outside player and they each use the same ball the entire time.
6. Rotate the players so both teams have the chance to play in the middle of the grid.
7. Move both teams to the middle; divide the grid into two with each team passing to their own team within their own grid area, keeping teams separate to begin.

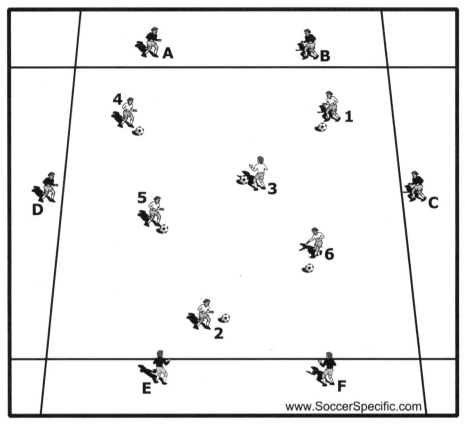

Diagram 88

1. Inside team players have a ball each now and have to look to find a free outside team player to pass to.
2. Set up the second touch with a good first touch. This develops the awareness of which players are free to pass to. Each team plays inside for 2 minutes, making as many give and go's with the outside players as possible.

Progression: Each time they pass it to outside players they have to receive it back and turn and find another player to pass to.
This ensures lots of situations where they have to receive and turn to practice the skill.

3. **Coaching Points:**
   a) Quality first touch of outside player.
   b) Decision making of inside player in terms of when and where to pass and technique (quality) of pass.

The Coach can create conditions:
a) Get a turn or dribble in before passing.
b) All in (many) touches, 3 then 2 touches.
c) Play 1- 2 with inside player then go outside.
d) Do a crossover with outside player rather than make a pass.

Inside player passes to outside player and closes down quickly, simulating a defensive movement. The receiver has to make a good first touch away from the pressure i.e. to either side of the pressuring player and they swap positions.

1. This is a good session because everyone is working but they get short intermittent rests, so maintaining quality.
2. **Competitive:** Have players count the number of successful passes they make in a given time and see who makes the most.

A GAME SITUATION

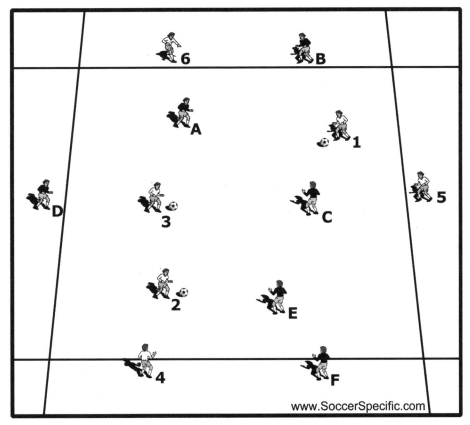

Diagram 89

1. Numbers team can only pass to numbered players on the outside. Letters team the same, only passing to lettered players on the outside.
2. **Progression 1:** Play 1v1s in the middle. Passive defense to begin, the defending players shadow the attacking players as they receive and turn and move.
3. Make it competitive. A lot of receiving and turning under pressure can occur now in the playing area.
4. **Progression 2:** Have a 3v3 small sided game in the middle.
5. Rotate the players.

COACHING CLINIC SESSION PLAN 16

(For age 8 years and older)

OBJECTIVE: RECEIVING, CONTROLLING AND TURNING WITH THE BALL IN FOURS STARTING WITH NON – COMPETITIVE PLAY

1. Support in a diagonal position, not in a straight line (off at an angle).
2. Receivers face the player with the ball (eye contact) so they know the receiver is ready.
3. Receiver moves to the ball to avoid anticipation of a defender intercepting or away to create space to come back into (if the player on the ball has time).
4. Receiver is "aware in advance" of where the space is to turn. Body position half turned to receive moving the ball on the first touch (changing direction). Use upper body to create an element of surprise or disguise.
5. Get your body between the ball and your opponent (screen the ball).
6. On receiving and changing direction with the first touch, change pace (away from a defender).
7. Use your arms to protect yourself and keep your knees bent for good balance.

Coaching Points and Methods of Turning:

a) Check off, receive and turn inside and face up to defender in one movement off the first touch.

b) Receiver backs into the defender and receives ball to feet, then spins defender using his body as a screen.

c) Turn away with outside / inside of each foot.

d) Turn inside or outside using the inside or the outside of the appropriate foot.

e) Turn without the ball to pull defender short, creating space behind, spin quickly and take the ball behind the defender.

f) Run defender off away from the ball then check back into the space created to receive.

g) Progression – The outside players can pass directly to each other (3 and 4 above) presenting more options for the player in possession in the middle.

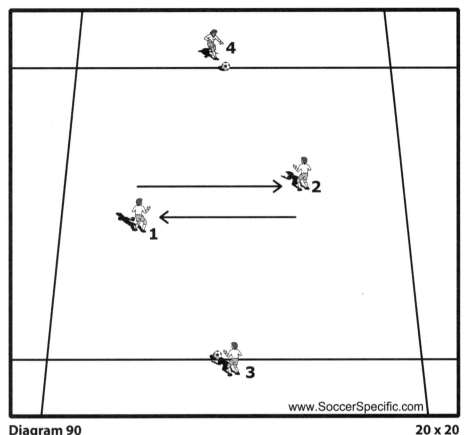

Diagram 90   **20 x 20**

1. Two balls going at once. (2) receives from (4) and passes to (3). At the same time (1) receives from (3) and passes to (4). The players switch across to the other side and work the other way.
2. This is a continuous movement exercise and the players have to get a rhythm going to make it work effectively. Use the previous coaching points in the three player set up.
3. Players must observe where the ball is coming from, where the other player in the middle is so they do not collide, and where the player is they are passing to BEFORE THEY RECEIVE THE BALL.

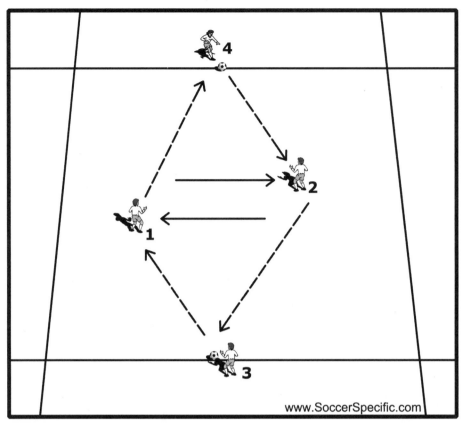

Diagram 91

1. Two balls going at the same time. Players must maintain the rhythm of the movement.
2. Once they pass the ball the middle players switch sides to receive the ball back again and continue the transition.
3. Ensures they use both feet to transfer the ball.
4. SAME IDEA as the awareness session in three's only we are going both ways at the same time with four players working.
5. Rotate the players.
6. Same build up as the awareness in three's session; use that information as a reference.

Going Competitive
1. To maintain interest in the exercise you can make this a competitive situation. For example, players must count the number of times they receive, turn and pass the ball accurately in 2 minutes. Each set of four players can compete against each other or each pair within each four can compete.
2. They will learn that if they sacrifice accuracy for pure speed the pass may not reach the target and so the number of times they are successful will be less. A balance will develop between accuracy and speed of play and as they get better at it the two will improve in unison.

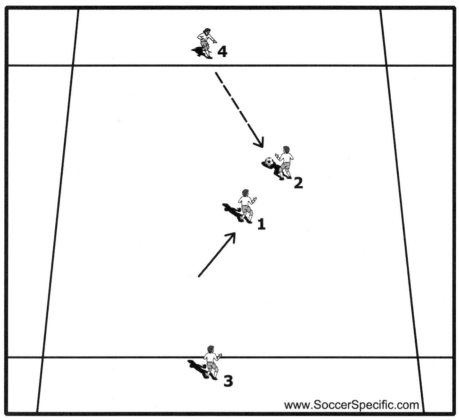

Diagram 92

1. **Coaching Points:**
   a) The quality of passes
   b) The angle and distances of support
   c) Beating the defender (various methods as discussed).
2. No opposition to begin.
3. (4) passes to (1) who receives, controls and passes to (3). (2) receives from (3), turns and passes to (4) and so on. Rotate the players in the middle.
4. Have the other player in the middle be a passive defender.
5. Middle players can switch sides to receive and turn.
6. Turning inside and turning outside using inside and outside of the foot (practicing with both feet).

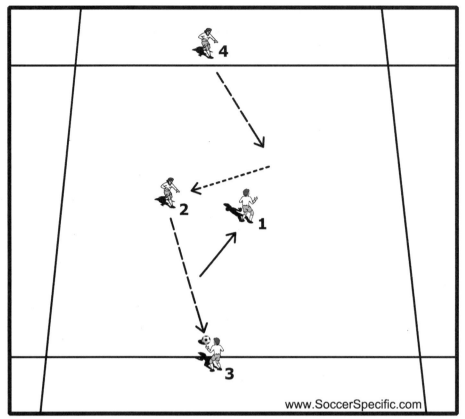

Diagram 93

1. Once you have gone through the progressions make the game competitive with a 1v1 in the middle as above.
2. Introduce a defender - (1) must receive and turn and pass to (3). (2) tries to stop the play and if successful can pass back and move again. Work both ways.
3. Whichever player has the ball in the middle works with both outside players until losing the ball, then the other player works with the two outside players.
4. **Progression:** Outside players can pass to each other, by-passing the inside player who can link up on the other side following the pass.
5. **Competitive:** Have a time limit (2 minutes for example) and have players count the number of successes they get in that time in terms of receiving, turning and passing to their teammate against their opponent. If you have 4 sets of 4 players for example, you can make this into a knockout competition with each winner of the 4 sets playing each other, then two sets of winners down to the final two players to find the ultimate winner. You could have a runners up knock out competition too so everyone gets ample opportunity to practice but in a competitive environment.

COACHING CLINIC SESSION PLAN 17

(For age 8 years and older)

OBJECTIVE: PRACTICING PASSING AND SUPPORT PLAY IN FOUR'S AND AIDING DEVELOPMENT OF AWARENESS "OFF" THE BALL

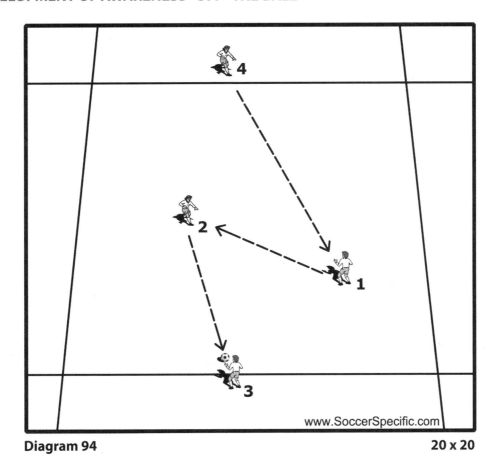

Diagram 94   **20 x 20**

NON – COMPETITIVE TO BEGIN

1. **Coaching Points:**
   a) Quality of passes
   b) Angles and distances of support
   c) Awareness of the positioning of teammates before receiving the pass (looking over the shoulder to see what is behind before receiving the pass)
   d) Timing of the interchange of players.
2. (3) passes to (1) who passes one or two touch to (2) who passes one or two touch to (4). Letters team work at the same time. Players need to be aware of where their own teammate is and where opponents are so they don't collide.
3. **Develop:** Have outside players switch with the inside passer. (2) passes to (4), (2) goes out and (4) comes in with the ball. You can mix it up by having the inside player pass to any outside player.
4. It is important that each player works an angle off the passer in advance of the pass e.g. (2) is receiving off (1) so moves to support as (1) is receiving off (3). Outside players must move along the line so inside players have to look to find them, before the inside player receives the pass.

5. Depending on numbers, put three in the middle on each team where they all must pass the ball to each other before it goes outside again (see over).

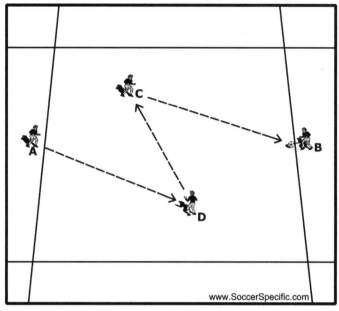

Diagram 95

PROGRESSIONS IN PASSING AND SUPPORT PLAY IN FOURS

Each team of four is playing through each other. We have here one ball per team of four, each going in the opposite direction and across each other.

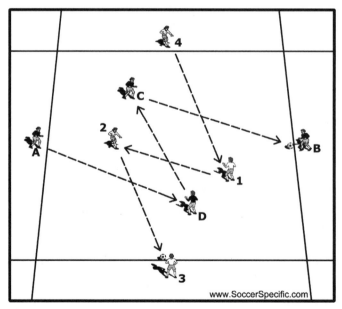

Diagram 96

Competitive: Now we have a 2v2 in the middle with players passing to their own teammates on the outside.

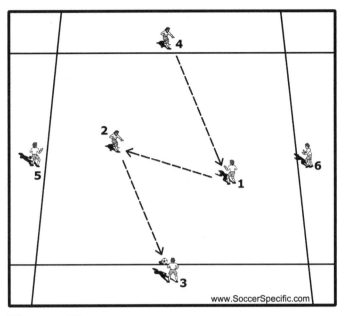

Diagram 97

If you only have 6 players you can adapt this clinic and play two in the middle and four on the outside. Inside players can pass to any of the outside players and then switch with them. (2) passes to (4) and goes out, (4) comes in. One and two touch passing where possible is what we are aiming for here.

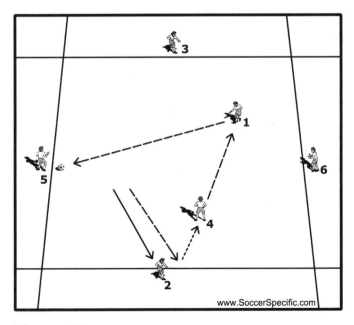

Diagram 98

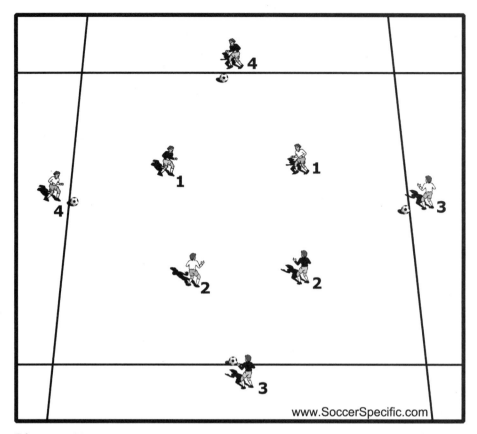

Diagram 99

1. Inside player receives from one outside player and passes to another free outside player.

2. Outside player moves the ball side to side to keep working until a pass is on. Rotate. Use different turns using all coaching points. Determine touches on the ball for quickness of turn.

3. **Going Competitive:** Have each player count the number of successful passes in a given time and see who makes the most.

4. Progression: Have the number 2 players play against each other and the number 1 players do the same. This time (unlike the basic 4 player set up as previously shown) because there are more players in the area their awareness off the ball of where other players are must improve to prevent them running into each other, but at the same time they must beat their opponent in the 1v1 situations.

5. They also need to be aware of which players on the outside do not already have a ball, so again peripheral awareness is being developed. They have to look for the free player on the outside to pass the ball to as two of the players will have balls already.

6. Progress this to a competition, winners against winners, and losers against losers.

COMPETITIVE GAME WITH EQUAL NUMBERS OF PLAYERS PER TEAM
TWO VERSUS TWO

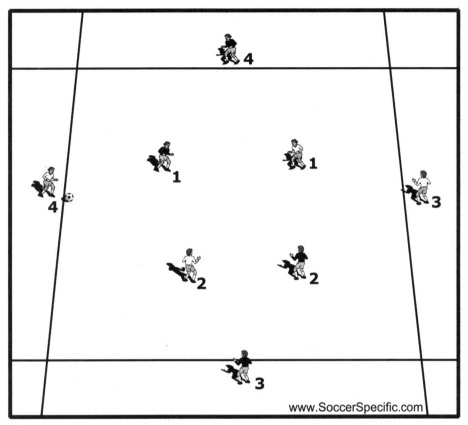

Diagram 100

GAME SITUATION

1. Now we move onto a game situation and one ball only. Each team has to get the ball to an outside player of their own to score. Once the ball goes to the outside player, that player comes inside to join the game; the passer goes outside to become a new target. This is now a competitive 2v2 game in the middle.

2. The idea is a quick transition from one end of the field to the other, few touches, quick play. Reward a point for one touch passes and for getting the ball to the target.

3. Quick rotation of players allows for a brief respite for each player when they are a target which means they can maintain a high tempo during the practice. Teams are playing in opposite directions.

4. **Progression:**
    a) Outside player receives the ball and brings it in, inside player who passed the ball goes out to become the new target.
    b) Limit it to 3 touches then 2 touches then 1 touch, but only if it is on to do so, and then finally 1 touch whatever the situation (this last one will REALLY test their awareness).

COACHING CLINIC PLAN 18
(For age 8 years and older)
OBJECTIVE: IMPROVING AWARENESS OF SPACING AND MOVEMENT "OFF" THE BALL

MOVEMENT OFF THE BALL KEEPING BALANCE IN ZONES
TWO TEAMS OF FOUR PLAYERS IN FOUR ZONES

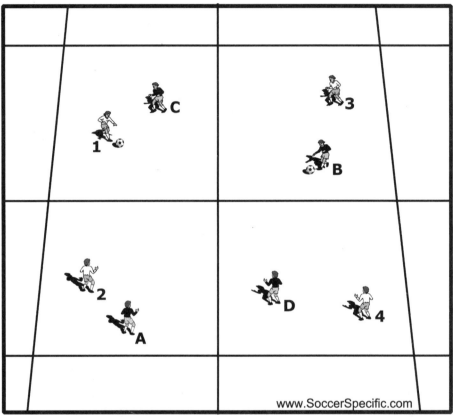

Diagram 101   **20 x 20**

1. One letter player and one number player in each zone to ensure movement on and off the ball. Players pass then move, move with the ball or just move off the ball.
2. In diagram 102 (1) passes to (4) who runs with the ball into another zone. This forces (3) to change zones. (2) moves up a zone forcing (1) to move down to keep the balance between all four zones.
3. Players need to look around and find a space to go in. If an area is free then a player can go into it. This is designed simply to get players appreciating how to find space in an area and can be used as a useful warm up. Conditioning zones within an area starts the process of finding space. As we develop the sessions they become more dynamic with few if any restrictions on where to go within the designated area.
4. **Coaching Points:**
    a) Quality Passing (accuracy, pace and timing)
    b) Support Positioning: Movement off the ball after passing and to get in position to receive
    c) Observation and identification: of where space and teammates are to pass to or receive from or to move into space to help the player on the ball pass to another player.

- 164 -

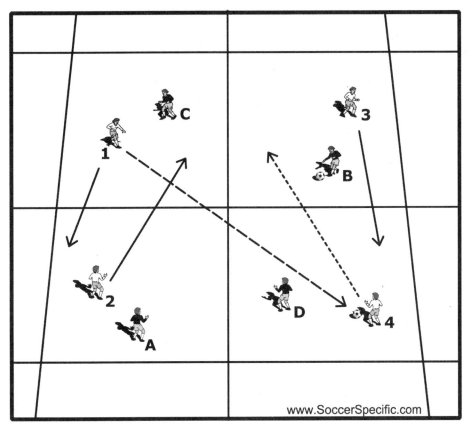

Diagram 102

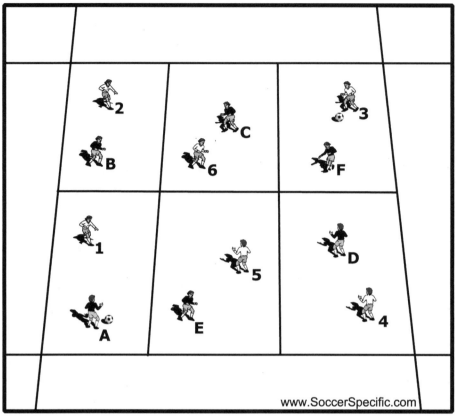

Diagram 103   **30 x 30**

1. This is a six zone game with more potential movement from the players due to more choices of area to move into. Observation has to be sharp here.
2. Opposite, showing the movement of one team only, there is constant interchange of players between zones ensuring they get the idea of moving with and without the ball.
3. **Competitive:** Have each player count the number of passes made in a given time. Obviously moving the ball one touch will make it faster.
4. **Game Situation:** Possession game emphasizing movement off the ball through setting conditions of players moving into other zones once they have passed the ball and players off the ball interchanging between the zones to get free to accept a pass. Players must make these movements and these should be in their thoughts at all times, as that is the Condition / Theme (zone transfer).
5. The coach cannot penalize players for not being in different zones all the time because this is impossible in such a dynamic game, but the theme will help the players focus on the need to move on and off the ball and should help them to make sure they do it.

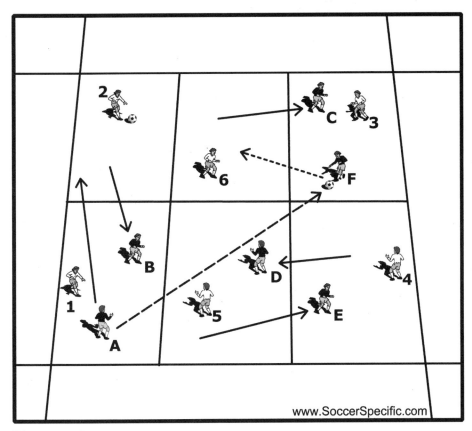

Diagram 104

COACHING CLINIC SESSION PLAN 19

(For age 9 years and older)

OBJECTIVE: FURTHER DEVELOPMENT OF AWARENESS AND OF MOVEMENT "OFF" THE BALL

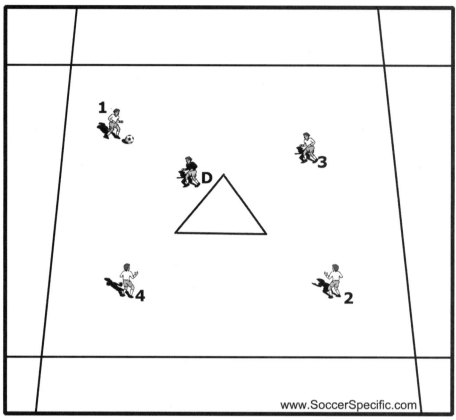

Diagram 105   **20 x 20**

1. Here is an interesting way to work on passing, movement off the ball, fitness and looking for the penetrating pass. Start with a 20 x 20 yard grid and have a 4 yard equilateral triangle in the middle made up of cones. There are 5 players in the activity – 1 defender and 4 attackers. The 4 attackers try to maintain possession while also looking to score goals by playing the ball through the triangle to their teammates. The defender is NOT allowed inside the triangle so he must be constantly working his way around the triangle trying to cut off the penetrating passes. See the diagram above for the set up.

2. The thing that makes this such an interesting activity is the required movement off the ball by the offensive players. On every pass they are moving in order to get into a better position to either make a penetrating pass or to receive one. As opposed to the norm in possession games when players wait till they receive a ball before thinking what to do next, in this game the players have to be thinking ahead of the passes because it's not good enough to just play the ball through the triangle, a teammate has to be there and receive the ball for it to count.

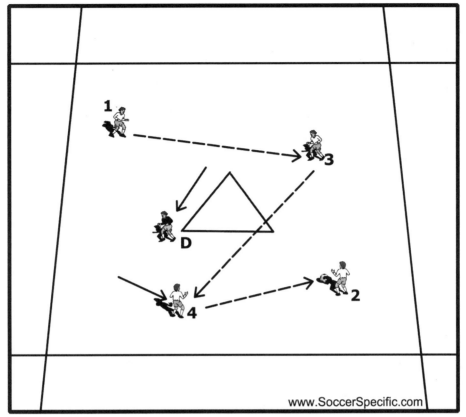

Diagram 106

3. Play this game for a 5 minute period with each player having a one minute turn on defense. It gets the players working hard, thinking and competing while having fun trying to beat their teammates. The player who gives up the fewest number of goals on defense wins the game.

4. There is a tendency in this game for the offensive players to get too close to the triangle, which takes away the passing angles (just like in a regular game where they come too close to the middle). This is easy to correct and is a good learning opportunity for the players. Above, (D) stops the immediate pass from (4) to (3) through the triangle so (4) passes to (2) and (1) makes a run off the ball to receive the next pass through the triangle and a goal is scored. (D) tries to get back and around to prevent this.

5. **Coaching Points:**
   a) Creating Space for yourself or for a teammate through movement off the ball
   b) Quality of Passing (weight, accuracy and timing)
   c) Quality of Control and first touch
   d) Effective possession

6. **Progression:** Change to 4v2, or 2v2v2. Keep the overload initially until players improve before you move on. Experiment with numbers, increasing the difficulty of the session as you go.

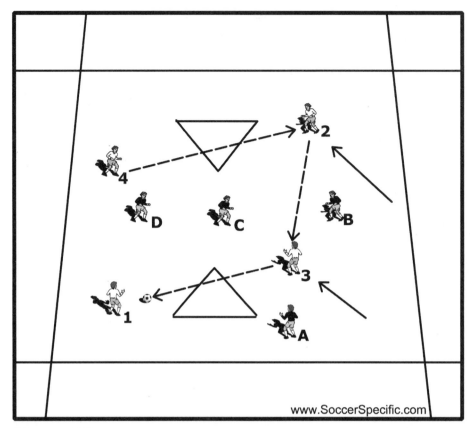

Diagram 107

1. **Coaching Points:**
   a) Head Up (looking into the other player,s eyes)
   b) Ability to look at the player AND see the ball also in their peripheral vision
   c) Good first touch to set up the second touch / pass
   d) Technique of Passing
2. Increase the area to 30 x 30 and have a 3v3 or 4v4 game (as above) and two triangular goals. (Numbers team attack one goal and letters team attacks the other.
3. **Progression:** Each team can score through both goals but it must be a pass and receive from one player to another through the middle of the triangle. This brings more switching the point of attack into the game.
4. Condition it where once you score through one you need to try to score through the other. You can't go back to the goal you scored in previously until possession has changed and you have regained possession again. Players can also score a goal by keeping possession and making 5 consecutive passes without an interception.

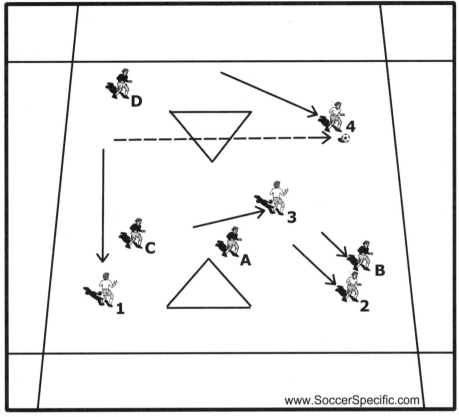

Diagram 108

1. Here (4) receives the pass into space from (1) after (2) has created the space with a run away from it.
2. Looking ahead, (3) makes a run into space to now help (4) and gets away from marker (A).
3. (1) makes a blind side run behind (C) to help (3) if he should receive the next pass, either as a pure pass or a pass through the goal to score.
4. Lots of movement off the ball by the players to either get it themselves or to help another player receive the pass.
5. I have made it look easier by not having defenders always track the runs but I do this to help emphasize how the movements off the ball can work.
6. Progress to using three, then four goals.

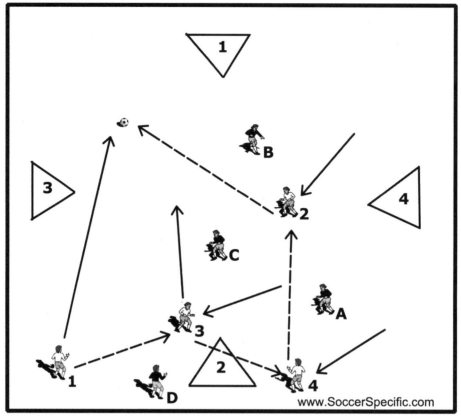

Diagram 109

1. Using four goals now and increasing the area to a 40 x 40. The numbers team attack goals one and two, letters team attack goals three and four.
2. Above (D) blocks the straight pass so (3) makes an angle for a pass from (1); (3) receives it and scores a goal passing through the triangle to (4).
3. (4) sees (2) in position for the next pass as the ball is traveling and plays him a one touch pass into space.
4. (1) is already on a run off the ball to attack the other goal and give (2) a new passing option. (3) also is on the move after passing to join in the next build up.

COACHING CLINIC SESSION PLAN 20
(For age 8 years and older)
OBJECTIVE: IMPROVING AWARENESS THROUGH A SIMPLE NUMBERS CONDITIONED GAME: INTRODUCING THE THREE TEAM AWARENESS GAME

AWARENESS NUMBERS GAME: PASSING IN SEQUENCE

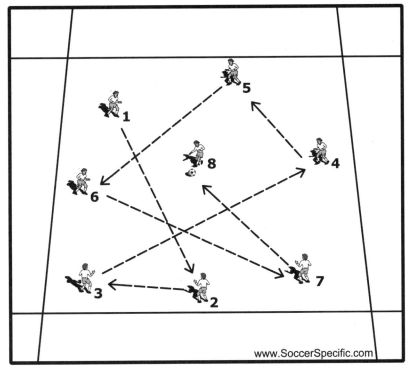

Diagram 110   **30 x 30**

1. Two Teams: 6 Players and only 1 ball to begin. Players must pass in sequence i.e. 1 passes to 2; 2 passes to 3; 3 to 4 and so on to 6 who passes to 1 and we begin again. You can have players static to begin then get them passing and moving.
2. Player receives from the same person and passes to the same person each time. This develops great awareness of time, space and player positions. There is continuous work on and off the ball.
3. Awareness of the location of the player you received from as well as the player you will pass to. Because of this players begin to anticipate the pass to them and where it is coming from. Also they must look to where it is going (where is the player they are passing to?).
4. We are trying to create a situation where players are looking two moves ahead not just one. For instance as (1) is about to pass to (2), (3) should be looking to support (2) for the next pass already, looking two moves ahead before the ball leaves (1). At the same time (3) should be looking to see where (4) is.
5. Peripheral Vision Development results from this.
6. **Progression:** Use two balls then three balls at the same time. Start with a ball at (1) and (4) then at (1), (4) and (6). To keep the sequence going players must move the balls quickly with few touches, hence their peripheral vision development improves dramatically. As soon as they have passed one ball off the next one is arriving, so quick thinking is needed to make the correct decisions.

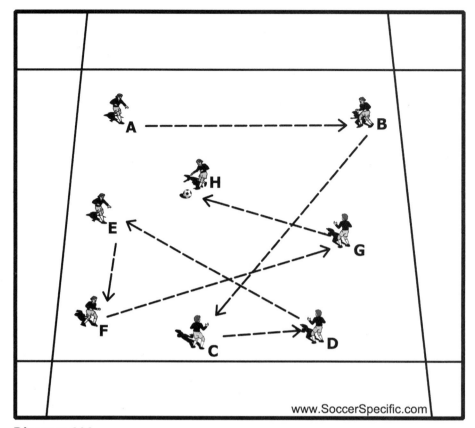

Diagram 111

1. The team above can be brought into the same zone to work in as the first team, each with a ball.
2. **Coaching Points:**
   a) Awareness of where the pass is coming from before receiving the pass
   b) Getting into position to help the passer make a successful pass
   c) Awareness of where the player to pass to is before receiving the pass
   d) Open Body position to receive the pass to enable a resulting one touch pass if necessary
   Progression 1:
   e) Awareness of the position of the player receiving the pass, before the person who passes to you receives it (thinking two moves ahead). If you are player number three, you are watching player number one passing in anticipation of player two passing to you.
   Progression 2:
   f) One and two touch condition to see who has good awareness.

Try the one touch condition and insist they stay with it. Who is good at it and who needs work?

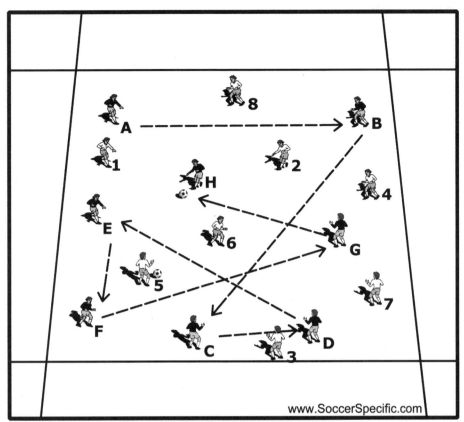

Diagram 112

1. You can begin with two teams in the bigger zone (combined zones of each team) and then have them play in the one zone where it's tight and more difficult to work in.
2. Obviously the players move but for simplicity of explanation I have shown it this way.
3. Player (A) is ready to begin the passing of the letters team.
4. **Competitive:** One ball per team, have a player count the number of passes a "team" makes in a given time period.

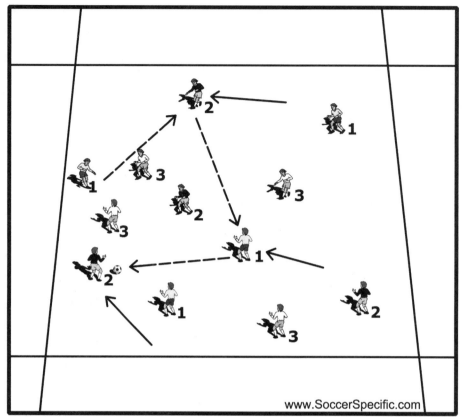

Diagram 113   **40 x 40**

1. Working with three teams (numbers depends on how many players are available, e.g. 4 v 4 + 4 or 5 v 5 + 5 etc). Teams (1) and (2) work together to keep the ball from team (3). If team (3) regains possession the team who gave it away becomes the defenders. The defenders' reward is they keep the ball and link with the other team. Rules: Once possession is gained, to establish who gave the ball away the defender who won the ball puts his foot on the ball to stop play and the coach can call out the team who gave it away. Play begins again, working on transitions.

2. **Develop:** Increase difficulty for attackers by:

   a) Reducing the zone size.

   b) Decreasing the number of touches on the ball for each player.

   c) Conditioning the passing to be only to the other attacking team's players e.g. (1) only pass to (2) and vice versa, therefore only half the number of passes are available per player.

   d) Using two balls, so that as they pass one ball they are now increasing their awareness and vision by looking for the other ball coming to them.

   e) Asking players to take off their pinnies so they really have to look and can't rely on color identification.

   f) No talking or pointing, so players have to rely on their own vision.

   g) Prohibiting verbal communication

COMPETITIVE NON - DIRECTIONAL THREE TEAM AWARENESS POSSESSION GAME
(4 v 4 v 4)

Diagram 114

1. **Further Progressions:** Making it more competitive, have each team be the defending team for a certain time span. If they win the ball they then give it back to the combined attacking teams. Count the number of times they win the ball. The defending team that wins the ball the most times wins the game, or alternatively the combined teams which give up the ball the fewest times win the game.
2. Attacking players individually count the number of times they give the ball away as an indication of how well they can maintain possession under pressure.
3. Begin with unlimited touches, then break it down to 3 touch, then 2 touch with one touch passing the goal if it is on to do so.
4. **Coaching Points:**
   a) Open body stance to allow a yard or more of extra space away from defenders by letting the ball run across the body into preconceived space.
   b) Looking before receiving to know in advance of the receiving pass: where the defending players are, where the space is, where teammates are free to receive a pass, how many options there are to move the ball on.
   c) Movement OFF the ball is a priority both to receive it and after passing it.

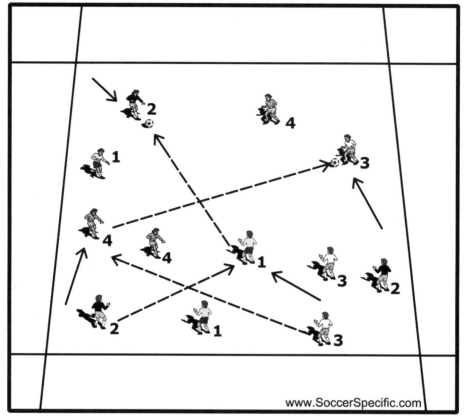

Diagram 115

1. This is a great game for forcing players to observe what is ahead of the ball so that they know what they need to do with the ball "before" they receive it. Players (1) and (2) work together and players (3) and (4) work together.
2. Players must pass in sequence i.e. 1 passes to 2; 2 passes to 3; 3 to 4 and 4 to 1 and we begin again. Players are static to begin then start passing and moving. Player receives from the same person and passes to the same person each time. This develops great awareness of time, space and player positions. This is continuous work on and off the ball.
3. Awareness of: the position of the player you receive from and the player you're passing to. Because of this players begin to anticipate the pass to them and where it is coming from. Also they must look to where it is going (where is the player they are passing to?).
4. We are trying to create a situation where players are looking two moves ahead, not just one. For instance, as (1) is about to pass to (2), (3) should be looking to support (2) for the next pass already, looking two moves ahead before the ball leaves (1). Peripheral Vision Development results from this.
5. (3) should recognize if he needs to move into a space early or late based on this observation, but know in his mind already what the next best option is. Moving into the space too early in a game situation, for example, may result in being marked too easily. But knowing in advance "when and where" to move is an advantage and this game helps players develop this thought process.

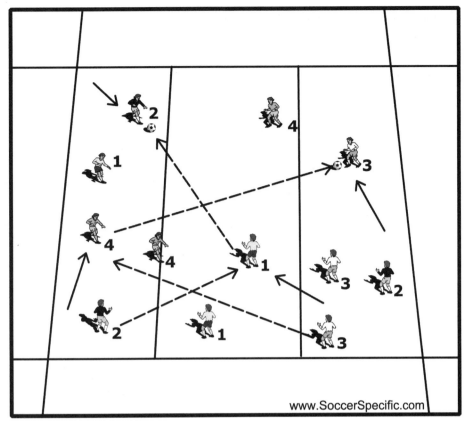

Diagram 116

1. Ask players to make it difficult to find them by incorporating lots of movement off the ball to test their teammate's vision.
2. **Progression:**
   Use two balls then three balls at the same time. Start with a ball at (1) and (4) then at (1), (4) and (6). To keep the sequence going players must move the balls quickly with few touches, hence their peripheral vision development improves dramatically. As soon as they have passed one ball off, the next one is arriving, so quick thinking is needed to make the correct decisions.

   Divide the field into thirds. Players have to make a pass in one third then move to another third to receive the next pass. This can cause players to pass long or pass short and vary the range and distance of the passes and the support.
3. Here (3) passes to (4) and moves into another zone to receive the next ball. This ensures players get the idea of passing and MOVING off the ball, not passing and then standing. (2) does the same with a pass to (1), then moves into another zone supporting the next ball.

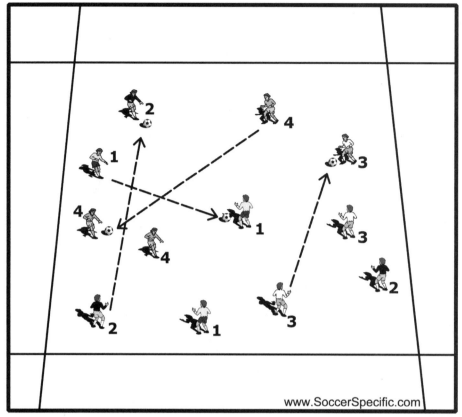

Diagram 117

1. **Competitive:** The same idea as the introductory session only the players count the number of passes they make in a given time as a team. Compare the totals. They can't pass back to the same player they received from.
2. Introduce several small goals for the players to pass through and count the number of goals scored. Ensure the players arrive at the goal (timing of the run) as the ball is passed through the goal (timing of the pass).
3. Players must not stand by a goal waiting for a pass because in a game they would not stand still waiting to receive the ball.
4. **Progression:** Increase the number of balls per team (two balls per team). Combine two teams and have them passing to the other color with three balls going at once, the variations can be numerous.

COMPETITIVE DIRECTIONAL THREE TEAM AWARENESS GAME INTRODUCING GOALS AS TARGETS

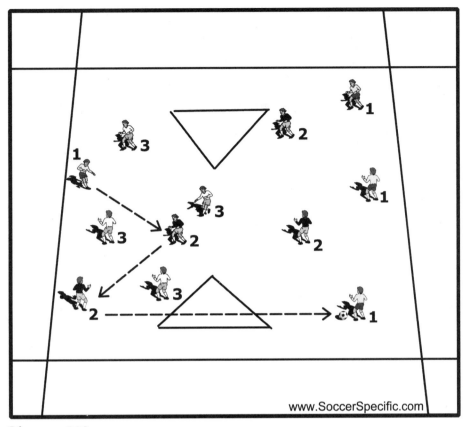

Diagram 118

1. Here is an interesting way to work on awareness training and passing, movement off the ball, fitness and looking for the penetrating pass. Add triangular goals to score through. This means the game continues after a goal is scored as the ball must be received and possession maintained by another player on the other side of the triangle to count as a goal. This ensures continuous play.
2. It is a more directional method of playing and more specific to the game in general. The defenders are NOT allowed inside the triangle so they must be constantly working their way around the triangle trying to cut off the penetrating passes.
3. Team (3) defends while teams (1) and (2) work together. The combined attacking teams can attack both goals alternatively. Attacking both goals encourages "Switching the Field".
4. Ultimately reduce the game to two equal teams for the greatest challenge and begin with as many touches as needed, reducing the number of touches as players improve and are able to keep possession effectively. Reducing the number of touches inevitably increases their awareness and forces them to look for options earlier and improves and speeds up their decision making. This should result in more effective possession play.

COACHING CLINIC SESSION PLAN 21

(For age 9 years and older)

OBJECTIVE: TAKING THE AWARENESS NUMBERS GAME INTO A MORE MATCH-LIKE ENVIRONMENT

NON – COMPETITIVE AWARENESS NUMBERS "GAME" WITH TEAMS: PASSING IN SEQUENCE
Divide the players up into three teams

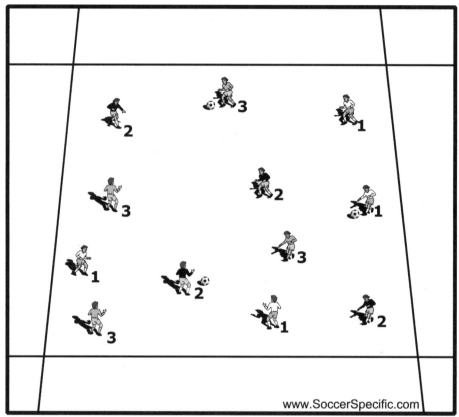

www.SoccerSpecific.com

Diagram 119   **30 x 30**

1. Using 3 teams. Within each team each player is numbered off. Teams (1) and (2) work together (with two balls) and team (3) works alone (with one ball). Players must pass in sequence i.e. with teams (1) and (2) working together 1 passes to 2; 2 passes to 3; 3 to 4; 4 to other attacking team's 1 and so on, while team (3) players pass 1 to 4.

2. Awareness of: the position of the player you receive from and the player you pass to. Because of this players begin to anticipate the pass to them and where it is coming from. Also they must look to where it is going (where is the player they are passing to?). We are trying to create a situation where players are looking two moves ahead, not just one.

3. For instance, as (1) is about to pass to (2), (3) should be looking to support (2) for the next pass already, looking two moves ahead before the ball leaves (1). Peripheral vision development results from this. Develop: Reduce the number of touches players are allowed each time they receive a pass, all in to begin, then three touch, then two touch then one touch if it is on to do so. This speeds up the decision making process and forces them to look earlier to find their next passing option.

SEMI – COMPETITIVE AWARENESS NUMBERS GAME: PASSING IN SEQUENCE

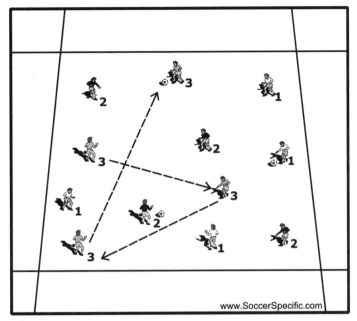

Diagram 120

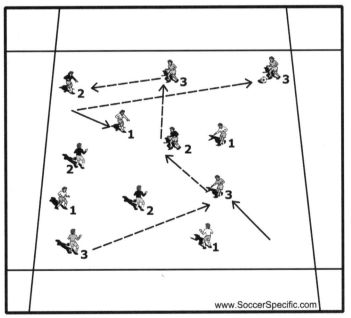

Diagram 121

Coaching Points:

a) An Open body stance is needed to allow a yard or more extra space away from defenders by letting the ball run across the body into preconceived space.

b) Looking before receiving to know in advance where the defending players are, where the space is, where teammates are free to receive a pass, how many options there are to move the ball on.

c) Movement OFF the ball is a priority both to receive and after passing.

- 183 -

AWARENESS NUMBERS GAME WORKING IN THREE ZONES

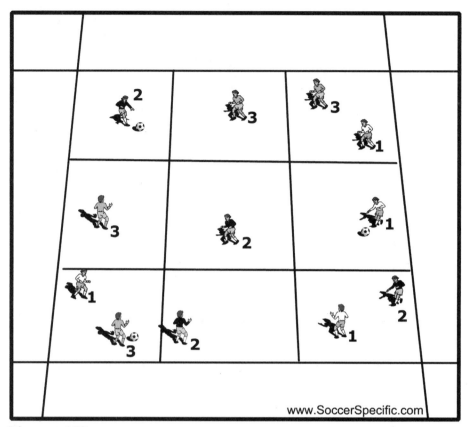

Diagram 122

1. Condition the players to pass and move by setting the rule that they need to move into another area once they have passed the ball.
2. Divide the field into sixths and have the players make a pass in one area then move to another area to receive the next pass. This can cause players to pass long or pass short and vary the range and distance of the passes and the support as they are required to move once they have made their pass.
3. Here we are using three teams of four players.
4. Here players pass and move into other zones to receive the next ball. This ensures players get the idea of passing and MOVING off the ball.
5. Have players pass to space, targeting a zone next to the player they are passing to in order to force that player to move to the ball.

COACHING CLINIC SESSION PLAN 22

(For age 9 years and older)

OBJECTIVE: WORKING ON PERIPHERAL VISION THROUGH THE SPECIFIC PERIPHERAL VISION COACHING GAME

A 40x30 area is organized as shown in the Diagram below. Six players are used within the activity. Repeat the setup to accommodate the entire team.

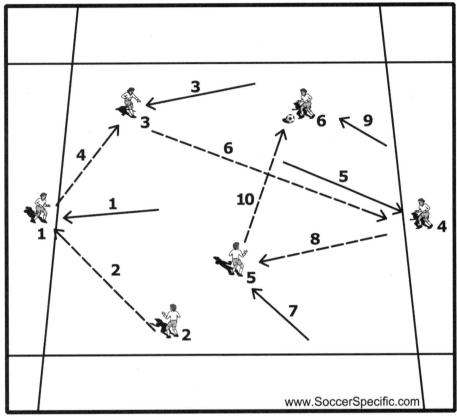

Diagram 123   **30 x 30**

This is a simplified set up to get initial understanding. Increase numbers as previously e.g. two teams of six. We started earlier with one ball and six players, so each person on the ball had five passing options.

Now we must identify one and only one pass and must try to make it. That pass is to the person who runs outside the zone. This player is the free player (unmarked). The session goes as follows and numbers are used only as a reference, the players can pass to anyone, in any order, but always looking for that vital run by a player to the outside area:

1. Player (1) runs outside the area (perhaps after several passes within the zone).
2. Player (2) on the ball sees the run and must pass to (1).
3. As (1) is about to receive (3) moves into a position to support him, showing anticipation and awareness.
4. (3) has already seen the run by (4) and passes. (4) brings the ball back in and the game continues. (4) passes to (5) who has moved into position in anticipation and (5) passes to (6) who has done the same. This is an indicator of how quickly players recognize the run and consequently make the pass.

5. Players are beginning to look one and two moves ahead of the ball. It doesn't need to happen so quickly in terms of the next player running outside but it serves as an example. The run can be likened to a penetrating run into the attacking third where the player hasn't been picked up or tracked and is in a great position to attack and score if the passer sees him and makes the pass.

6. **Coaching Points:**
   a) Decision: Movement of the player running out of the area to initiate the move
   b) Do the other players see the run?
   c) Most importantly, does the player receiving the pass see the run?
   d) Decision by this player to make the one pass needed to the outside player
   e) Quality of Passing: A one or two touch pass to the outside player for speed of action to show the run was spotted.
   f) Weight of pass to the next passing player so he has the choice of making a one touch pass if he has seen the run
   g) Does the receiving player on the outside see the runs of others to make the next pass?
   h) Support Positions: Other players already making movements to give the receiving outside player options to move the ball quickly with good support in terms of angles, distances and timing.

SPECIFIC PERIPHERAL VISION COACHING SESSION

Further development, ideas and ideals of this practice leading to the introduction of defenders but in an attacking overload situation.

1. Within the zone there are many passing options but as soon as a player makes the run outside that is the pass to make. Coach can determine the tempo of the game e.g. to avoid too many running out at the same time the coach can signal to an individual player to move out without the others knowing so only one at a time goes out.

2. Once the free player is outside and waiting for a pass, see how many passes are made inside the zone before someone sees him and makes the pass. This is an indication of which players play with their heads up (good peripheral vision) and which don't, (poor peripheral vision or even none at all).

3. The fewer touches on the ball the player needs to get the ball there the greater his anticipation of the run. (One touch is the ultimate aim: as the ball is traveling to the player, another player makes his run out; the receiving player sees the run and makes the pass first time).

4. More touches means more reaction time needed, which makes things easy for the defenders.

5. Initially the coach may see several passes made within the area until someone sees the player who made the run outside; this will happen less and less as you practice and as the players improve their peripheral vision.

6. The exciting part of this is when the coach sees one of his players make the right pass quickly in a game situation due to the work they have done in this session.

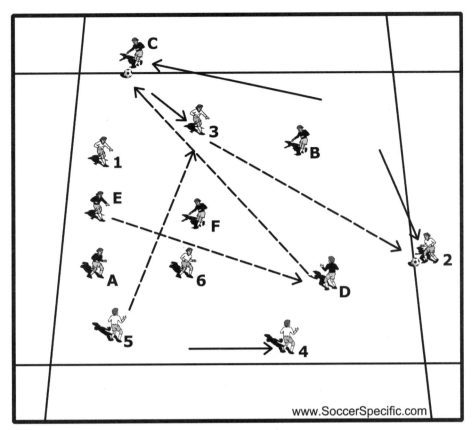

Diagram 124

1. Here we have two teams playing in the same area, player (5) passes to player (3). Player (2), as the ball is traveling, runs outside the area. Player (3) has to see this movement and make the next pass to (2). If (3) makes it with a one touch pass, it shows he had his head up and saw the run as the ball was arriving and made the quickest pass possible. Player (2) then brings the ball back into play and the passing sequences start again.

2. Likewise player (E) on the other team passes to player (D), player (C) runs out of the area and the set up continues.

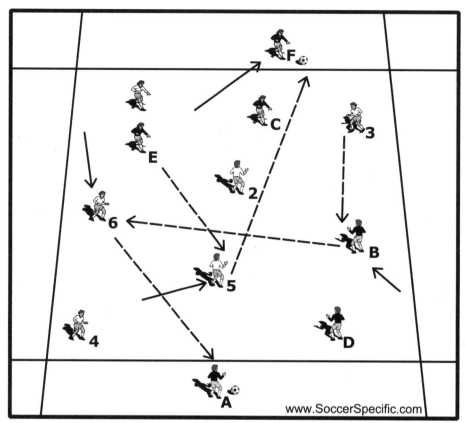

www.SoccerSpecific.com

Diagram 125

1. **Progression:** Passing to opposite colors, so now a red player (numbers team) is looking to make a pass to a gray player (letters team) running out of the area and a gray player is looking to make a pass to a red player running out of the area. This really sharpens up the awareness capabilities of the players. Here Grey (E) passes to Red (6) and Grey (F) makes a run outside the area, (6) spots the move and makes a one touch pass to (F).
2. Likewise Red (3) passes to Grey (B) who spots the outside run by Red (2) and passes to him.
3. This is all designed to sharpen the awareness of all the players so they keep their heads up with and without the ball and are therefore able to observe their options as quickly, efficiently and as effectively as possible
4. The ultimate challenge is to ask them to play 1 touch only and make it work.

GAME SITUATION

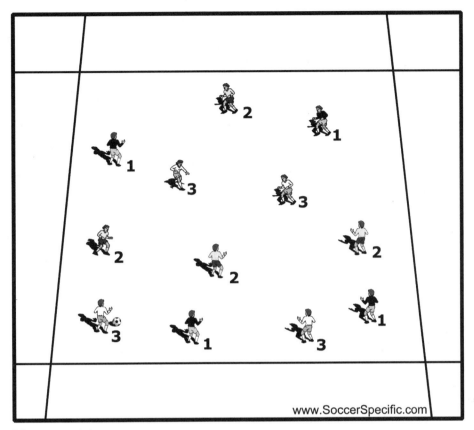

Diagram 126

1. Three team game, two teams combine and play together against one team. It is always best to begin with an overload situation to help them make it work. Once they are successful go to two equal numbered teams.
2. Count how many times the combined teams give the ball away in a set period of time. Have each team be the defending team.
3. The winner is the team who defend and have the most gains during their time defending (can include winning possession, forcing opponents to kick the ball out with pressure etc). If they win possession they give it back to the two attacking teams (or reward them by letting them try to keep possession).
4. **Develop:** Include running out of the area in the game and if a player does this and receives a pass successfully it cancels out two give aways. Defending players can't track them outside the area.
5. This will encourage players to make outside runs as there is a reward and it will also test the peripheral vision of the players on the ball and how quickly they identify that particular run. This must happen in less than 6 seconds or the player who made the outside run must come back into the game.
6. Numbers and letters team work together. It is an 8v4 overload.
7. (2) makes a run out of the area, (A) sees the run and passes. (2) brings the ball back in and the game continues.

8. You are looking for players to anticipate where (2) needs support and move into position to help.
9. Here (1) runs off the defender to create space for (C) to run into and support (2). (B) also makes a run between the defenders to offer close help. Other players need to move off the ball to get into open positions for the first pass or in anticipation of the next ones.
10. Finally, equal number teams but with the same rules.

COACHING CLINIC SESSION PLAN 23
(For age 9 years and older)
OBJECTIVE: DEVELOPING PERIPHERAL VISION AND AWARENESS TRAINING
INTRODUCING MORE BALLS INTO A COMPETITIVE GAME

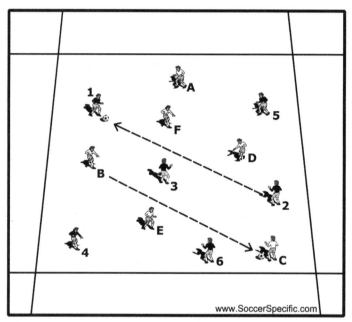

Diagram 127   **30 x 30**

1. **Coaching Points:**
   a) Looking before receiving, developing Peripheral Awareness
   b) Quality of first touch
   c) Quality of pass
   d) Support movements off the ball
   e) High Concentration due to multiple balls and multiple options
2. Players passing and moving in the usual format, rotate between passing to their own color and the opposite color to test them as a warm up. Start with one ball, add another, then another. Practice with several balls so players need to be aware of several options.
3. Once they begin to show improvement, introduce a competitive element to the game. Have 1 ball to begin and make it a possession game of 6 against 6. Introduce another ball (to the team not in possession) so each team has to keep possession of their own ball while trying to win possession of the other ball.
4. It may be that a particular player is involved in trying to win a ball back but has to be aware that other teammates have possession of the second ball and he may have to adjust his thinking and positioning instantly if a player looks to pass the second ball to him. This helps the mind prepare for instant transitions from attack to defense and defense to attack.

5. Players need to be prepared to change their focus; one second trying to win a ball but the next making themselves available to receive another ball from a teammate already in possession.

6. On changing from a defender to an attacker by receiving the second ball, this player must think about where the other players are who are free to pass to in order to keep the momentum of the move going. Going back to the Awareness principles, this player has to know where the ball is going before receiving it to have the best chance of keeping possession of this second ball.

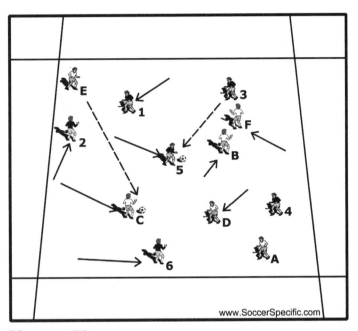

Diagram 128

7. The next stage may be that the team that wins back the first ball now has 2 balls to keep possession of. This means the players are constantly looking around the area. As soon as a player receives and passes on one ball he is looking to receive and pass the second ball and so on.

8. Above, each team has a ball to keep possession of and at the same time they are trying to win possession of the other team's ball.

9. **Observe:** (C) and (D) make movements to support (E) to keep the ball, at the same time (B) and (F) close down (double team) (3) on the other team in possession of the other ball.

10. Observe; (1) and (2) close down (E) to win back the ball and (5) and (6) move into space to support and receive a pass from (3).

11. Develop by playing with 3 balls. Awareness must be really sharp now with so much to think about; which balls we have in our possession and consequently where we have to position to keep possession but also which balls we haven't got and how we need to work to try and win them back.

12. Decision making now is being tested to the fullest capacity. Do I support the balls we have? Do I defend to win possession of the other team's balls? Do I change mid-stream as the opportunity presents itself? Each player needs to be aware of all these options.

13. When we go back to one ball with two teams playing simple possession, the Awareness instincts of the players should be more developed and sharp as a needle.

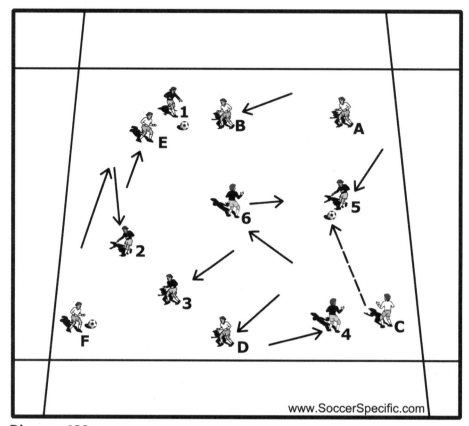

Diagram 129

14. Above (E) and (B) close (1) down but (E) wins the ball. (B) at the same time sees that (C) needs help and moves from defending against one ball to supporting another. (C)'s pass in the meantime is intercepted by (5). (6) moved to support (1) initially who then lost the ball so (6) switched to support (5) who had just won another ball.

15. (2) moved to support (1) on the ball, (1) then lost it so (2) changed direction to help (3) pressure (F) who had possession of another ball and so on.

16. It looks complicated but when you get into the session you can see how it works and how players need to constantly learn to transition in their minds and in their actions.

17. Experiment with the size of the area. It will be easier to introduce this in a bigger area with more space to work in, maybe a 50 x 40 yard area. A bigger area means also that it is easier to identify what is happening with each ball as they can be spread apart more. It is almost like three individual games going on in the same area but they become intermingled as possession changes and players change their roles as defenders to attackers and vice versa in an instant.

COACHING CLINIC SESSION PLAN 24

(For age 10 years and older)
OBJECTIVE: DEVELOPING TEAM PLAY THROUGH A DIRECTIONAL FOUR TEAM AWARENESS GAME WITH SIXTEEN PLAYERS: PART A

This is an interesting way to practice and develop the concept of awareness. This works with various numbers of players but here we are using 16. It is becoming more directional in content with players working up and down the field of play as in a game situation.

I believe these two clinics can easily be broken down further to four to six individual clinics as there are so many developments and progressions within the idea once you have included the warm up, some fast footwork, the actual theme of the clinic, the small sided game and the cool down. It can depend on how quickly the players take on and learn the ideas from this session and how long it takes them to be able to use them effectively. My advice is to focus on this particular directional theme for more than just two sessions because the players will have a lot of information to process. Just the game itself at the end of this clinic plan can constitute a full new session itself.

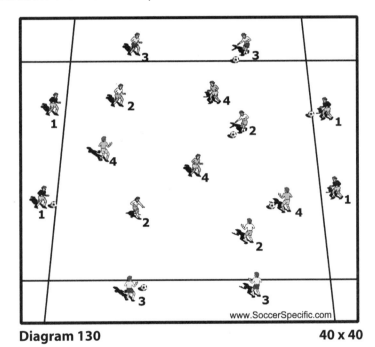

Diagram 130   **40 x 40**

1. (2)s pass to (1)s and (4)s pass to (3)s. The two groups work across each other. Four teams working.
2. A directional clinic now working across each other, needing to know where teammates are but also where the other numbered players are in the middle. This improves awareness and the peripheral vision of the players.
3. This is a good lead-in to everyone being free in the area and passing and moving, which will come later.
4. Players need to look before they receive, see what the options are in advance of the ball.
5. You can start with one ball per team and work on team shape within the clinic. For example, the target player must pass to the furthest forward player (so they need to see this before they get the ball) who lays it off one way diagonally, this next player passes it across the area diagonally forward again (forming a diamond pattern to make it work). Then they pass it into the next target on the other side.

6. **Progression:** Make it all one touch passing.
7. **Coaching Points:**
    a) Awareness of where your own players are and where the other team's players are before receiving the ball
    b) Awareness of where the spaces are to move into before receiving the ball.
    c) Quality of the first touch: First touch into the path you are taking to get the ball to the outside player or one touch transfer if possible
    d) Support positions of teammates off the ball
    e) Playing through the other team in the opposite direction, testing positional ability
8. Directional movement as in a game

LIKEN TO WORKING THROUGH THE THIRDS OF THE FIELD

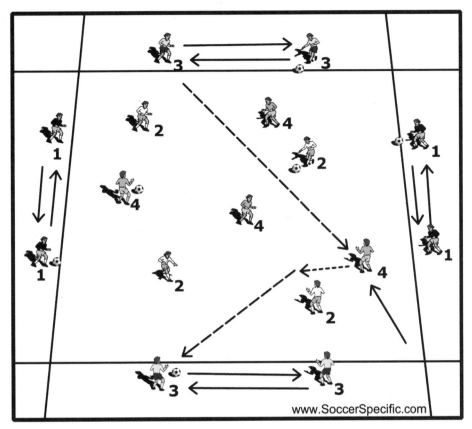

Diagram 131

1. Three or four balls per side. Players on the outside constantly switch positions past each other so they are moving targets (as in a game players are on the move) and also to keep them working and on their toes. They can also pass a ball between them to keep the game flowing. Therefore, the inside players are passing outside to a moving player, into their path, and so into space.

2. Think defending line: midfield line:attacking line so if the ball is with a (3) player they are the defensive line, the receiver (4) in the middle is the midfield line and the player to pass to on the other side is the attacking line. The players are working the ball through the team from the back to the front.

3. Discourage players from passing up and down in straight lines. Above is an example of diagonal passing and movement. Once this movement has been completed the player in question must look for another ball to work with at either end of the field.

4. Players must identify a free player to pass to "before" the pass is made. They also need to be aware that by the time they get the ball and are ready to pass the situation may have changed and so they are able to adjust with good awareness and find another player who may have just become free.

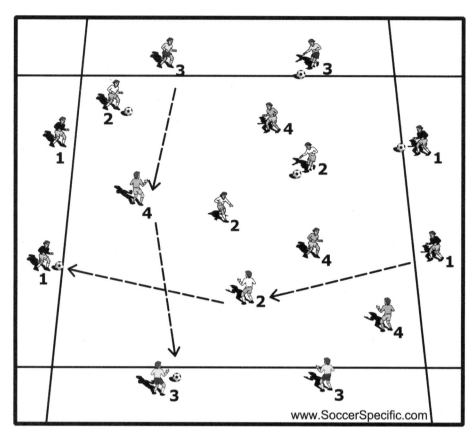

Diagram 132

1. Try to avoid players just passing in straight lines as above.
2. A midfielder receiving with his back completely turned to his intended target will have a difficult time seeing where defenders and his intended target are positioned until he turns. This inevitably results in extra time and extra touches, which often result in a loss of possession. Turning side on will help but opening up the angle to receive will work better.
3. One of the number (4) players above has closed down his own space by getting too close to the passer (3), so he has less room to work in. Ask players not to get too close to the passer as in a game a defender can effectively mark both of them.

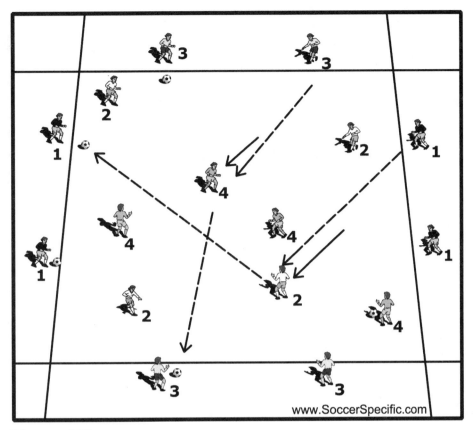

Diagram 133

Progressions:

a) Passing in straight and / or angled lines
b) Running in straight and / or angled lines
c) Mixing up the two (above (4) makes an angled run off the ball to receive, receives an angled pass and makes a straight pass to the target). (2) makes an angled run off the ball to receive and makes an angled and diagonal pass to (1) in one touch.
d) Players pass to the end players only, to begin transferring the ball from one side to the other. If both players on the other side have balls at their feet then liken it in a game to the strikers being marked and you have pressure on the ball preventing a forward pass so you have to go back to where you came from, either to the other player you did not receive the pass from or back to the same player.
e) Passing inside the area to teammates in the build up, not just to the outside players.

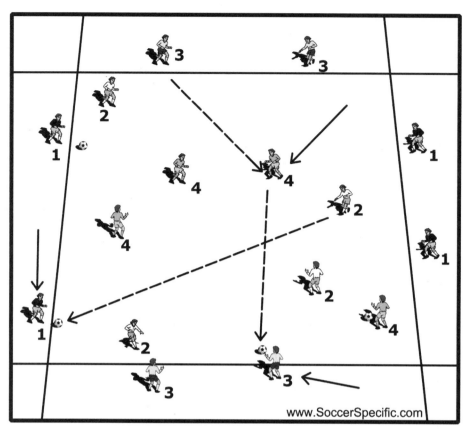

Diagram 134

f) Outside players can pass to each other on the same side to keep the ball moving and keep the inside players aware of where the ball is.

g) Outside players switch positions with and without a ball. If without the ball then they are now moving targets as it would be in a game.

h) All players communicate with each other to help make each movement and pass successful (above as (4) receives the pass, (3) calls to let him know he is free to receive the next pass).

i) Ask inside and outside players to pass to space to move players into better positions to receive the pass. Above, (2) passes to space to force the outside player (1) to move to receive the pass. (3) passes to space to move (4) into the path of the pass. (4) and (1) respectively can help (2) and (3) by pointing to where they want the ball if they identify the space to pass it to first.

COACHING CLINIC SESSION PLAN 25

(For age 10 years and older)

OBJECTIVE: DEVELOPING TEAM PLAY THROUGH A DIRECTIONAL FOUR TEAM AWARENESS GAME WITH SIXTEEN PLAYERS: PART B

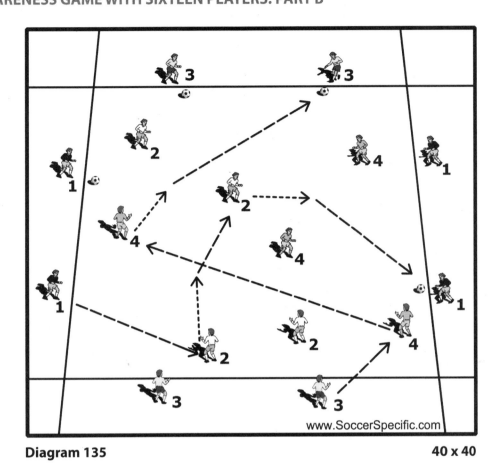

Diagram 135   **40 x 40**

1. Playing through the midfield with another inside player to reach one of the targets.
2. Each player takes one touch to take the ball in the direction he wants to go and the second touch is a pass to the next player.
3. It may be a one touch pass that is needed depending on the distances involved. It may be he needs more touches on the ball because no one is immediately available to receive a pass. Or you may condition it that he needs to do a dribble of some sort in the middle before passing to the next player. There are many variables you can introduce to suit your needs.

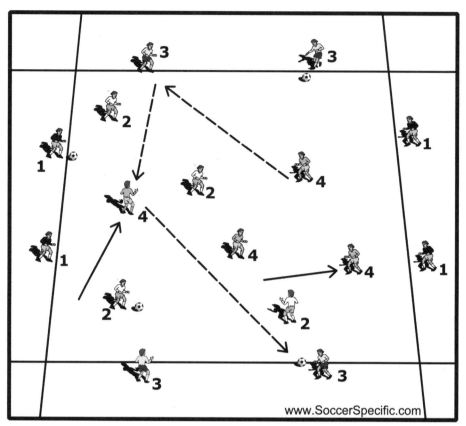

Diagram 136

1. Encouraging players to look ahead of the play. Here (4) passes to outside player (3) and another (4) player is supporting (3) for the next pass, working a triangle of support.
2. (3) needs someone to pass to, (4) has already moved into position to receive.
3. As (4), who is receiving the pass from (3), gets into an angled support position ensuring an open body stance, he has to have these things in mind before receiving the pass:
   a) Where is the space to go to in order to receive the pass from (3)?
   b) Who is free at the other end to make the next pass to?
   c) Where is the space to take my next touch, or can I pass it one touch to (3) on the other side?
4. As this pass is coming in to (3), another (4) player is already looking to support the next pass going back.

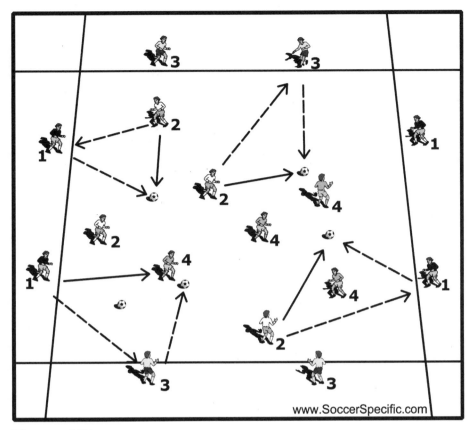

Diagram 137

1. The ball starts with the inside players. They must play 1- 2's or a give and go with an outside player.
2. Passes to an outside player should be played so that the ball can be passed back in one touch so it is a genuine give and go. The inside player must support at an angle to have an open body stance to go the other way and to be able to see what is ahead before he receives the ball.
3. Check they do not close down their own space when they pass so they can't see what is behind, or which target player on the other side is free (or not free). If this happens, more touches are required to move the ball and get into position to go the other way.
4. (4) above plays a give and go with (3), checks off at an angle with an open stance to receive back and goes the other way having identified already who is free on the other side. (2) plays the 1-2 with (1) then runs the ball back across the field to do the same with (1) on the other side.

SWITCHING POSITIONS WITH THE OUTSIDE PLAYER

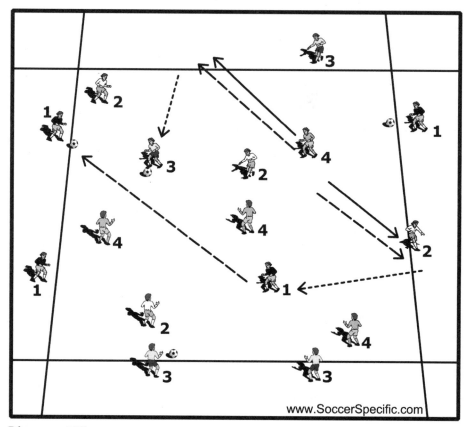

Diagram 138

1. Now to involve everyone in the middle, have the players switch positions after they pass to an outside player.
2. (4) passes to (3) who takes the ball back in with a good first touch to then look to pass to another player and get the ball to the other side.
3. Likewise (1) receives from (2) and runs the ball into the middle to continue the movement, and (2) runs out of the area to be an outside receiver. (1) then passes to another (1) player and switches with him.
4. As shown above, players (1) and (2) can pass to either numbers (1) and (2) because it will be both numbers now on the outside, not just the one number. The same is true for players (3) and (4). So it is still a directional session working up and down the field of play.

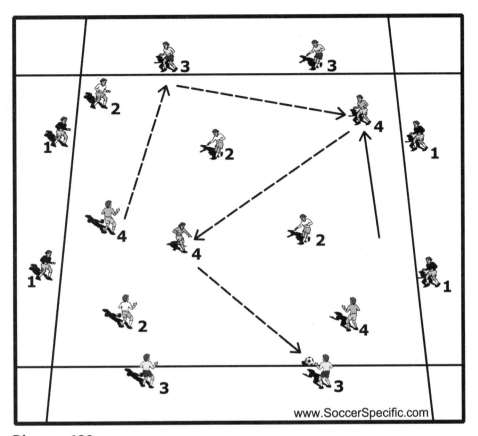

Diagram 139

1. Now we take the session into a game. (2)'s play against (4)'s.
   Start with four 1v1's, a ball each pair (4 balls) then build to two 2v2's then go to a 4v4 game.
   Number (2) players need to pass to number (1)'s on the outside to score, (4)'s pass to the
   (3)'s. 1v1 is very intense so to maintain quality keep it fairly short.
2. Now playing 4v4 the (2)'s work with (1)'s on the outside and score by completing a pass to
   the outside players. They then have to get the ball to the other side to score again. (4)'s work
   with the (3)'s on the outside so teams play in opposite directions.
3. **GAME:** Play to 10 goals then rotate the players so the (1)'s play against the (3)'s.
4. Rotate the teams so the (1)'s play against the (2)'s and the (3)'s against the (4)'s.
5. Here the number (4) team have scored one goal at one end then switched the play to the
   other end by quick accurate passing to score another goal.

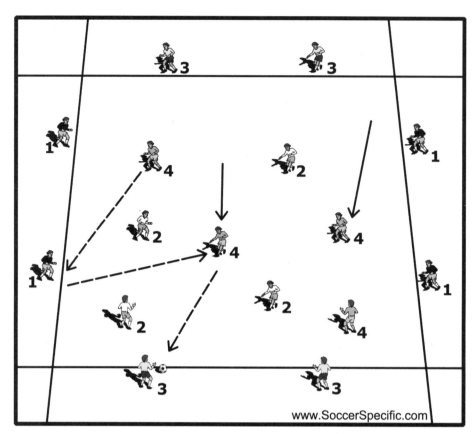

Diagram 140

USING SUPPORT PLAYERS ON THE OUTSIDE

1. Same game idea but while the (2)'s have to get the ball to the outside (1)'s they can use the (3)'s as support players.
2. Likewise the (4)'s get the ball to the (3)'s to score but can use the (1)'s as support players.
3. This takes a lot of thought for the players and keeps them focused.
4. As the ball goes to (1), other (4) players need to be getting into position to help the outside player on the ball. Player (1), outside and on the ball, has to be looking to see where the next pass can go before receiving the ball.
5. Here the number (4) player has moved to help (1) make a good pass and keep possession by passing to (3) and scoring. The other (4) player is already on the move to support (3) and attack the other way..

Diagram 141

1. Developing the idea, now two teams play together and switch positions when they score a goal.
2. (4) passes to (3) who can bring the ball back in and (4) can go outside to be a target player.
3. Progression: Introduce scoring a goal by making a successful one touch pass to encourage the players to think quickly and make instant decisions when they receive the ball.
4. Have outside players switching positions so they are moving when they receive the pass.

COACHING CLINIC SESSION PLAN 26

(For age 11 years and older)

OBJECTIVE: AN AWARENESS OF THE SPACE TO EXPLOIT USING THE SHADOW STRIKER

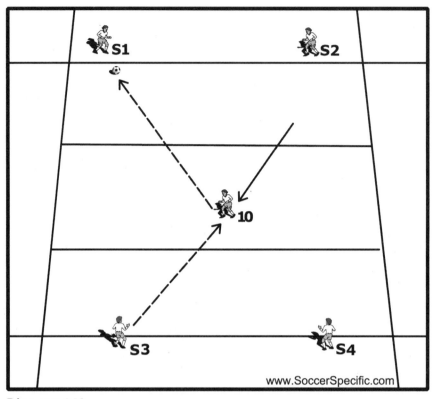

Diagram 142

Playing with a shadow striker requires a good player with a vast amount of awareness to know when and where to drop off and receive, which means being aware of markers and also where teammates are. The need for awareness was never emphasized more than in this type of role for a player and many of the best players in the world play this position between the midfield and the strikers.

1. Server S3 feeds the shadow striker (10).
2. (10) turns and feeds S1 at the far end.
3. S1 feeds S2, striker switches with another S (S3 or S4) and the cycle continues.
4. **Technical Coaching Points:**
   a) Support angle / distance of (10)
   b) Receiving skills of (10)
   c) Passes into and from (10)
   d) Awareness of (10)
5. **Progression:**
   a) S's change sides before receiving a pass from (10).
   b) Introduce another striker.
6. Liken the thirds to the attacking third, middle third and defensive third so the shadow striker is dropping back from the attacking third to the middle third to receive the ball.
7. You could also liken this to a midfield player dropping short to receive from the back players.

8. This is a great all round clinic for many skills, including: Passing quality and the weight and angle of the pass, Movement off the ball, Creating and finding space, supporting positions (particularly angled support); decision making without pressure to begin, transition, and ultimately Awareness on and off the ball.

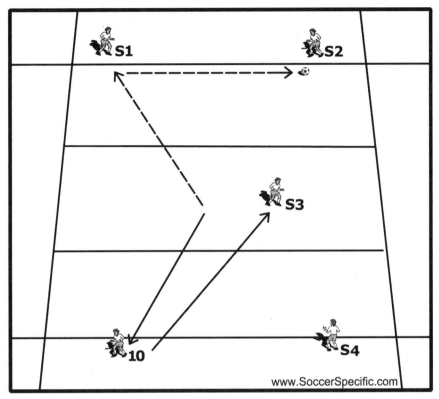

Diagram 143

1. Here (10) has passed to S1 who plays the ball to S2 to change the angle of the pass to the next shadow striker S3.
2. As (10) lays the pass off he chooses a player to switch with. This player, in this case S3, then goes to receive from S2 and the cycle continues.
3. All the players get the chance to make the necessary runs as the shadow striker in the middle and into the middle third.
4. Here, S1 acts as the second striker in front who has received a pass from (10).
5. Once this pass has been made, S1 and S2 become essentially midfield support players going the other way, and (10) and S4 are target second strikers.
5. Who the middle player passes the ball to determines which player the middle player switches with to ensure there is an angled support. Here the ball will eventually finish up at S2 so the logical player to switch with is S3 as shown to maintain the angled support. If the switch was to be with S4 then that player needs to ensure he does not support a pass from S3 in a straight line by working an angle to receive, making a run to the center of the field, not straight at S2.

FRONT STRIKER / SHADOW STRIKER

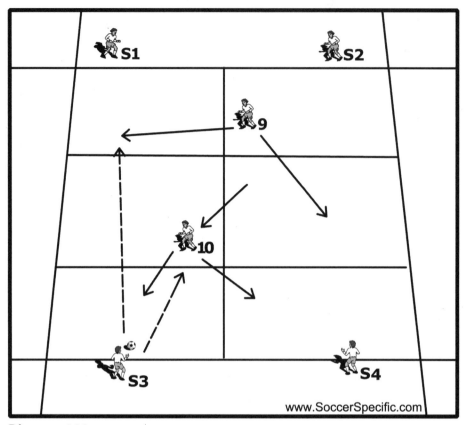

Diagram 144

1. Central area coned off into thirds. We have six players (4 servers, 2 players). The S's serve to each other then into either (9) or (10).
2. Both (9) and (10) must touch the ball before it is transferred to the other side.
3. (9) and (10) must be aware of each other's positions. They must never be in the same third of the field to ensure one goes short and one long.
4. Working on receiving skills and release skills.
5. Avoid supporting in a straight line, working angles off each other to support.
6. **Progression 1:** Play the ball into the second striker or front striker who then lays it off for the shadow striker, instead of going to the shadow striker first. In this way, it is all passing the way you are facing.
7. **Progression 2:** One S player can move into the area as a supporting midfield player and receive passes from (9) or (10).

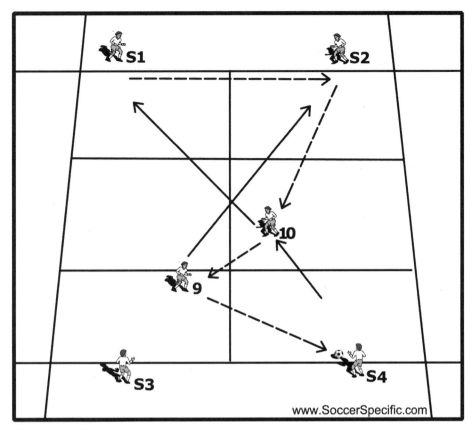

Diagram 145

1. The play starts at S1.
2. All players have the opportunity to be the two strikers, the front striker and the shadow striker.
3. When (10) and (9) have combined and passed the ball to S3 or S4 they switch with S1 and S2 who become the two strikers going the other way.
4. One player has to go short into the midfield third to be the shadow striker and one stays up top in the attacking third as the front striker.
5. Have them both make diagonal runs to get into position because this will make them more difficult to pick up in a game.

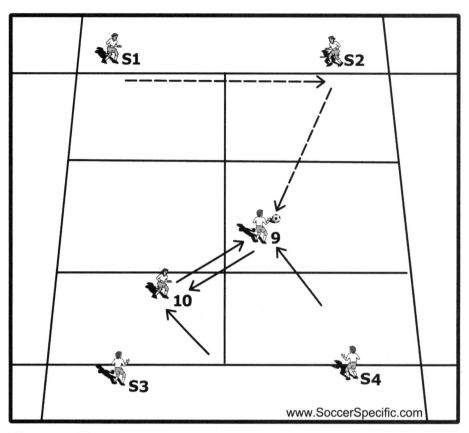

Diagram 146

1. Here the timing of the runs is too early so the two strikers switch positions to make the timing right. In a game this will make it more difficult for defenders to mark them with this constant movement off the ball to receive.

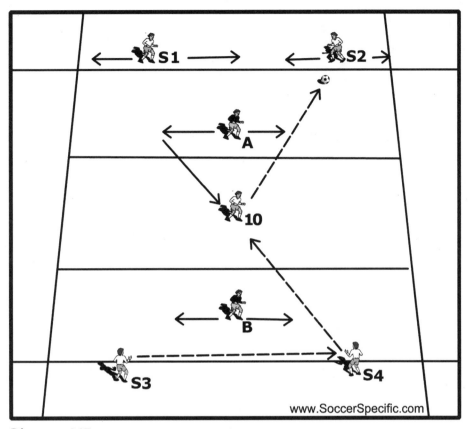

Diagram 147

1. (A) and (B) work along the lines to try to intercept the passes made by (10). Here S1 and S2 can move along the line to open up the angle to receive from (10). The defenders (A) and (B) must stay and defend in their own third initially.
2. **Progression:** Defenders (A) and (B) can come forward and oppose (10), but only after (10)'s first touch. This means (10) has time to receive and turn and pass successfully so the pressure is essentially passive.
3. (10) feeds an S target player and then switches with S3 or S4, therefore alternating the shadow striker.
4. **Technical Coaching Points:**
    a) An Awareness of the positions of (A) and (B) before receiving the ball.
    b) Passing past opponents
    c) Attacking opponents with the ball; running with the ball, wall passes
6. All players change positions as the exercise continues.

INTRODUCE DEFENDERS AND THE POINT STRIKER

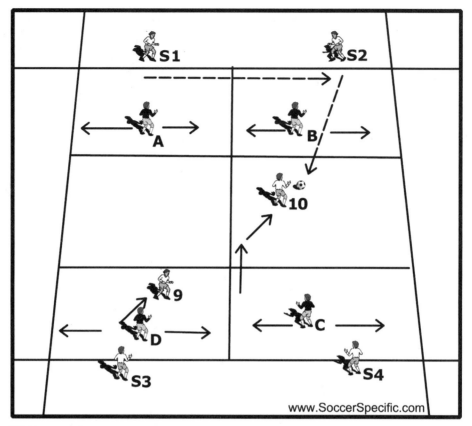

Diagram 148

1. **Progression 1:** TRY THIS WITH ONE DEFENDER IN EACH SIDE FIRST TO GAIN SUCCESS. Defenders must stay in their own thirds and can only intercept the pass.
   Try to have the players combine. If the single defender in the first progression closes down (9) (knowing (10) and (9) have to combine) and it becomes false, then have it where (10) can receive and pass directly to an S player.
6. **Progression 2:** Add two defenders each side. This will ensure one defender tries to get into the passing lane to stop this and might in fact release (9) for a pass.
2. S players on the outside must move along the line to open up the possibility of the pass from (9) or (10).
3. In this case (A) and (B) can intercept the pass to (9) or (10).
4. (10) must maneuver into the middle third and get free to receive, but also into a position between or either side of (A) and (B) to open up the angle for the pass from S2.
5. (9) stays in the attacking third and so can be challenged by (C) or (D).
6. The idea is for (10) to drop deep to become the shadow striker and get free from the marking of (C) or (D) as neither can encroach into the middle third.

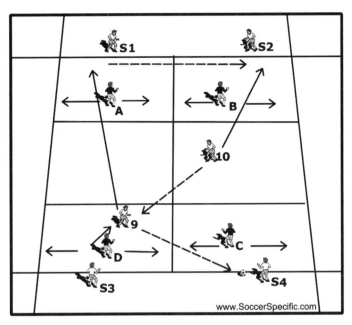

Diagram 149

1. Here (9) and (10) combine and pass to S4 then switch with S1 and S2.

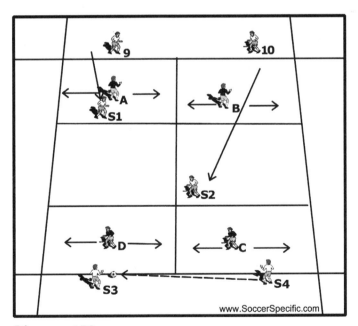

Diagram 150

1. (10) and (9) combine and pass to S4. Defenders (C) and (D) try to intercept the pass.
2. (10) and (9) then have to switch back with S1 and S2 who become the next two strikers going the other way.
3. Timing of this change is possible because by the time the ball has been transferred from S4 to S3 the timing should be right.
4. Again, one player becomes the shadow striker and one the front striker, staying in different thirds to ensure there is depth between them.

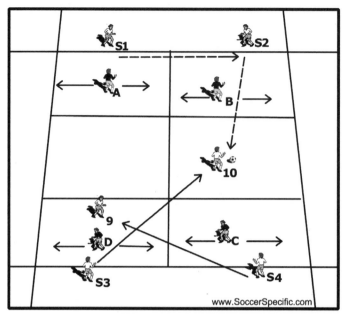

Diagram 151

1. Here they both make diagonal runs to receive the pass. The pass could go to player (9) or player (10) first.

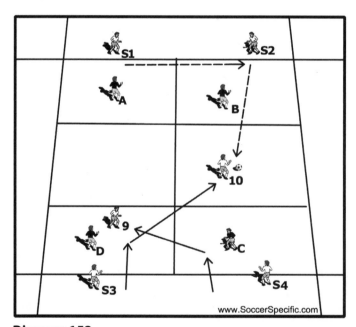

Diagram 152

1. Or they could both come back in straight lines then switch late and fast to make their ultimate diagonal runs, to lose markers in a game situation for example.

COACHING CLINIC SESSION PLAN 27

(For age 10 years and older)

OBJECTIVE: A TRANSITION GAME DEVELOPING THE PLAYERS' ABILITY TO RECOGNIZE THE IMMEDIATE CHANGES FROM DEFENSE TO ATTACK AND ATTACK TO DEFENSE AND TO ACT ON IT QUICKLY

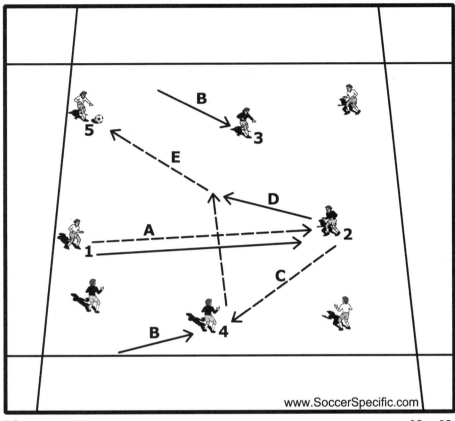

Diagram 153   **40 x 40**

Two teams / one ball, passing to anyone.

1. Passer (1) plays the ball to the receiver (2). (1) then becomes a defender and must pressurize receiver (2).

2. Receiver (2) must work a 1 – 2 around the defender (1) with a support player. Try to establish support on both sides of the receiver so there are two options available to support (3 and 4).

3. Work on angles and distances of support (triangular support), timing of the pass depending on the closeness of the defender, quality of pass, preferably off the front foot to aid the disguise of the pass.

4. Receiver plays a 1-2 with support player (4), passes to a new receiver (5) and becomes the new defender and the cycle begins again.

5. **Routine:**

   a) 1 passes to 2 and pressurizes.

   b) 3 and 4 move to support 1 (thinking two moves ahead).

   c) 2 passes to 4.

   d) 2 runs around 1 to receive (give and go).

   e) Now 2 passes to 5 and becomes the defender.

6. **Progression:** Increase number of balls, passing to opposite color only, but support from same color i.e. pass opposite, support same. Quick decisions required.
7. Passer plays the ball to receiver and closes down as a defender; receiver must move the ball away first time or draw defender in and move the ball off at an angle away from the pressure.

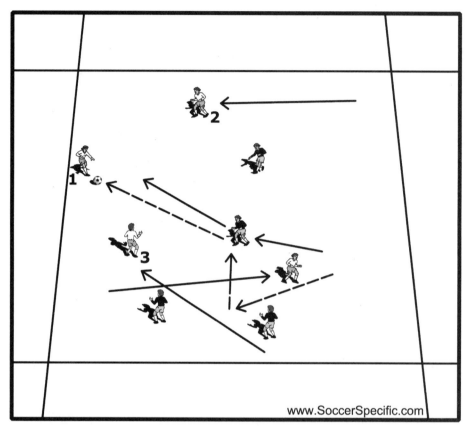

www.SoccerSpecific.com

Diagram 154

1. Here player 1 receives the pass in the next phase of the movement, being closed down by the passer. Players 2 and 3 now must move to support player 1 in order to enable him to play a give and go around the closing defender. And so the cycle continues.
2. **Coaching Points:**
   a) Quality passing
   b) Quick pressure following the pass
   c) Movement off the ball by supporting players (angle and distance of support)
   d) Awareness of the receiver to see the options before receiving the ball
   e) Good touch and pass by the receiver of the first pass
   f) One touch pass from the support player around the defender with good angle, pace, accuracy and timing
   g) Timing of the run of the receiver to accept possession of the ball
3. **Competitive:** Take it into a regular game, emphasizing movement off the ball to support the player receiving the ball.

COACHING CLINIC SESSION PLAN 28

(For age 9 years and older)

OBJECTIVE: COMBINING AWARENESS TRAINING WITH SHOOTING AT GOAL AS THE END PRODUCT: DRIBBLING / TURNING COMBINATION PLAYS AND FINISHING

Diagram 155

1. Players can go by number, play a 1 – 2 with the coach and shoot or dribble around the passive defending coach. Get dribbling and control in one grid plus a shot at goal in the other. Players can count the number of goals they each score as a target.
2. **Progression:** Have a player in the coach's position who must come short to the ball to receive and turn and shoot, the passer then takes his place. Coach can be a passive defender.

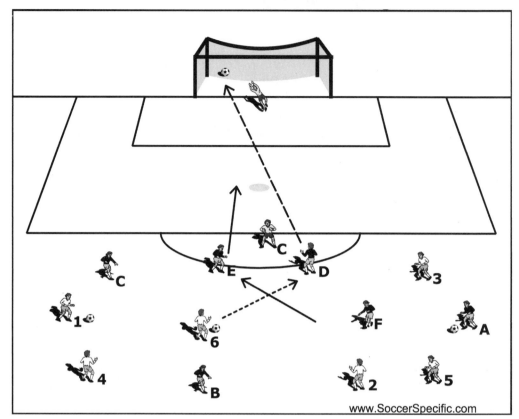

Diagram 156

3. Defending and Attacking – 1v1 situations. One player starts as a defender. Another with a ball must beat him and score, then become the defender for the next one.
4. **Coaching Points:**
   a) A **positive attitude** to beat the defender
   b) Beating the defender with a trick or pure pace
   c) Quality shot at goal
   d) Follow in for possible rebounds

COMBINATION PLAY WORKING IN TWO'S

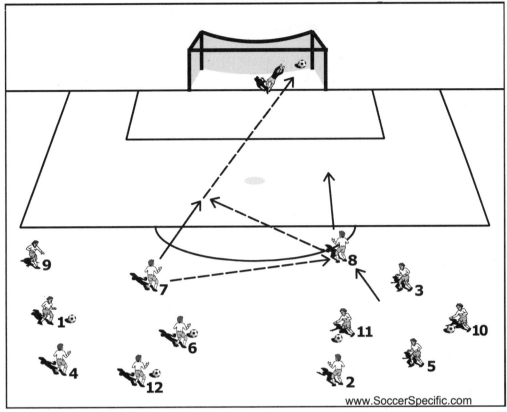

Diagram 157

5. Combination Play (in 2's) – The same passing and moving awareness session but this time a player on the ball makes a decision to pass to the coach, who lays it off for a supporting player without a ball to shoot (or cross if pushed too wide). Follow in for rebounds. If two players with a ball each go, then the one who is last to go must turn back and join the group.

6. **Coaching Points:**
   a) Timing and angle of the run by receiver (7)
   b) Timing and quality of the pass by passer (11)
   c) Quality one or two touch pass by receiver (7)
   d) Timing and angle of the run by the new receiver (11)
   e) Quality of the shot by the receiver (11)
   f) Both players should follow in for rebounds just in case!!

7. **Progression:** The coach is a passive defender; in the above example (11) plays a 1 – 2 around the coach with (7) to shoot on goal.

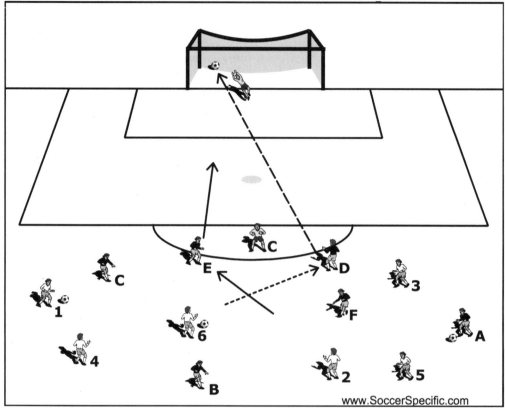

Diagram 158

1. Two Teams - Passing to own teammates but attacking the goal alternately (this allows the ball to be shot at goal and the player to get back to the group before the same group goes again).
   Attacking in one's (1 – 2 with coach or dribbling around the coach to shoot).Change by passing to the opposite team only.

2. Combination play - In two's (a player without a ball from the same team must support and make a 1 – 2, an overlap run, crossover or diagonal run to receive and shoot or act as a decoy). Coach acts as passive opposition. (D) makes a diagonal run, (E) makes a diagonally opposite run. (D) can shoot and use (E) as a decoy or pass to (E) to shoot and follow in for rebounds.

3. Progression – Passing to opposite colors and only an opposite color can support in two's (improves peripheral vision and awareness, identifying when the break is on and who it's with).

4. All the players are constantly working, passing and moving (no standing in lines awaiting a turn) then have to decide when and where to go.

5. **Coaching Points:**
   a) Passing and Support play.
   b) Decision – When and where to attack.
   c) Technique – of the pass (timing, weight and accuracy).
   d) Timing of the runs.
   e) Execution of the shot – Accuracy and Power.
   f) Rebounds.

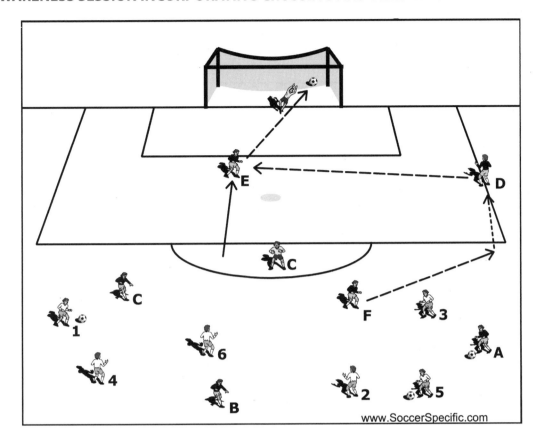

Diagram 159

1. Crossing and finishing exercise playing a ball wide to the supporting player to receive a cross back. Players are constantly passing and moving. They must recognize when and where to break forward in two's and attack the goal.
2. **Coaching Points:**
   a) Passing and Support play
   b) Decision - When and where to attack.
   c) Technique of the pass (timing, weight and accuracy).
   d) Timing of the run to receive the cross.
   e) Angle of the run to receive the cross.
   f) Quality of the cross (timing, height, pace, and direction).
3. Once two players have performed their move and they collect a ball and join back in with the group, the next two players must go through the decision making process of when to attack the goal and so on.

COACHING CLINIC SESSION PLAN 29

(For age 10 years and older)

OBJECTIVE: FURTHER DEVELOPMENT OF THE FINISHING GAME USING TWO GOALS AND INCREASING THE NUMBER OF OPTIONS

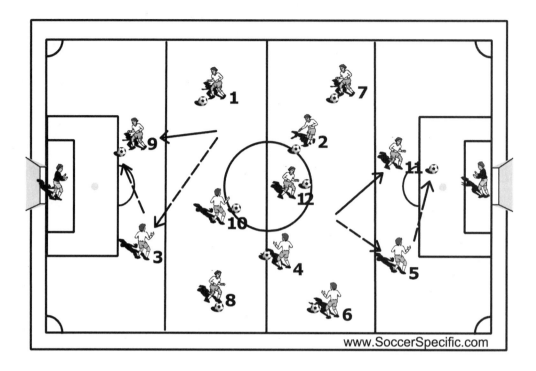

Diagram 160   **60 x 40**

1. Change the set-up to working to two goals instead of one so there are choices going both ways.
2. More action, more shots on goal, faster transitions all occur in this session.
3. You can use this progression for all the sessions that involve attacking one goal only.
4. Begin with a simple pass to a player and a shot, playing a one-two with a player to score a goal and then move into the combination plays and so on. (3) and (5) collect the balls that have just been shot and join in the group again and (9) and (11) become the wall pass players playing the 1-2 with the next players.
5. If need be you can increase the length of the area you are working in.
6. **Coaching Points:**
   a) Decision - When and where to pass and combine with the striker
   b) Decision - Which goal to attack
   c) Recognizing the moment to link up with the striker
   d) Quality play of the give and go with a one touch layoff and shot at goal
   e) Scoring the goal

Diagram 161

1. Here we are getting into the passing and moving play before the players work their way to get a shot at goal. The emphasis is on passing and moving rather than dribbling and turning (when they had a ball each) and the shot on goal.
2. Look to develop the session using two goals to attack in the same way we did using only one goal to attack.
3. **Coaching Points:**
   a) Awareness of the player without the ball - when and where to make the run OFF the ball to receive the pass and shoot at goal.
   b) Awareness of the player making the pass - of the run of the player looking to receive
   c) Timing, pace, accuracy and angle of the pass to make it easy for the receiving player to run onto
   d) Finish with a shot on goal.
4. Use your imagination to create new set-ups for the players. The crossing and finishing one is an example where each team goes the opposite way to attack.

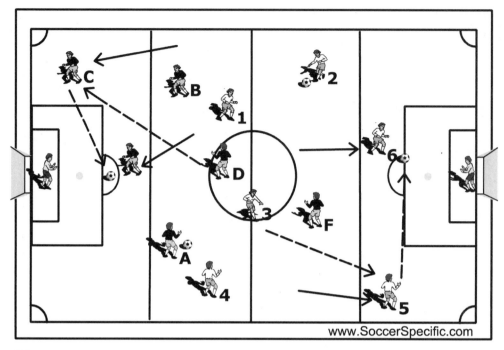

Diagram 162

1. Crossing and finishing game. Each team attacks the opposite way.
2. One ball for each team to begin. Once that ball has been used for the move the coach passes another one in.
3. **Progression:** Two balls per team, passing and moving, then players making runs wide and receiving to cross.
4. Develop the idea by adding:
   a) Two players attacking the cross
   b) One recovering defender
5. As soon as the move is over the players go back into the middle to play again.
6. Decisions to be made by each team: Do I run wide to cross? Do I attack the ball from the cross? Do I track the player going the other way? The player on the ball has to see the outside run and make the right pass. Players off the ball have to make runs into the box to receive the cross and also watch the opposite end and defend.

Diagram 163

1. **Competitive Game:**
   Now we have a game in the middle. Players must get 3 passes in, which is then a cue for a player to attack in a wide area.
2. Use different ideas to develop the game:
   a) No defenders can encroach into the attacking third so the attacking players are free to attack
   b) One striker, then two, can attack the goal
   c) As soon as the attack is over another ball goes in from the coach and the team who were defending get the ball in a 6 v 4 and try to get three quick passes in to attack.
3. Count the number of goals each team score in a given time, or first to 5 goals wins.

COACHING CLINIC SESSION PLAN 30

(For age 10 years and older)

OBJECTIVE: IMPROVING AWARENESS IN ONE TOUCH FINISHING INSIDE THE BOX - ANGLE, WEIGHT AND TIMING OF THE PASS IN THE BOX

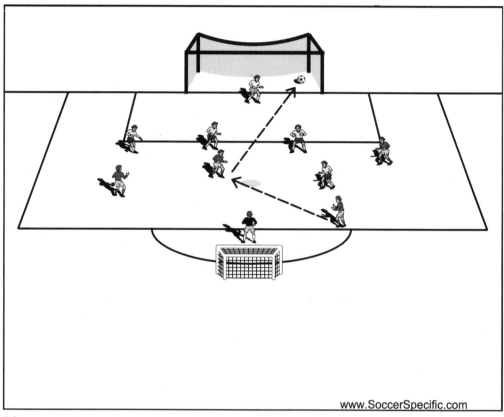

Diagram 164

Great awareness of teammates and opponents in a very tight environment is essential here. The passing and movement is very quick and as often as possible one touch so players really need an awareness of what to do with the ball before they receive it. Otherwise, the move will break down. Players need to identify when to pass and when to take the quick shot and should also know where the keeper is positioned before they shoot.

Coaching Points:

1. Quality of Passing - Concentrate on the weight, timing and angle of the pass. Under-hit the pass to draw the receiver to the ball and into a position to shoot and get free of the defender. This technique is used to allow the receiver to hit a one touch shot at goal. Weight of pass must be light to allow this. This is the opposite of what coaches normally tell players: "Don't pass the ball short or under paced because it can be intercepted".
   In the diagram above, a short under-hit pass draws the player towards the ball to get free from the defender and, half turned with a side on stance, hit a one touch shot.
2. Positioning and Crossing Technique - creating width to cross.
3. Balance in Attack - (near post / far post / middle of goal).Positioning from crosses, timing of runs (late and fast), changing of positions to move defenders, angles of runs, contact on the ball.

4. Observation: of players' positions in the small area they are working in (teammates and opponents), and especially the positioning of the keepers so they know where to shoot.
5. Finishing Technique – Position of the feet to receive. One touch finishing.

POSITIONING FROM CROSSING

Diagram 165

1. The keeper plays the ball wide and the attackers get in position to meet the cross near post, far post and centrally behind them for the pull back.
2. Try to finish one touch.
3. The game is constant attacking play both ways. To make it competitive, count the number of goals scored. Encourage the players to shoot on sight.
4. Teaching transitions from one moment defending to the next moment attacking, this exercise improves the concentration of the players.

POSITIONING FROM CROSSING

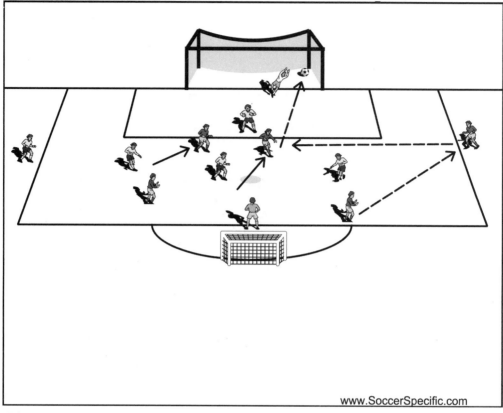

Diagram 166

1. Introduce 2 players on the outside who stay outside the playing area. No one can tackle them so they are guaranteed to get a cross in.
2. This could be a quick play session focusing on crossing and one touch finishing, the emphasis being on a two touch maximum in wide areas, ensuring a quick cross into the scoring area.
3. Players know they only have 2 touches when it goes wide so they work quickly to get into position, expecting the early cross.
4. This should improve quick decision making as everything is done at pace.

COACHING CLINIC SESSION PLAN 31

(For age 10 years and older)

OBJECTIVE: IMPROVING QUICK FINISHING INSIDE AND ALSO AROUND THE BOX

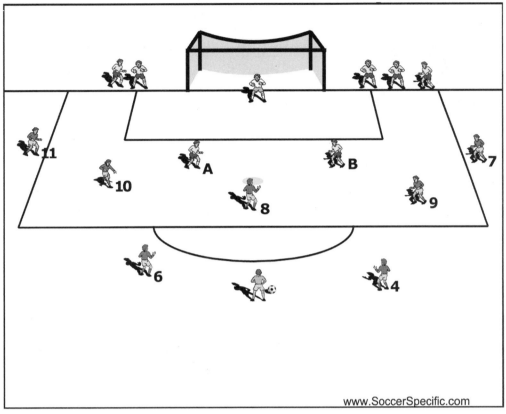

Diagram 167

Coaches Notes:

1. Similar to the last clinic, great awareness of player positioning is needed in this one. But the attack is based more around the box and going into it.

2. This is a Functional practice, a 3v2 with support players involving Receiving, Turning, Dribbling and Shooting. First priority of the striker is "Can I shoot?" Composure in the box is the key factor, defenders don't want to concede a penalty so strikers have more time than they realize.

3. No conditions to start but support players stay outside the box. If defenders win the ball they play to the coach or just clear it to outside players. Start again with a new ball to the strikers. Strikers try to receive the ball at an angle so they are half turned and facing the goal so they can get a quick shot in. Others take up positions off this for rebounds etc.

4. Outside players can be passing a ball around to keep active and when the play is finished inside the box whoever is on the second ball passes it in to restart.

5. Looking for quick shots, working off rebounds, combination work, 1 – 2's, quick movement to create space, support play.

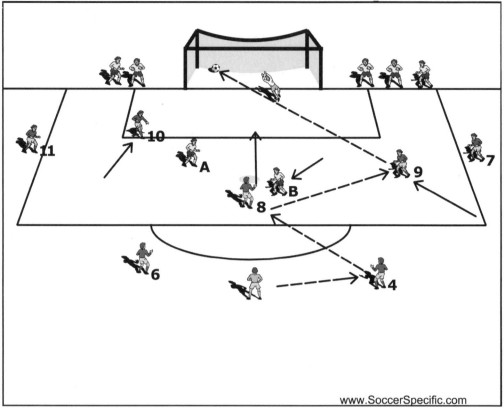

Diagram 168

1. Make it a competition between two teams. Each team has 15 attempts at goal, see who can score the most goals. Attacking team continue each attempt until the ball is out of play or a goal is scored or the opponents win possession. Rotate the defenders to keep them fresh.
2. Here the coach passes to (8) who lays it off for (9) who shoots and scores. (8) and (10) follow the shot in for any rebounds.
3. **Coaching Points in Shooting:**
    a) P**ositive Attitude** to shoot, quick shooting.
    b) Awareness of positioning of players and the keeper before receiving the pass, thus knowing options in advance of the ball.
    c) Receive on the Half Turn if possible (create space for yourself), take the chance
    d) Accuracy and Power (accuracy first). Be composed
    e) Shooting High or Low (low is best because it's more difficult for the keeper)
    f) Selection of Shot (driven, chip, side foot, swerve etc). You can use defenders to shoot around for placement. Check keeper's position (if time!)
    g) Near Post or Far Post (can depend on keeper's position, also if you shoot and miss at the near post the ball is out of play, if shooting at the far post and it's missing, the keeper may palm it to a striker following up, a striker may intercept it on its way and score, (it may hit a defender and go in)
    h) Rebounds (follow all shots in)

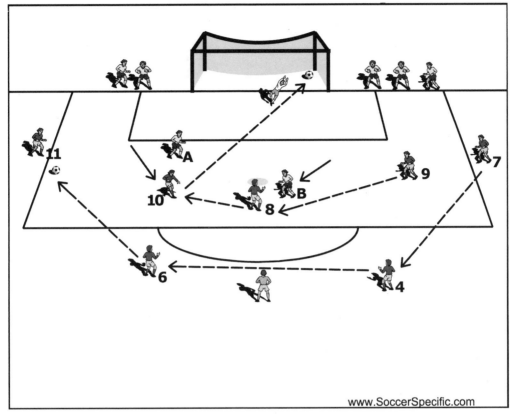

Diagram 169

1. (8) passes to (10). The pass is under-hit to draw (10) away from defender (A); into space and towards the ball. The shot has been taken and a goal scored. At the same time the outside support players are passing the next ball around, keeping active and ready to pass into the box to begin the next play. As soon as the first play is finished the second play begins from where the second ball is at that particular time. Players must be ready to begin the next play.
2. This session with two balls involved helps the players' observation and concentration. The players inside the box need to be aware that only three of four outside players are available at any one time to support. Also, once the play is over they must tune in quickly to the next one and be able to see quickly where the next ball is coming from and take up their positions accordingly.
3. The outside players must be able to recognize when they need to support an inside player when the outside ball is played to them and when it needs to be played in for the next play.
4. Lots of decisions to be made, all leading to quick thinking and observation away from the ball as well as on it.

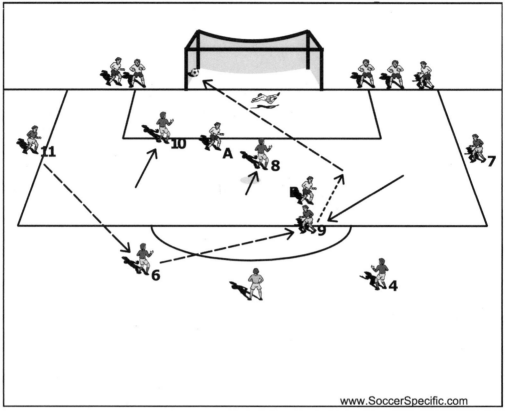

Diagram 170

1. Examples can be a pass to (9) who beats (B) and shoots, (8) and (10) follow in for rebounds. (9) opens his body stance and comes off the shoulder of (B) to create space and an angle to receive the pass. He can shoot first time using the momentum of the pass or make a good first touch past (A) and take the shot in two touches. First touch by (9) may be back across (B) coming inside for the shot or a one touch finish using (B)'s position as a guide to bend the shot around. Strikers can use support players in link up play if for instance they receive but can't turn.

2. **Progression:** Condition the strikers to three touches, then two touches, then say do it one touch, but only if it is on to do so.

3. Support players can change from two to one touch as they won't have a lot of time on the ball in a game. This ensures both strikers and support players are thinking quickly and trying to recognize situations early.

4. Have wide players crossing the ball when they get it so players inside take up a position to receive from the cross.

5. Central midfielders pass or shoot.

POSSIBLE PASSING OPTIONS

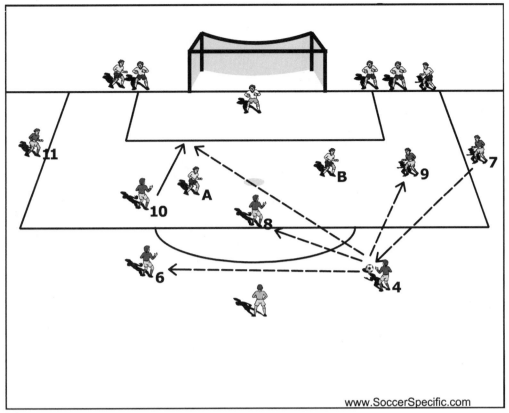

Diagram 171

1. **Progression:** Support players on receiving can pass to other support players to change the direction of the attack. They can also shoot directly at goal and strikers work their positions off this, again for possible rebounds.
2. As you gain success in a 3v2 situation, even with one and two touch conditions, bring another defender in and play a 3v3. Rotate players regularly to ensure quality as this session can be tiring.
3. Introduce offside. This helps defenders and forces strikers to time their runs and support positions (You can work on your defenders to improve them in this session).
4. 3v3 but either team can score if they get possession. This is helpful if you only have attacking players at your session and you want them all to work on finishing. Server calls team name that he will pass to, that team's players adjust their positions to receive, and the other team adjusts to stop them and regain possession.
5. **Develop:** Support players have a ball each and are numbered off. The coach calls a number of a server and players react off it. Thinking processes are remembering where the ball is coming from and what to do when you have the ball or the opposition have it; quick decision making.

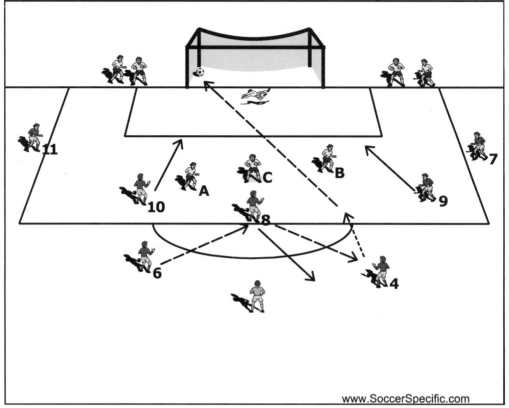

www.SoccerSpecific.com

Diagram 172

1. Outside players can shoot for themselves. Develop the idea of switching positions from the outside to inside and visa versa. For example, when the pass is made from (8) to (4), the players switch positions, one going out the other coming into play to link up with the other inside players.
2. (4) may come into a good position to shoot at goal as above. This not only good because the switching movement happens in a game, but from a coaching point of view it keeps everyone involved in the game.

Overview
1. 3v2, 2v2, 3v3, varies depending on success. Vary the number of touches on the ball as well.
2. Outside players can pass another ball while action is inside (two balls working).
3. Have both teams attacking the goal. Outside players can pass to each other and also shoot for goal (support the strikers).
4. Outside players switch positions with inside players on receiving a pass from them. Bring in outside players so numbers are even inside the box. This is intensive work, good for seeing who can make quick decisions, who has good control of the ball etc.
5. Position players inside the box, two strikers centrally and two players wide and supporting midfielder inside the edge of the box centrally for lay offs so they are working from a shape.

3 v 3 ATTACKING AND DEFENDING GAME

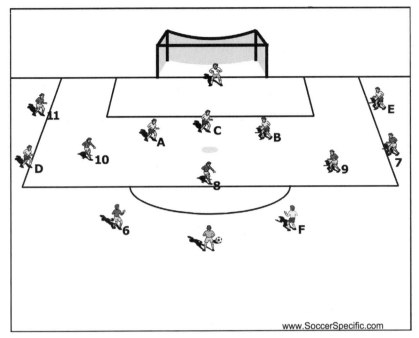

Diagram 173

1. A 3v3 game in the middle, one team attacks the other defends. How many goals can the attacking team score in 5 minutes?
2. If the defending team win the ball they pass to their own players on the outside (same as winning and keeping possession in a game) who then give the ball to an outside attacking player and the sequence begins again.
3. Rotate the teams and each team gets a chance to attack for 5 minutes. Add up all the goals scored for either side in the 20 minutes for a combined winning team.
Alternatively have two goals at opposite ends so it is more like a game situation.
4. Rotate the players within each team.
5. **Progression 1:** One touch play to speed up decision making; this now tests the foot and body preparation as well as the awareness principles of looking before receiving.
6. **Progression 2:** A 3v3 game but both teams have the chance to score a goal. The coach serves the ball in to each team alternately so they know if they have to create space or mark up. They can use the outside players as support but only their own teammates. Both teams can attack and both teams can defend, hence constant transitions from defense to attack and attack to defense. The three moments in the game now come into play; when we have the ball, when they have the ball and when the ball changes hands. This play is good for quick decision making because of the constant transition.
Server passes alternately, telling players first so each team knows how to position (defensive or attacking positioning).
7. **Progression 3:** A 3v3 game. When a team wins the ball they have to pass it to an outside support player to begin their attack, developing quick transition. This is particularly good for strikers to practice in regaining the ball and getting rewards for doing so. This ensures the attacking team on losing the ball change direction and become the defending team to win it back and the defending team on winning the ball pass it out and then change direction to become the attacking team. Great for quick transition and fast play and you can limit the number of touches on the ball to further speed up the play.

COACHING CLINIC SESSION PLAN 32

(For age 10 years and older)

OBJECTIVE: DEVELOPING ONE AND TWO TOUCH PASSING AND MOVING IN RESTRICTED SPACE ENSURING QUICK DECISION MAKING

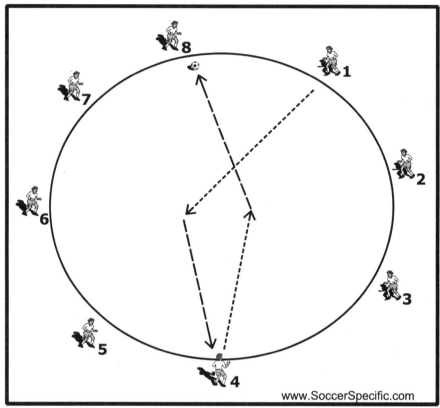

Diagram 174   **30 x 30**

1. The circle is approximately 20 yards across. To help develop the players' awareness instincts, ask them to call out the name of the player who they will be passing to before they receive the ball. This ensures they look to see who is free before they receive the ball so they know in advance who is free to receive.
2. One ball. (1) runs and passes to (4) and takes his place. (4) takes the ball, runs and passes to (8) and so on.
3. **Progression:** introduce two, then three, then four balls all going at the same time. "Awareness" of where each player is running is needed here so they don't collide and also where potential free players to receive are "before" you make the run and pass.
4. **Coaching Points:**
    a) Good communication between the players.
    b) Quality of the pass (timing, accuracy and weight).
    c) Good first touch by the receiver.
    d) Progression – Passer becomes a passive defender who puts the receiver under pressure. The receiver must move the ball away at an angle from the pressure on the first touch.

RUNNING WITH THE BALL

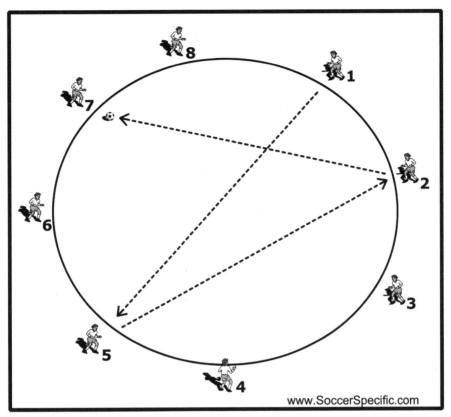

Diagram 175

A) Running with the ball technique:
   a) Head Up – look forward, observing options "before" receiving the ball using (Awareness!)
   b) Good first touch out of feet, 2-3 touches maximum, not dribbling.
   c) Run in a straight line, the quickest route.
   d) Running Style, use the front foot to control the ball using the laces.
B) **Decision:** Where is the player taking the ball? In this case to (5) but (5) must try to decide as the ball is coming, not after he has it. Identify who is free early on.
C) **Communication:** Call the name of the player you are running the ball to.
D) Timing of take-over: (1) does not pass the ball to (5) but allows (5) to take it using the momentum of the ball. (5) must use a good first touch to get the ball out of the feet.
E) **Progression:** Two balls going at once, then three.

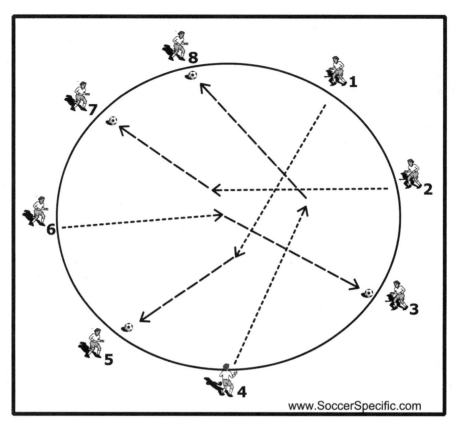

Diagram 176

1. You can divide the teams into two and have half the players working and half resting. Work a set time then change the players. Here the players are running with the ball then passing and then will get it back to go somewhere else to another player to work with.

2. Change the emphasis on the movement: running with the ball, performing a clever dribble or turn, pass to an outside player, do an overlap and get the ball back, play a give and go and do a turn when receiving it back, etc.

3. There are many ways to develop this idea to get lots of touches on the ball: practicing running with the ball, receiving and turning with the ball and dribbling with the ball, combination plays, give and go's, overlap runs and so on. The coach can use his imagination to make this work.

PLAYING 1 - 2'S

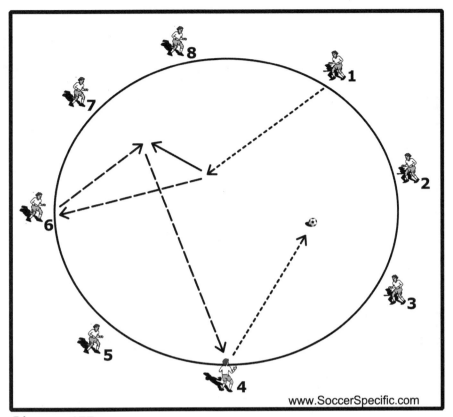

Diagram 177

1. (1) runs with the ball and passes to (6) who plays a 1–2 then (1) passes to (5) who then can carry the move on. (1) takes (5)'s place.
2. Progression – Use two balls at the same time. Awareness of other players in the same spaces comes into play in the movement of the inside players.
3. Coaching Points as in previous exercise.
4. If (1) passes to (6) and supports to the right of (6) then the pass is going to the left to (5), making sure we are working angles of support and passing and it lets (5) know the next pass is going there.

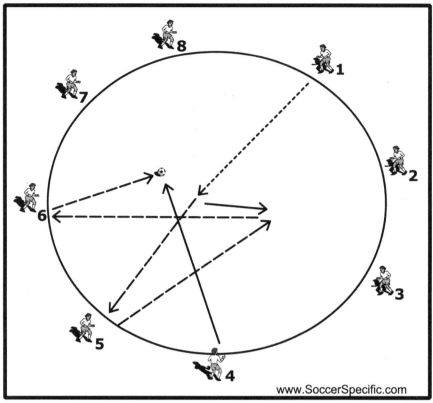

Diagram 178

1. (1) runs with the ball and plays a 1–2 with (5), then passes to (6). At the same time, (4) makes a run to receive the ball off (6)'s pass.
2. (1) takes (4)'s place. This exercise is about movement off the ball and thinking a move ahead of the game.
3. **Coaching Points as previously but include:**
   a) Timing of the support run off the ball to receive the pass.
   b) Timing of the pass into space, not to feet.
4. Initially, when the player passes back, he always goes to the same side (right or left). This gets the players into the routine.
5. **Progression:** (1) can pass to either side of (5) after receiving the ball back so it can be (4) making the pass and (6) making the run. This keeps the players concentrating.
   Develop the practice by having two balls and two players going at the same time.
   Use as few touches on the ball as possible to ensure it moves quickly, even try to limit it to 1 touch only..

OVERLAP RUNS

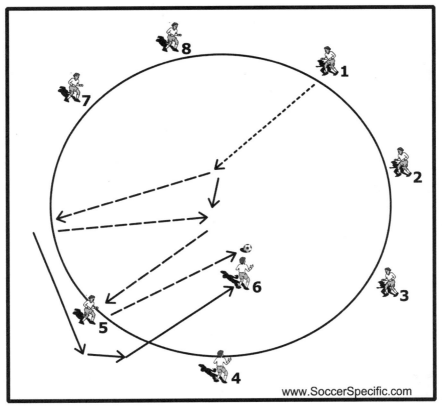

Diagram 179

1. (1) runs with the ball and plays a 1–2 with (6), then lays the ball off to (5). At the same time (6) makes an overlap run around (5) to receive the pass in front. (1) takes the place of (6). Develop the usual way. Coaching Points as the previous exercise but this time the support run is in the form of an overlap.
2. Timing of the overlap run is important, as is the timing of the pass into space in front of the overlapping player to receive.

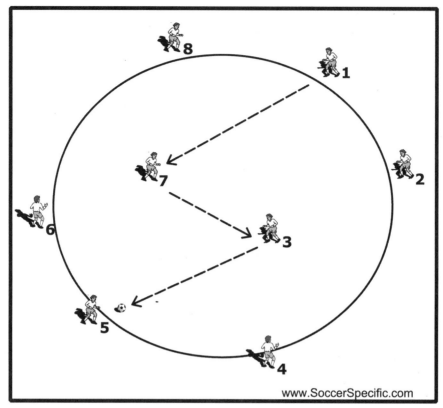

Diagram 180

1. As the ball is going to (7) he has already looked to see where (3) is. (3) has already moved into a support position to be ready to help (7) and at the same time is viewing the field to see who is available to receive a pass on the outside. As the ball travels to (3), ask him to call the name of the player he intends to pass to before the ball gets to his feet. To do this he needs to look at (7) as the ball arrives, look to see who is free, then look back to see the ball coming.

2. (7) moves to an angled support position to receive the pass from (1). (3) makes an angle off (7) to receive the ball then passes to (5).

3. **Coaching Points:**
   a) Body shape when receiving;
   b) Quality of pass (weight, timing and accuracy)
   c) Support angles
   d) Good first touch.

4. **Progression:**
   a) three players working together in the middle. Try one touch and two touch play
   b) Two pairs working together in the middle with a ball each pair.

5. Pass in the same sequence each time into the middle players. Awareness is required as players must know where the other players are, both on the outside and in the middle, where they can get in the way of each other in the two team situation.

6. Creating awareness of where the other pair is, forcing players to look away from the ball and observe their surroundings.

COACHING CLINIC SESSION PLAN 33

(For age 10 years and older)

OBJECTIVE: DEVELOPING ONE AND TWO TOUCH PASSING AND MOVING IN RESTRICTED SPACE ENSURING QUICK DECISION MAKING IN A COMPETITIVE ENVIRONMENT

ONE v ONE

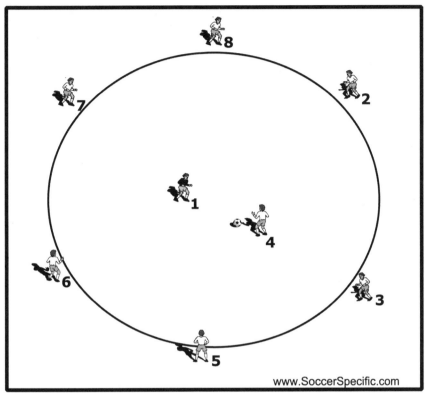

Diagram 181   **30 x30**

Introduce Opponents.

1. 1v1's – This is now possession play (keep ball) in the middle to start. Outside players play two touch but must release it quickly to keep the pressure on inside the circle. This is high intensity work. Rotate players. Inside players get as many touches as they like, practicing dribbling skills in 1v1 situations, passing and moving off the ball to work combinations with teammates.

2. Inside players cannot tackle outside players but can intercept passes from them. Outside players can move side to side to improve their support angles. Emphasize passing to both space and feet.

3. This is technically a 7v1 in favor of the player in possession.

4. Here we have a 2v1 - Two then one touch on the outside. We can work on the attacking players' passing and support techniques; or the sole defender on defensive skills.

5. **Coaching Points:**
   a) Quality of passing (accuracy, timing and weight).
   b) Angles and distances of support.
   c) Movement "off" the ball.
   d) Communication.

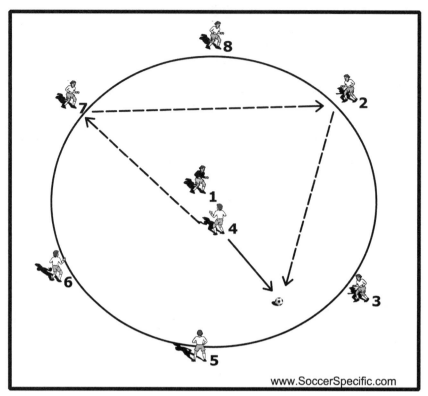

Diagram 182

1. Players can pass the ball around the outside until a pass is on to an inside player. You can restrict the number of continuous outside passes as the main work has to be done by the inside players to keep them involved.

2. Players on the outside identify who they are passing to as the ball is coming to them. They can call a player's name to pass to "before" they get it so the inside player in possession knows which player to work off next to receive the ball from again. Or as the ball is coming to (7), player (2) may call and ask for the next pass to make (7) aware that he is open and available. Good communication is the key to this.

3. Here (4) passes to (7), who as the ball is traveling calls out (2)'s name. This is a cue for (4) to then change position to receive the next pass from (2) early and in space. One or two touch play on the outside will mean this is quick passing and it will help (4) get possession again early and in space away from defender (1), who hopefully has been left flat footed.

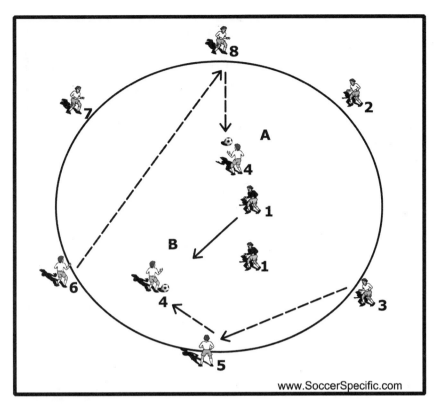

Diagram 183

1. Avoid players closing their own space down by getting too close to the player on the ball. At figure A, (4) is not only too close but also has gone in too straight and thus cannot view the full field nor see where the defender is.
2. Correct movement would be off at an angle to receive facing forward and inside if possible to see the whole field. Figure B shows this. If the defender blocks the pass to (4) then the passing channel is open for (5) to pass elsewhere and (4) will work his position off the next pass.
3. Try to receive the ball facing inside so you can see the full area and all of the players. An open body stance will help this. In figure A (4) can see (8) but little else of the other players or the field. In figure B, (4) can see most of the players and most of the field when receiving the ball or moving to receive the next pass if (3) passes it elsewhere.

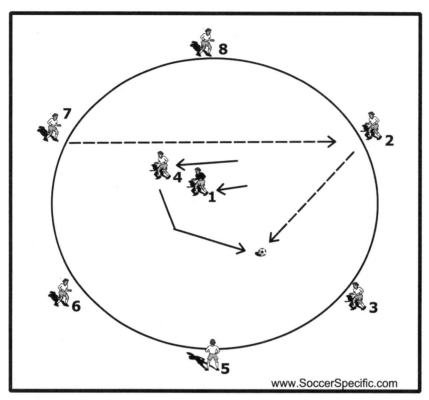

Diagram 184

1. Here (4) comes to receive a pass, (1) is marking tightly. (7) can pass the ball to the opposite side of (4), away from the side (1) is defending.

2. (7) can also put a little more weight on the pass. (4) lets it run across his body with a feint to fool (1) and it runs to (2) who then can lay the ball off back to (4) who has turned away from (1) to get free to receive the next pass.

3. This movement creates space behind for (4) to run into off the next pass. (4) has to be aware of the position of (2) "before" the pass. (2) has to be ready to receive and expect the ball from (7).

4. A one or two touch pass from (2) into space for (4) ensures the movement and passing is rapid and gives the defender (1) less time to react.

5. Try to get faced up to the defender when you receive the ball instead of playing with your back to him. This gives the attacking player the advantage.

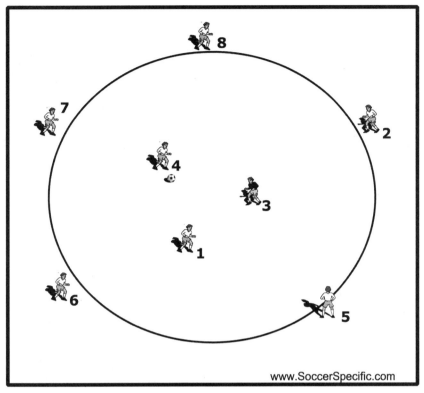

Diagram 185

1. Here we have an overload of a 2v1 in the middle. (1) and (4) must keep the ball away from (3) using the outside players as support.
2. If (3) wins the ball then that player has an incentive to use the outside players to try to keep possession.
3. **Develop:** If an inside player gives the ball away, that player then becomes the defender against the other two players.
4. Players (1) and (4) must make it as difficult as possible for defender (3) to win the ball. If it becomes too easy using the outside players then limit them to one touch each and have the two inside players limited to two touches, then one touch so the challenge becomes greater.

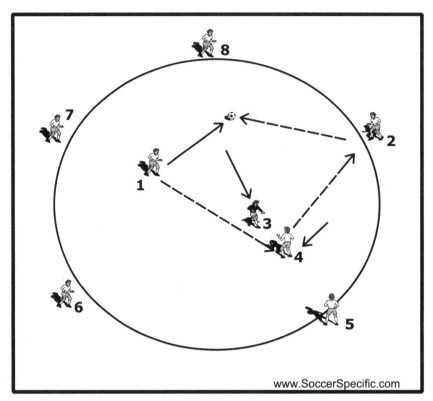

Diagram 186

1. You can also limit the number of times the ball is played around the outside players. For example, the ball has to come back into an inside player every two passes. Play around with this until you can get a balanced situation putting the two inside players under enough pressure with restrictions, to make it demanding but also giving the defender a fair chance to win the ball back.

2. Here (4) creates an angle for the pass from (1) by moving into space that (1) can see. (4) then lays a pass off to (2) who passes into space to draw (1) to the ball and take him or her away from (3). Too often player (4) may stand in a position behind (3) so (1) can't see them. This really emphasized the need for movement off the ball to support a player on it.

3. Awareness is being trained here for all the players both in the middle and on the outside. As the ball is traveling to (4) he needs to call the name of the player he is passing to before he receives it, then (4) has to be aware of where to pass it next, in this case into space for (1)

TWO v TWO

Diagram 187

1. A 2v2. (1) and (4) against (2) and (6). Building to a 3v2 and so on depending on numbers. Use outside players as support for both teams.
2. Inside players can have free play then develop to three then two touch to improve speed of decision making.
3. Outside players play two touch then one touch.
4. This is technically a 4v2 in favor of the team in possession.
5. Keep rotating players, putting them with different partners. This is physical work but players get a break on the outside to recover ensuring quality work inside the circle.
6. An alternative is to have two teams and the inside players can only pass to their teammates on the outside. This gives them fewer choices and increases the difficulty of the exercise.

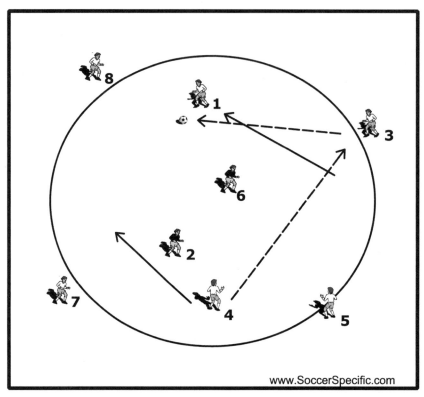

Diagram 188

1. Using the outside players – an example would be as above where (6) has gotten into the same passing lane as (3). (1) shapes up to receive a pass but lets it run across his body through to (3) and then makes a movement to support the next pass from (3).
2. This results in dummying defender (6) into thinking (1) will receive the ball and so (2) pressures (4). The movement results in (1) getting free from the marking of defender (6), using (3) to receive the next pass into space.
3. In the meantime (4) will be on the move to support the next pass from (1) and thus getting away from the marking of defender (2).
4. Initially have no restriction on the passing so the players can pass around the outside of the circle until an inside player is available to receive the ball.
5. **Progression:** As the players improve, put conditions in where there can be only three, then two passes between outside players, then the ball must be passed to an inside player. The two inside players must link up with a pass before the ball goes to an outside player again.

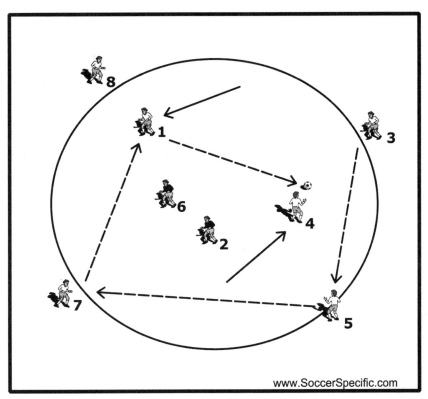

Diagram 189

1. The ball is being passed around the outside of the circle. After two passes it must go to an inside player. The inside players have to work hard to get into a position to receive the pass knowing the next pass has to be inside to one of them.
2. If it is (6), as above, who receives the pass, then (4) must work off the ball to get into a position to support (6), particularly if the condition is that a pass must be made inside the circle between the two inside players before it can go out again.
3. This is a great session for working on movement off the ball for players to support each other in tight spaces as well as developing technical skills on the ball in tight spaces.
4. Introduce a free player who works with both teams when in possession to develop the practice into a 3v2.

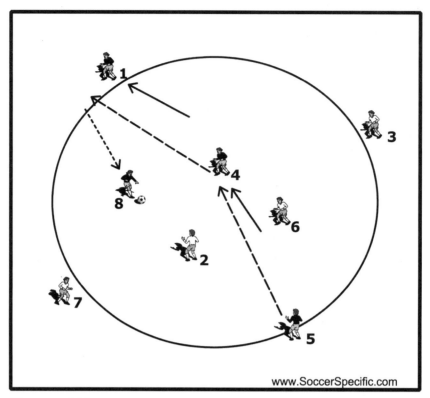

Diagram 190

1. It is a 2v2 in the middle, players can only pass to their teammates on the outside to keep possession, so half the number of options as before.
2. **Develop:** The outside player who receives the pass from the inside player now keeps possession and goes into the middle and switches with the inside player who initially passed the ball outside.
3. Outside player coming into the circle with the ball can run it in and keep possession or pass it to their teammate one touch. Constant changing of positions here means players are always on the move both on and off the ball.

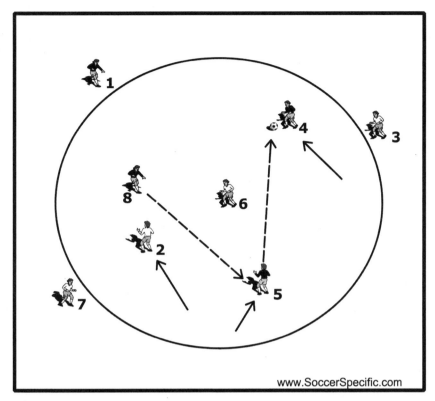

Diagram 191

1. Now we have an overload situation as in the 2v1 previously. You can bring in this set up before the 2v2 if you desire as it is easier to gain success with it than in the 2v2 and equal numbers.
2. To make it a bigger challenge to the players, condition the number of touches they have in the circle to three, then two touch, then one touch if it is on to do so. Try to split the defenders with a pass between them.
3. If the defenders win the ball, because they are outnumbered, allow them to be free with no restriction on touches and encourage them to keep the ball using the outside players themselves now. This is their reward for winning back the ball.
4. The variations on this set up are numerous and it just takes a little imagination to develop new ideas from this.
5. Progress the idea from 1v1, 3v1, 2v1, 2v2, 4v2, 3v2, 3v3 and so on depending on the numbers of players you have to work with. The area can change as you increase the number of players in the middle.
6. Use the clinic to improve support play or improve defensive play (when the players are out-numbered for example).

COACHING CLINIC SESSION PLAN 34

(For age 11 years and older)

OBJECTIVE: DEVELOPING THE PLAYERS' ABILITY TO SWITCH THE PLAY, BE AWARE OF TEAMMATES AND OPPONENTS POSITIONING BEFORE RECEIVING AND THEN CHANGING THE POINT OF ATTACK

Individual Coaching Points:

    a) Look before you receive – where are teammates / opposing players?

    b) Open body stance – side on to where the ball is coming from.

    c) Check towards the ball – a dummy to fool the defender in a game situation.

    d) If time and space are available, let the ball run across the body – switching play without needing to touch the ball. If the space is covered move the ball in another direction with a good first touch.

    e) Pace of the pass – must be such that the player receiving the pass can let the ball run across his body and maintain possession of it.

    f) Change direction – switching from one side to the other.

1. Players often get into the habit of taking the ball back to where they are facing because of a closed stance and where the ball has just come from. These sessions are to help players get the idea of opening up their body stance to be able to switch the play in another or the opposite direction and thus get a better appreciation of the use of the whole field of play.

2. This is the basic beginning of the Awareness session where we first have all the players moving freely, passing and moving within their own team.
   Divide the group into two teams. Begin with one ball being passed around each team and as they become proficient introduce another ball to increase their Awareness qualities.

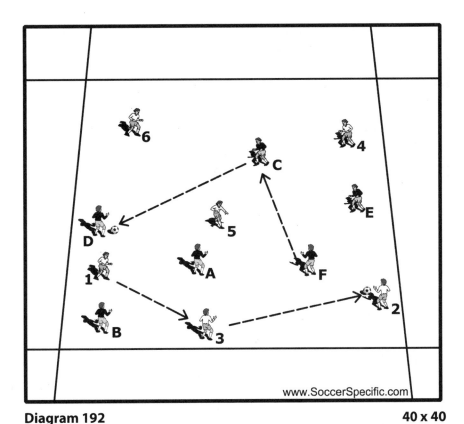

Diagram 192   **40 x 40**

3. Often in games players have the opportunity to switch the direction that the ball is traveling but choose to take it back to where it came from and often this is back into where the opponents are strong, instead of opening their stance up and changing the field to where the opponents may be weak and your team is stronger. It is like the players are wearing blinders.

4. These sessions are designed to help the players develop the capacity to look around and identify the moment they can switch the field. The presentation is based on a field set up where you can develop the session in different ways with built in progressions and as little need to change the basic set up as possible.

5. To begin have the teams play throughout both grids to spread the play out and get the players comfortable and composed. As they improve, you can change it to playing in one grid only so there is less room to work in and things happen more quickly. This is a test of their Awareness ability.

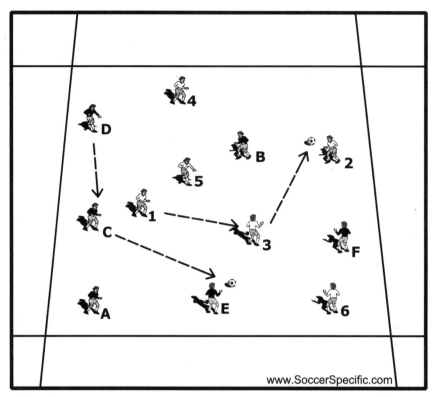

Diagram 193

6. Introduce the concept of switching the direction of play. The receiving player lets the ball run across his body to change the direction of play. The weight of the pass is important here. He can also move the ball off at another angle to change the direction of play. One method is without a touch on the ball, the other is with a touch.

7. This is to counter the situation in a game where a player takes the ball back to where it came from, mainly due to a closed body position and thus not opening up the field of play.

8. Players must recognize where to change direction to and what their options are before they receive the ball. The other team's players act as non-competitive opposition by getting in the way, filling the same spaces.

TEAM GAMES PRACTICING AND DEVELOPING AWARENESS
USING GOALS AS A SUPPORT REFERENCE

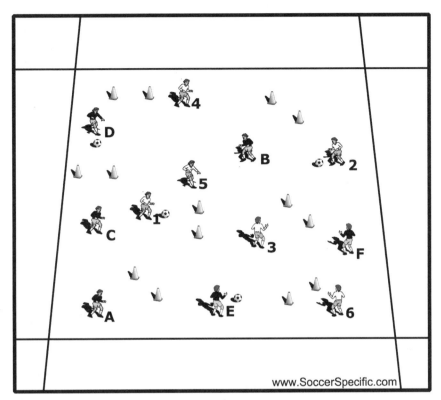

Diagram 194

1. The goals are spread out and act as a reference to help the players spread out, switch play, pass and support each other.
2. They must make their passes through the goal. This condition forces the players to find a goal (and space) to pass and to receive through. Once they receive the ball they must then find someone else to pass to. The support players spread out to receive by moving into space (where the other goals are).
3. Two teams working in the same area means congestion, so decisions have to be quick on where, when and how to pass and receive.
4. Move into an overload situation so there is opposition to increase the pressure on the players. Have an 8v4 in the above workout, still using the goals as points of reference for support positions. Count the number of passes made through the goals. Develop – score a goal by dribbling through the goal also.
5. Eventually have equal sides and make it competitive counting passes through the goals as a goal and perhaps have the first team to ten goals will be the winner. All your previous work trying to teach them how to play in less pressurized situations (over a long period of time) to relax them ultimately leads to you testing them in full scale match play. The progression to this must be gradual.
6. **Coaching Points:**
   a) Look before you receive – where are teammates / opposing players.
   b) Open body stance – side on to where the ball is coming from.
   c) Check towards the ball – a dummy to fool the defender in a game situation.

d) If time and space are available, let the ball run across the body – switching play without needing to touch the ball. If the space is covered, move the ball in another direction with a good first touch.

e) Pace of the pass – must be such that the player receiving the pass can let the ball run across his body and maintain possession of it.

f) Change direction – switching from one side to the other.

6

THE AWARENESS COACHING METHOD AND
"THEMED" SMALL SIDED GAMES

HOW TO PRESENT A SMALL - SIDED GAME

This is a game of less than 11v11. It can be any number, from 3 v 3 through to 9 v 9. The most common set-ups to establish team coaching themes are 4v4, 5v5, 6v6 or 8v8. I have included examples of these set ups.

Session Plan

1. Only coach one team at a time.
2. Try to work with all the players on the team you are coaching, affecting each performance in a positive way.
3. Stay with one theme / topic at a time. Don't jump from one to another during the session, this will only confuse the players.
4. Divide the field into thirds: defending, middle, attacking third, for easier points of reference. Cone the thirds of the field off to show the boundaries.
5. Use specific start positions to get the session going.
6. Develop your theme using the key coaching points and use them as a base for referral to check you have covered them in the session.
7. List the key points in the order you perceive them in the process of building the session. For example, in defending, pressure on the ball comes before support. Once you let the game go free, key points can be highlighted in any order depending on if the previous key point was performed correctly and didn't need to be addressed.
8. Move from simple to complex as you develop the session. For example, in the theme "Defending from the Front", coach individual play within the team concept first (working with one striker), move to coaching a unit of players (it could be the two strikers working together), then extend the numbers (it could be working with the strikers and midfield players), then finish with coaching the whole team (strikers, midfielders, defenders, keeper).
9. You may work the other way around depending on your session theme. For example, if your session is "Playing from the Back", you could start with the distribution of the ball from the keeper (individual) to working with a wide defender receiving from the keeper (individual), developing the theme with each individual defender. Then move onto the defending unit and the keeper combined (unit), then introducing the midfield players (combined units), and finally introducing the strikers (whole team).
10. This is individual, then unit, then team. This builds the session from simple to complex in a logical order.
11. This is just an example of how it can be done in a logical order; it is up to the individual coach to develop his own method to suit his own style of coaching.
12. Once the defending team have won back the ball they have 5 passes (or whatever the coach decides) to score a goal, then the game restarts with the defending team having to win back the ball again. This is because we are working on defending and don't want the team to spend a lot of time with the ball on attacking play. By giving them the chance to attack once they have won the ball, they have a reward for good defending.

SMALL-SIDED GAME PRACTICES
INCORPORATING AWARENESS PRINCIPLES

COACHING CLINIC SESSION PLAN 35
(For age 6 years and older)
OBJECTIVE: DEVELOPING TEAM PLAY AND INDIVIDUAL "THEMES" THROUGH 3v3
AND 4v4 SMALL SIDE GAMES (PART ONE)

Three v Three: A Basic Triangular Shape

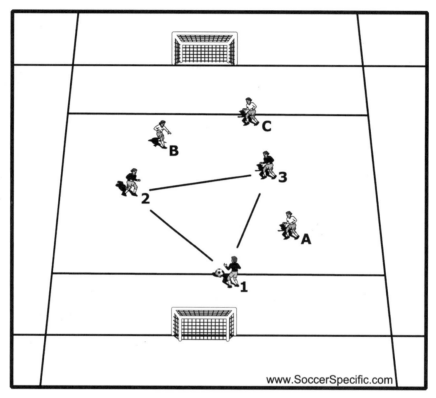

Diagram 195   **35 x 20**

1. Using the principles of the Awareness Program is imperative to get the most success out of this small-sided game concept.
2. The 3v3 small-sided game is the perfect introduction to learning triangular support shape in terms of angles and distances and establishing the supporting positions of the players.
3. Playing 3v3 without keepers presents an opportunity to develop the keeper-sweeper concept. The keeper and the supporting defender (sweeper) learn to handle the ball close to the goal and use their feet away from the goal (you can have a designated area if you like within which they can handle the ball).
4. Avoid the situation where a player from each team stays back in goal; encourage them to get involved in open play.
5. Move to 3v3 plus keepers as a natural progression when the time is right. Having three permanent outfield players provides the players with more options on the field of play.

SMALL-SIDED GAME 4 v 4 DEVELOPMENT

SMALL-SIDED GAME PRACTICES
Incorporating Awareness Principles

Four v Four: A Basic Diamond Shape
(Most 4v4 games are played in 35 x 20 yards size fields)

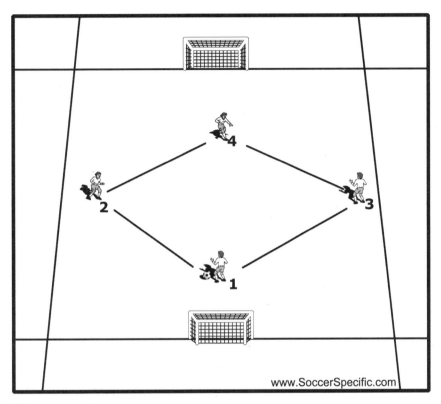

www.SoccerSpecific.com

Diagram 196

1. There are no set positions but there is a positional theme to work from which is the diamond or kite. Begin with one team working up and down to each target alternately taking shape from this. Introduce another team and have them playing through each other.
2. You can have two keepers in goal (or coaches) as targets to pass to, and then players reverse their direction of play, attacking the opposite goal. Keep it continuous using the other team as non-competitive opponents to play through.

3. **Coaching Points:**
   a) Correct Positioning when attacking and defending.
   b) Maintaining Possession and dictating the direction of play by running with the ball, passing and dribbling.
   c) Forward passing where possible but if not then positioning for back or sideways passing.
   d) Movement as a team forward, backward, sideways left and right.
   e) Communication – verbal and non verbal (body language).
   f) Techniques involved – Controlling and Passing, receiving and turning, dribbling, shielding and shooting. Defending principles are practiced too.

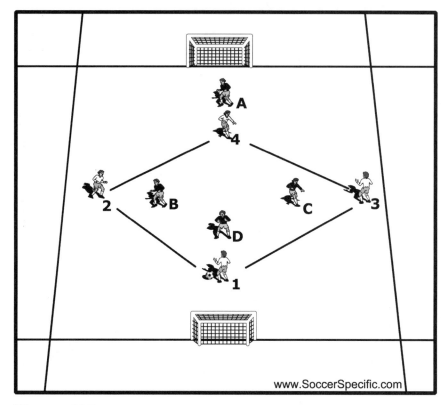

Diagram 197

1. This is the set up for the eventual 4v4 (or a 5v5 plus keepers) competitive game situation. The above coaching points are important to use as guidelines to what you are trying to achieve in this coaching practice.
2. The attacking four spread out as wide and long as they can to make it difficult for the defending team to mark. Maintenance of a rough diamond shape ensures good angles and distances of support wherever the ball may be.
3. The use of the Awareness principles is very important in the development of this game and you can ensure they are applied by conditioning the game by, for example, making it one and two touch play.

PASSING SUPPORT AND COMBINATION WORK GAME PLAN
(For age 8 years and older)

Four v Four – A Basic Diamond Shape
(The length of field is now 25 yards and the width 35 yards)

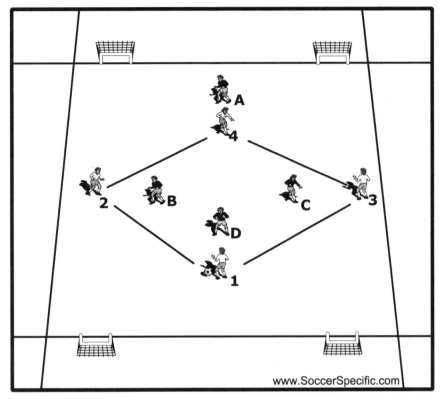

Diagram 198

1. You can start as in other practices with two teams playing through each other with a ball, each practicing switching play, attacking each goal in turn. Limit it to two touches to ensure quick decisions both from the player on the ball and the players off the ball who need to get in support positions early.
2. Using two wide positioned goals for each team to attack. This is designed to encourage players to spread out when they attack and switch play, changing direction if one route is blocked. It also encourages players on the ball to look around more, as there are two areas to attack.
3. Looking for quick transition and movement off the ball to create space but attacking the space only when it is on to do so. The first thought of the player on the ball should still be "Can I run or pass the ball forward".
4. **Coaching Points:**
   a) Creating Space – for yourself and your teammates.
   b) Decision – When, Where and How to pass the ball.
   c) Technique – The Quality of the pass (Accuracy, Weight, Angle).
   d) Support Positions of teammates (Angle, Distance and Communication). Players are supporting in front of the ball, to the side and behind the ball.
   e) Switching Play using width in attack.

COACHING CLINIC SESSION PLAN 36

(For age 8 years and older)

OBJECTIVE: DEVELOPING TEAM PLAY AND INDIVIDUAL "THEMES" THROUGH 3v3 AND 4v4 SMALL SIDE GAMES (PART TWO)

DEFENDING THE GAME PLAN

Four v Four: A Basic Diamond Shape

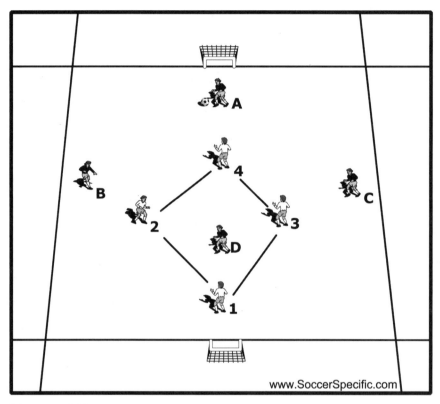

Diagram 199

1. The main idea here is for the defending team to condense the area the ball can be played into. The defending team form a diamond within the opponent's attacking diamond. (4) forces (A) one way and the rest of the team adjust their positions off this. (3) protects the space inside but can close down (C) if the ball is passed.
2. As the opponents move, the defending team must move to compensate. Also, if any pass is played behind (1), (2) or (3), that player should be first to the ball.
3. **Coaching Points:**
   a) Pressure – 1v1 defending to win the ball, delay or force a bad pass.
   b) Support – position of immediate teammate (angle, distance and communication).
   c) Cover – positions of teammates beyond the supporting player.
   d) Recovering and Tracking should the ball go past our position, recovery run to goal side of the ball and tracking the run of a player.

e) Double-Teaming – (A) passes to (C), (3) closes (C) down from in front, (4) follows along the path of the ball to close down from behind or slightly to the side. (4) closes in such a way as to obstruct a pass back to (A).

f) Regaining Possession and creating compactness from the back (pushing up as a unit).

3. The objectives of defending are to disrupt the other teams build up, make play predictable, prevent forward passes and ultimately regain possession of the ball.

4. Techniques include: pressuring, marking, tackling and winning the ball.

SHOOTING GAME PLAN WITH KEEPERS

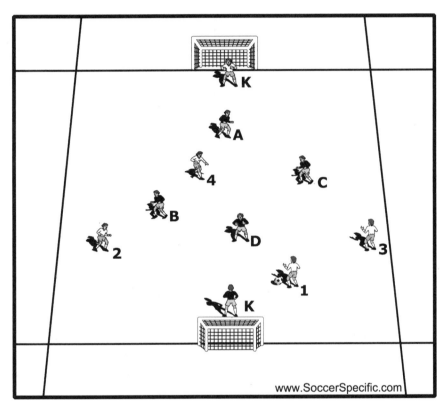

Diagram 200

1. Two large goals to shoot at to encourage success by scoring goals. Shorter field, so lots of shots on goal because players are nearly always in shooting positions. Initially have the two team / two balls set up with no opposition to enable players working both ways to get lots of shots in. Once a team has worked a position to shoot and has done so, that team's keeper sets up another attack.

2. Progress it to the competitive even sided game.

3. **Coaching Points:**
   a) Quick shooting.
   b) Rebounds.
   c) Transitions.
   d) Quick break counter attack.

4. Players must be particularly aware of where teammates, opposing players and the keeper are because the space to work in is small and the time they have on the ball is short.

5. Hence development of the mental side of the game in terms of the Awareness program, i.e. seeing situations quickly and acting upon them is very important to the player to help him have success by scoring goals. The shorter and sharper the practice then the less time the players have to make the correct decisions to be successful, the more important it is to train them to be able to cope with these pressure situations.

DRIBBLING GAME

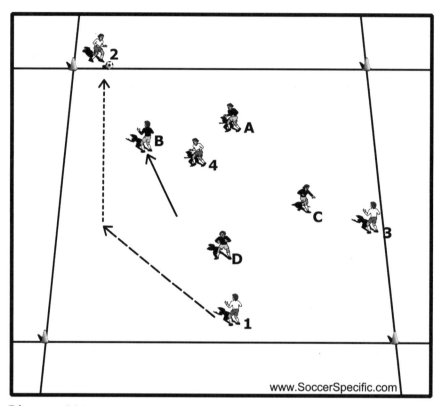

Diagram 201

1. No goals are used. To score, a player must dribble the ball under control over the goal line. We are looking to encourage 1v1's and work on improving ball control with quick movement. Players must decide when and where to dribble. This practice can be applied with the same principles with larger numbers of players such as a 6v6
2. **Coaching Points:**
   a) Creating Space – For you to receive the ball.
   b) Decision – When and where to dribble (less likely in the defending third, most likely in the attacking third).
   c) Technique –Tight Close Control on receiving the ball, use of body to dummy an opponent, ability to change pace and direction, established dribbling skills, a positive attitude to beat the player.
   d) Runs of Teammates – To support or to take opponents away to leave a 1v1 situation.
   e) End Product – beating an opponent in a 1v1 situation.

While with the Awareness program I am encouraging players to make quick observations and quick decisions often resulting in a player passing the ball early to avoid being caught in possession, it also helps players who are good at dribbling by enabling them to identify situations in advance to allow them to get in a good position to take a player on in a 1v1 situation. This could include opening the body up to receive and face up to an opponent, seeing the immediate opponent has no cover on so you can attack 1 v 1, seeing where the defender is early and identifying the best side to attack, seeing you have no support so have to attack 1 v 1 etc.

SMALL-SIDED GAMES 6 v 6 DEVELOPMENT:
(All 6 v 6 games are played in a 60 x 40 yards size area)

COACHING CLINIC SESSION PLAN 37
(For age 10 years and older)
OBJECTIVE: DEVELOPING TEAM PLAY AND INDIVIDUAL "THEMES" THROUGH A 6 v 6 SMALL SIDED GAME (PART ONE)

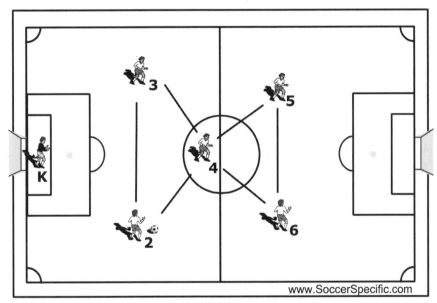

Diagram 202

1. The basic shape is a double triangle, again a positional theme where players are encouraged to interchange then return to a basic shape when the time is right. You could use a 2 – 2 – 1 formation also to allow a 2v1 overload at the defensive end.
2. As in the previous games, the coach needs to focus on the principles established with the Awareness program and get the players to apply them in the S.S.G. concept.
3. **Coaching Points:**
   a) Create Space - players spread out to be in position to receive the ball.
   b) Decision – when, where and how to pass.
   c) Technique – Quality of the pass (Accuracy, weight and angle).
   d) Support Positions – of teammates (angle, distance, and communication).
   e) End Product – shots on goal. Anticipate rebounds.

f) The themes you can concentrate on one at a time include: Creating Space as a team, Forward passes to Feet and Space, Switching Play as a team, Running with the Ball, One and Two Touch Play, Passing and Support Play, Diagonal Runs without the Ball (diagonal runs, Overlaps, blindside runs, under laps), Forward diagonal Runs to Receive, Receiving and Turning, When and Where to Dribble.

A 6 v 4 GAME OVERLOAD SITUATION

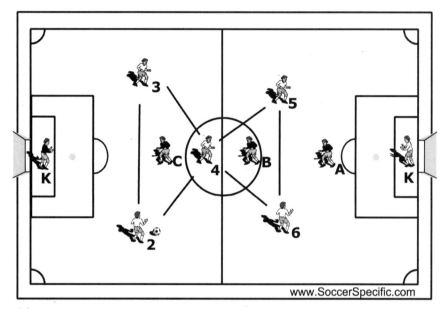

Diagram 203

1. Overload situation now with a 6v4 in favor of the numbers team. Ask the defending lettered team to play passively to begin to get the session going easily.
2. Then as we progress the defenders can't tackle but can intercept passes.
3. Next, ask the defenders to defend correctly and at 100% but the team in possession should still be able to make it work with the overload in their favor. More game-like now. If the defending team wins it they can attack.

OBJECTIVE: RUNNING WITH THE BALL IN A SMALL SIDED 6 v 6 GAME

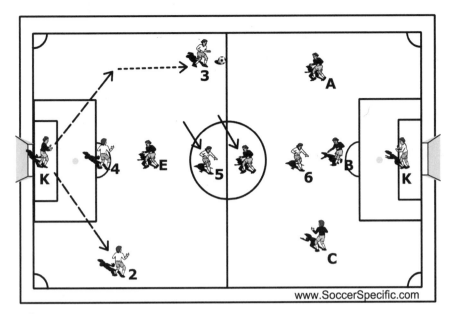

Diagram 204

1. Here the theme is running with the ball, particularly from the back. Use the progressions to get it going.
2. **Coaching Points:**
   a) Creating Space – Players breaking wide to receive the ball from the keeper.
   b) Decision – Can I run with the ball or do I pass.
   c) Technique – Key factors of running with the ball, head up, good first touch out of your feet, and run in a straight line (the shortest route forward) with pace, using your front foot to control the ball.
   d) Quality of Pass / Cross / Shot / Dribble at the end of the run.
   e) Support Positions – support in front, fill in behind.
3. When you get to a 6v6 set up it may be useful to change the shape of the teams to 3 – 1 - 1 from a 2 – 1 – 2 so there is a 3v1 overload at the back to help players run out with the ball. The space is usually in the wide areas for this movement. This allows for a greater chance of success until players are comfortable and confident in the exercise.

OBJECTIVE: SWITCHING PLAY IN A SMALL SIDED GAME OF 6 v 6

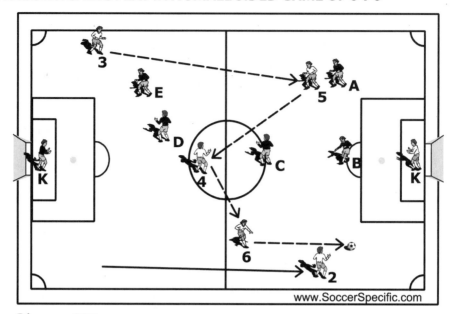

Diagram 205

1. As in all these 6v6 presentations the coach should use a progression method to build up to the competitive 6v6 game situations eventually.
2. Use the 2 – 1 – 2 system of play. The coach must decide how much of an overload is needed to build up to a 6v6 competitive game situation (6v2, 6v3 etc).
3. Use the 6v6 game with the two-team concept before going into a competitive 6v6.
4. **Coaching Points:**
   a) Creating Space as individuals and a team.
   b) Decision – When, where and how to pass the ball.
   c) Technique – Quality of the pass, can I pass it forward or do I switch the play.
   d) Support Positions – To switch the play (open stance to receive and pass).
   e) Switching the Play – From one side of the field to the other.
5. In the above example the team have attacked down one side of the field but been stopped from further progress by good defending so they have come back and switched the play to the other side. A great run by (2) on the overlap complements this move, making a 2v1 situation on the opposite side of the field from which they started the move.

OBJECTIVE: CREATING SPACE IN A SMALL SIDED GAME OF 6 v 6

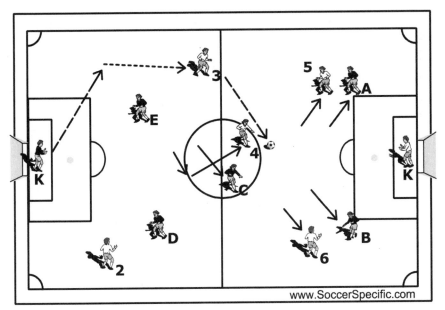

Diagram 206

1. Here the players work to get free of their markers with movement off the ball; they create space for themselves and / or for their teammates.
2. **Coaching Points:**
   a) Creating Space – Spreading out as a team.
   b) Decision – When, where and how to Create Space.
   c) Technique – of passing and receiving.
   d) Support Positions of players; angles and distances, movement off the ball.
3. In the above example (2) and (3) break wide to create space and offer two options to receive a pass from the keeper. (3) receives the pass and (4) runs off (C) to check back to receive the pass in space. (5) and (6) create space in front of the receiving player by making split runs to move (A) and (B) away from where (4) wants to attack and shoot at goal.
4. If either (A) or (B) do not track the two strikers and stay in the space in front to defend against (4) then (4) can pass to whichever player got free by not being tracked on their run.

OBJECTIVE: WHEN AND WHERE TO DRIBBLE IN A SMALL- SIDED 6 v 6 GAME

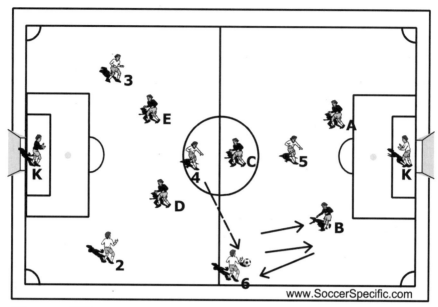

Diagram 207

1. Looking to create 1v1 situations in the middle and especially the attacking thirds of the field, focusing on good dribbling technique.
2. **Coaching Points:**
   a) Creating Space – Run the player off to check back and receive to feet. Body position half turned with the back to the touchline. Where the defender marks determines whether the attacker goes inside or outside.
   b) Attitude to Dribble – Aggressive / Positive.
   c) Decision – Does the attacker run, pass, cross, shoot or dribble?
   d) Technique of Dribbling - when it is on to dribble. How to dribble using moves.
   e) Safety and Risk Areas of the Field – where it is on to dribble.
   f) Runs of the players – to support or create space.
3. Here (6) runs off (B) to create space behind to come back and receive the ball to feet. (6) must shape up with his back to the touchline to be able to see the entire field and options available. If player (B) doesn't follow then (6) can get the pass in front and attack the goal; using (5) in order to create a 2v1.

COACHING CLINIC SESSION PLAN 38

(For age 10 years and older)

OBJECTIVE: DEVELOPING TEAM PLAY AND INDIVIDUAL "THEMES" THROUGH A 6 v 6 SMALL SIDED GAME (PART TWO)

OBJECTIVE: RECEIVING AND TURNING IN A SMALL SIDED 6 v 6 GAME

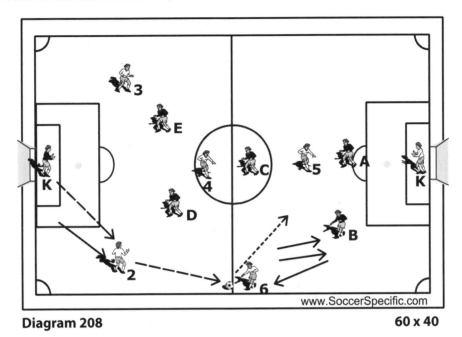

Diagram 208   **60 x 40**

1. Here the theme is receiving and turning, particularly in the middle and attacking thirds.
2. **Coaching Points:**
   a) Creating Space with movement off the defenders.
   b) Decision – When and where to receive and turn.
   c) Technique – How to receive and turn. The best way, if you have time, is to run your marker off and return to the space you have created for yourself by that movement.
   d) Quality of the Pass into the receiver for ease of control.
   e) Positions of Support of teammates in front and behind the player on the ball.
3. In the above example (6) runs the defender (B) off away from the ball to check back to receive the pass. (4) positions to support behind. (2) can also support (5), but if (6) has turned, (5) can make a run into a receiving position of support in front of the ball to take a shot or create a 2v1 situation with (6) by losing the marking of (A). If (6) is a very good dribbler, (5) can run off (A) away from the space in front of goal to leave (6) in a 1v1 situation.

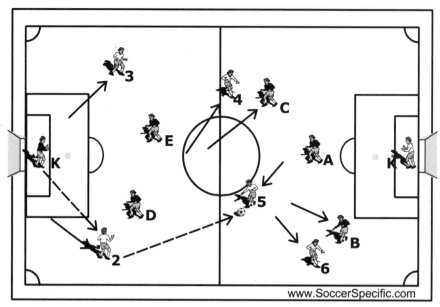

Diagram 209

1. The theme is making diagonal runs with or without the ball to receive or create space for a teammate. When it is a forward diagonal run the player making it must avoid running offside in a game situation.
2. **Coaching Points:**
   a) Creating Space.
   b) Decision – when and where to pass into the receiver.
   c) Technique – Quality of pass, particularly the weight, accuracy and timing.
   d) Angle and Timing of the Diagonal Runs both to create space and to receive the ball.
   e) Support Positions of the players.
3. In the above example (2) is on the ball to pass it forward. (6) makes a diagonal run away from the center, taking his marker (B) with him. (4) also makes a diagonally opposite run away from the central area, taking (C) away also. This leaves space for (5) to come short with another diagonal run to receive the pass. In receiving and turning, (5) may have run (A) off to check back if time was available,thus creating more time and space on the ball.
4. Another way to create space for (5) coming short to receive would be for (6) to make a run towards (5) and cut across the path of (5)'s marker (A) to hold up his run.

OBJECTIVE: FORWARD DIAGONAL RUNS TO RECEIVE IN A 6 v 6 GAME

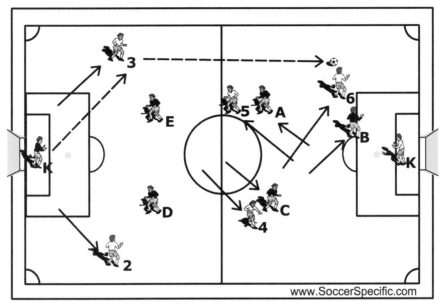

Diagram 210

1. Here (5) goes short, taking (A) with him. This creates space behind (A) for (6) to run into in order to receive the pass. (4) again runs off (C) to help clear the space.
2. Below, the strikers make opposite diagonal runs to get midfielder (4) in centrally.

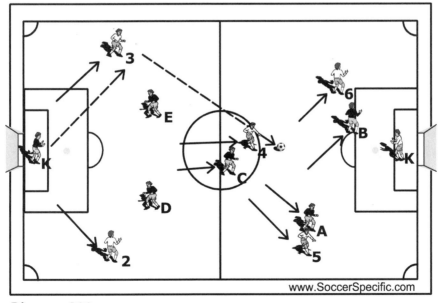

Diagram 211

3. Here (5) and (6) run off their markers, breaking wide to leave space inside for midfielder (4) to run into.

7

DEVELOPING THE AWARENESS COACHING METHOD THROUGH "THEMED" TEAM GAMES

COACHING CLINIC SESSION PLAN 39

(For age 11 years and older)

OBJECTIVE: DEVELOPING PASSING AND SUPPORT THROUGH THE DIRECTIONAL PASSING AND SUPPORT THREE ZONE GAME: PART A

RUNNING WITH AND WITHOUT THE BALL
LONG PASSING (Playing area is 60 by 40)

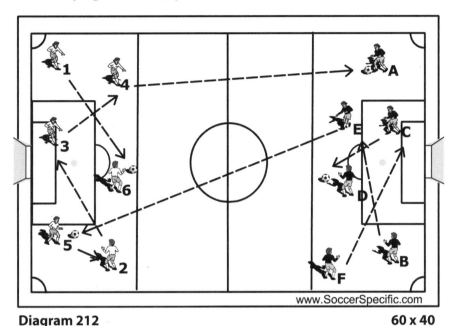

Diagram 212   **60 x 40**

www.SoccerSpecific.com

1. You can use various numbers of players at each end of the grid in this sequence.
2. Players pass and move in their own grid and pass to the opposite grid on eye contact or a verbal call. Balls are constantly changing grids; players have to have awareness in their own grid to receive but also awareness of when a pass is on from the other grid (must have head up and be constantly looking around to see this). If they don't observe where their own teammates are or those in the other grid are, they won't be successful with this, so they must play with their head up and have the ability to look away from the ball as well as at it, observing all the options, both in their own grid and the opposite grid.
3. Conditions – Ball can't bounce between grids for chipped or lofted passes, or must be driven along the ground with pace for quick passing.
4. Develop Running with the Ball across the grids. Pass and move within own grid then a player picks a moment to run and takes it.
5. Keep balance of balls in each grid. Can start with one in each; try to avoid two in one grid at once. Increase to two balls per grid.
6. Long pass then follow the ball (supporting the pass) into the other grid, so not only are balls being transferred but also players. Players must move as quickly as possible to support in the other grid.
7. **Coaching Points:**
    a) Awareness of the positions of players in both grids, thus ensuring the players have their heads up to see the pass.
    b) Movement off the ball to make themselves available in both grids to receive a pass.
    c) Quality of short passing in one grid and long passing into the other grid.

d) Depending on the theme, the development of awareness of when and where to pass, run with the ball, make a movement off the ball (third man run for example), receive and turn with the ball, and so on.

RUNNING WITH THE BALL

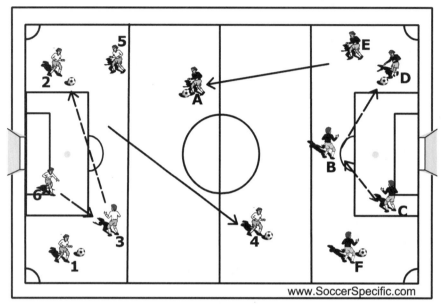

Diagram 213

1. The skill practiced here is specifically running with the ball, still identifying passing and moving options, but also looking to make a run when the time is right.

2. **Coaching Points:**
   a) Head Up – look forward
   b) Good first touch out of feet, 3-4 touches maximum, not dribbling.
   c) Run in a straight line, the quickest route.
   d) Running Style, use the front foot to control the ball using the laces.

PASSING THEN SUPPORTING THE PASS

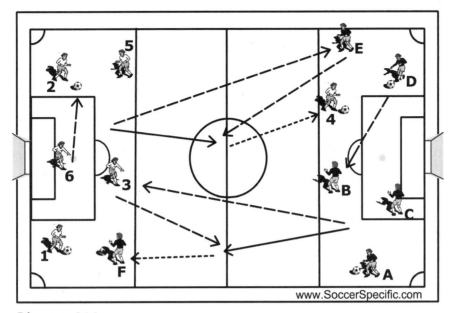

Diagram 214

This is like a player passing into a striker and receiving the pass back (one touch if possible for quickness of transition) and then running the ball forward into the attacking third.

COACHING CLINIC SESSION PLAN 40

(For age 11 years and older)
OBJECTIVE: DEVELOPING PASSING AND SUPPORT THROUGH THE DIRECTIONAL PASSING AND SUPPORT THREE ZONE GAME: PART B
THIRD MAN RUN DEVELOPMENT

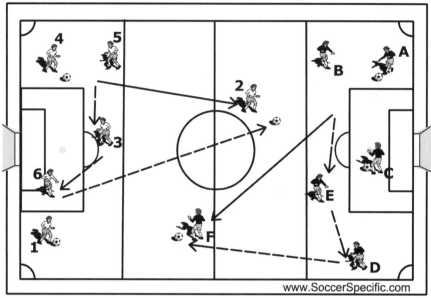

Diagram 215   **60 x 40**

1. Third man run development – A player makes a run into the neutral area between the grids; a player on the ball must see this quickly and pass to the player making the run. Try to drop the ball in front of the player to run onto. That player then takes ball into other grid. At the same time another player goes the opposite way. Start with one ball in each grid and build up.

2. **Progression:** the type of runs to be made, straight or diagonal runs. Diagonal passes and straight runs, and diagonal runs and straight passes as above or diagonal runs and diagonal passes. Equate the situation with how to make it difficult for defenders in a game to mark players who make different types of runs. Here above, (F) Passes to (E) but continues the run forward, (E) passes back to (D) who passes into the path of (F) continuing the forward run.

3. If a player makes a run and doesn't receive a pass then he works his way back into his own grid. Relate the move to a player making a forward run, not getting the pass, working back, drawing a defender with him and then another player makes the run into the space left to receive a through ball.

4. Receiving and Turning – a player moves out of the area and positions side on at an angle to receive and turn (looking before receiving) and take the ball to the other grid. Same happens on the other side.

5. **Coaching Points:**
    a) Timing of the 3rd man run off the ball into space
    b) Observation of the run by the player on the ball
    c) Pace, accuracy and timing of the pass in front of the receiving player

PLAYING GIVE AND GO'S

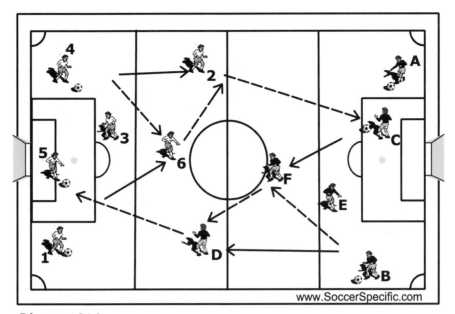

Diagram 216

1. Give and Go's (Movement in two's) - A player moves into the neutral zone (with a third man run off the ball) and another player on the ball passes to him. The passer then follows and receives a pass back (a 1– 2 move) and then passes the ball into the other grid. Both players move into the other grid and join in. Now the existing players in this grid must balance things up and look to break in twos the other way as soon as possible.
2. **Progression:** Introduce a defender in each grid. This is now a 4v1 and only one ball per grid.
3. As the number of players involved increases, so does the number of balls used. At times, two players can be making moves across the free space from the same grid at the same time, hence there is constant movement between grids. The players will get good at passing and moving and being able to look beyond the ball and at the same time making quick decisions the more they practice this session.

INTRODUCING DEFENDERS

Up to now there have been mainly ZERO OPPOSITION GAMES and SHADOW PLAYS to allow players to develop anticipation, awareness, vision and imagination regarding passing, receiving, support and composure on the ball. We can now introduce DEFENDERS to add pressurizing situations to test the players.

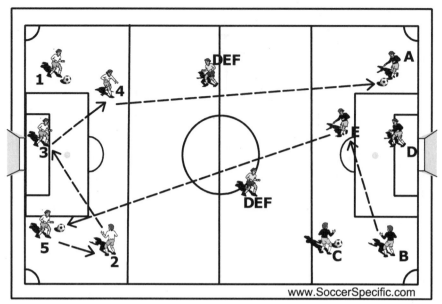

Diagram 217

1. Introduce defenders to put the players under pressure when they pass or run the ball across the middle of the field.
2. It can begin with 2 defenders, then 3 defenders to make it more difficult where defenders can intercept passes or tackle players with the ball.
3. This exercise includes:
   a) passing across the area,
   b) running the ball across the area,
   c) third man runs,
   d) passing then supporting the pass,
   e) playing give and go's,
   f) receiving and turning, and so on.
4. Adding defenders takes the session to a more competitive level. Now the players have to focus not only on passing, running and supporting in their own zone and into the other zone, but also on the position of the defenders and how to best get past them.
5. If a defender intercepts the ball they switch quickly with the player whose pass was intercepted.

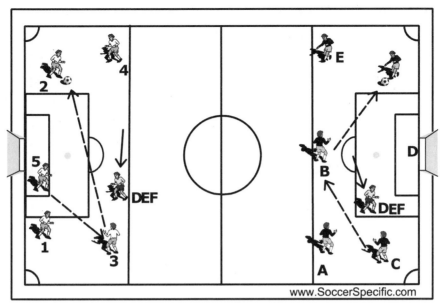

Diagram 218

1. Have a 5v1 in each zone, introducing defenders to make the situation competitive. To begin we can have one ball only, then introduce a ball each side.
2. Players need to get a certain number of passes in before it goes to the other side. It may be that at any one time there will be two balls in one side so this team must get a ball to the other side to balance it as soon as possible.
3. You can introduce running with the ball across the free zone into the other area, third man running and receiving, passing first then third man running, passing into the other zone then joining in following the pass and so on.
4. All this results in a more competitive environment with players being put under pressure to test their awareness more thoroughly.
5. Players should always strive to keep the balance with a ball each side.
6. If a defender wins the ball, the player who gave it away becomes the defender. Have defenders just hold a bib to identify them as defenders so the transitions are quick and effective.
7. **Competitive:** Add keepers and have a game.

COACHING CLINIC SESSION PLAN 41

(For age 11 years and older)

OBJECTIVE: SWITCHING PLAY AS A TEAM

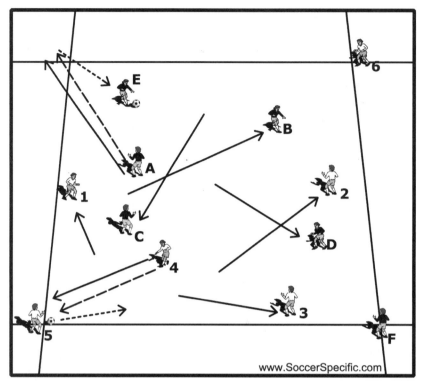

Diagram 219   **40 x 40**

1. Two teams, a ball each, playing to targets. Once they get to one target they must work to get the ball to the other target. As the player passes to a target they must change over with the target player who comes into play. As (4) passes to (5) and switches position, already the other players have spread out to attack the other target.

2. Teams play through each other and must have awareness of where their own players are and where the opposing players are as they pass through them. Emphasize a good first touch out their feet to set up the next pass or pass first time to a teammate. Players must look before they receive the ball.

3. Ensure as the ball is transferred from one end to the other that all players get a touch on the ball before it gets to the next target.

4. As the ball is passed to the target and the target player brings the ball out with a good first touch the other players must already be positioning themselves to be in support to transfer the ball to the other target. This means spreading out width wise and length wise to make themselves hard to mark such as in a game. Ensure they don't turn their backs and run away but keep looking at the ball and open their stance to receive a pass or at least offer an option. Show the movement across the field as they break out, diagonal runs for example (C & B), no breaking in straight lines and hence easy to mark.

5. Introduce opposition so the two teams play against each other and make it competitive by keeping score.

6. **Coaching Points:**
   a) Look before you receive – where are teammates / opposing players.
   b) Open body stance – side on to where the ball is coming from.
   c) Check towards the ball – a dummy to fool the defender in a game situation.
   d) If time and space are available, let the ball run across the body – switching play without needing to touch the ball. If the space is covered, move the ball in another direction with a good first touch.
   e) Pace of the pass – must be such that the player receiving the pass can let the ball run across them and maintain possession of it.
   f) Change direction – switching from one side to the other.

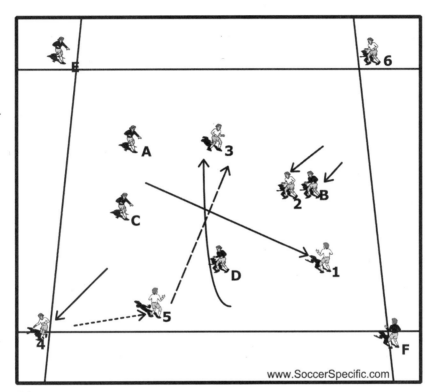

Diagram 220

1. (4) becomes the new target player with a pass to (5).
2. (5) runs the ball out and (1) and (3) make diagonal runs in front to lose their markers and get free to offer passing options to (5).
3. (2) runs away from in front of the target to get free to receive a pass, or take defender (B) away from the space (3) is running into.
4. In this situation the best action for (5) is a pass to (3) that can easily score by a pass to the target player (6).
5. **Coaching Points:**
   a) Quick transition from inside to outside player
   b) Immediate support positions of teammates (movement off the ball)
   c) Decision making by the player on the ball (pass, run, dribble)
   d) Score a goal by passing to the other target player

COACHING CLINIC SESSION PLAN 42

(For age 11 years and older)

OBJECTIVE: CHANGING THE POINT OF ATTACK THROUGH THE DIRECTIONAL FOUR GOAL SWITCHING PLAY GAME

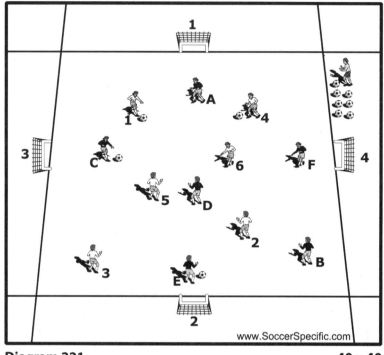

Diagram 221   **40 x 40**

Two teams passing and moving with a ball each team. Initially, have one team attacking goal (1) and the other team attacking goal (2). Coach calls "switch" and they attack different goals.

1. **Progression One:**

   Team (1) to (6) passes, trying to score in goal (1), then (2). Team (A) to (F) passes, trying to score in goal (3), then (4). They are still playing through each other but going in different directions. Next each team can attack two goals (opposite goals) at once.

2. Looking to switch play attacking two goals, players decide when to switch the ball and which goal to attack. Have a one or two touch shooting condition so the timing of the passing and the timing of the movement into position to shoot are correct.

3. **Progression Two:**

   a) Use two balls per team so they can attack two goals at once if necessary.

   b) Introduce goalkeepers in each of the four goals to make it more competitive. Have a constant supply of soccer balls to keep the game moving.

   We are looking to include all the main coaching points in this awareness session. Call "switch" so they attack the opposite two goals. We are developing quick decision-makers. Ultimately, have a competitive game between the two teams using the various rules and conditions above.

4. **Coaching Points:**

   a) Two directions to attack, so quick decisions are needed as to which way to go.

   b) Awareness of space in front and behind (if the player needs to change the direction of attack)

   c) Quick transition: scoring then changing direction to score in the other goal.

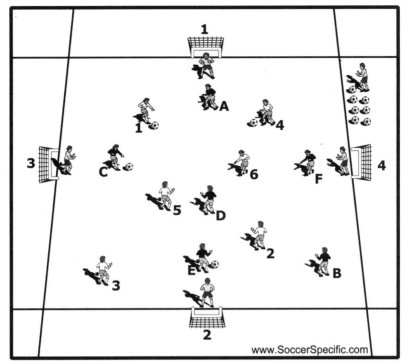

Diagram 222

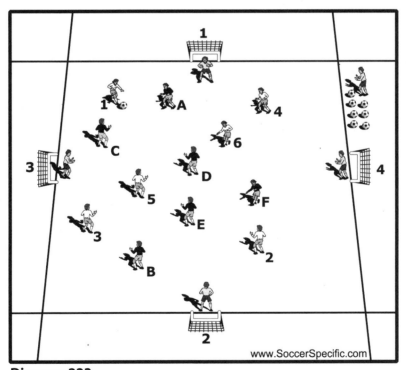

Diagram 223

- 291 -

COACHING CLINIC SESSION PLAN 43
(For age 12 years and older)
OBJECTIVE: DEVELOPING WIDTH IN ATTACK USING THE SWITCHING PLAY GAME
8 v 8   3-2-2

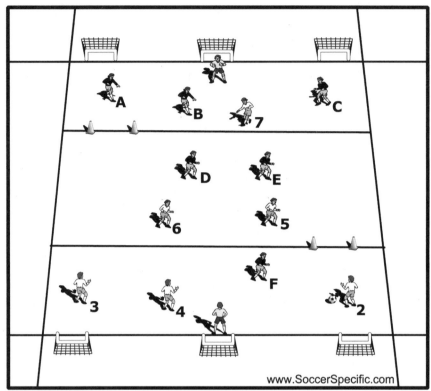

Diagram 224   **60 x 40**

1. Using three goals as reference points award one point / goal for scoring in the central goal and two points / goals when scoring in the wide goals. This should encourage them to spread the play using width in attack. If it is tight down one side, encourage them to switch the play and go down the other side.

2. Using the goals on the field, award a point / goal if they play through the goal, again encouraging using width in attack. They can dribble or pass through these goals. What you hope for is that if it is tight down one side and they can't score because the other team is defending well, a player may spread out to the other side to receive the ball with the idea that the team can score a point / goal by passing or dribbling through the other goal on the far side of the field (thus switching the play).

3. **Coaching Points:**
   a) Looking before receiving, knowing options on the ball in advance of receiving it
   b) Open body stance to receive to allow for changes in direction of play
   c) Letting the ball do the work with the open body stance allowing the ball to run across the body without having to touch it and thus changing the direction of play
   d) Weight of pass by the passer to allow the receiver to do this without losing possession of the ball
   e) Switching the play where appropriate

SWITCHING PLAY: FOUR SESSIONS IN ONE WITH PROGRESSIONS

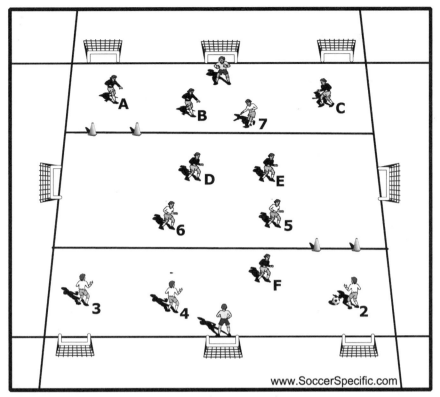

Diagram 225

1. Begin with four balls and the awareness session to introduce the idea of switching play and spreading out. No opposition, just two teams playing through each other using the other team as non- competitive opposition.
2. Once this has been practiced, make it competitive with two teams competing against each other with one ball only.
3. **Progression One:** Have the three-goal game with one point for a goal in the central goal and two for goals in the wide goals. Leave two cone goals inside the grid. When players pass or dribble through them they get a point.
4. **Progression Two:** Finish with a switching game using the four central goals on the four sides of the grid. Teams score in opposite goals so there are two goals to attack but they are opposite each other. One team can attack North and South the other East and West
5. All the sessions are designed to help players learn how to change the direction of attack and switch the play.

COACHING CLINIC SESSION PLAN 44

(For age 12 years and older)
**OBJECTIVE: TEACHING MOVEMENT "OFF THE BALL" THROUGH THE TRANSITION
DIRECTIONAL TARGET GAME
WITH 16 PLAYERS**

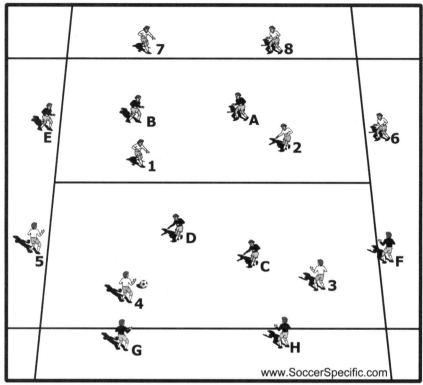

Diagram 226   **50 x 40**

1. **Rules:**
   a) Players must pass the ball to their target players to score. To score again they
      have to work the ball back into their own half of the field to be able to return.
   b) Target players have two touches, as do side players.
2. **Coaching Points:**
   a) **Creating Space** by running off the ball to receive or to help a teammate receive.
   b) **Quality of Passing**; long and short to targets and to teammates.
   c) Support play: working angles and distances incorporating switching play using the side
      players.
   d) **Receiving and Turning** in tight situations and dribbling in 1 v 1 situations.
   e) **Quick Decision Making** is required in this session because the numbers are small, the
      area tight and the transitions rapid.
3. **Develop:**
   a) No restriction on touches, then 3, 2 and ultimately 1 touch, but only if it is on to do 1 touch.
   b) All outside and target players have one touch only where possible
   c) Switch with target players as they receive the ball.
   d) Switch with outside players

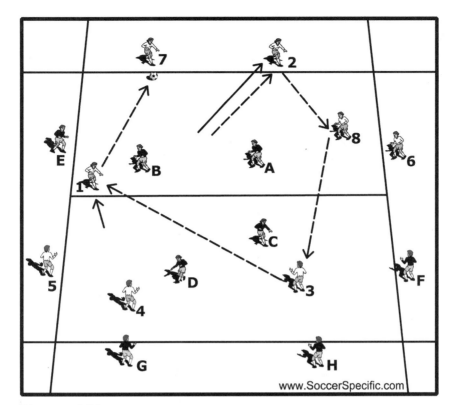

Diagram 227

1. Here is an example of the transition and movement off the ball to make it happen.
2. (2) passes to target player (8) who brings the ball back into the playing area.
3. (3) makes a run into the other half of the field on the blind side of (C) to receive the next pass. They need to get the ball into that half to be able to score.
4. (1) makes a forward run into space to receive the next pass off (3) and passes to target player (7) who can start the play again.
5. (1) switches with (7) and becomes a target player for the next phase of play.
6. **Observe the Attacking Team** – Recognize their movement off the ball. For example to work the ball into their own half see if the players make runs early in there as soon as the ball is at a target, some should support short and some long so the target has choices.
7. **Observe the Defending Team** – see if they are sucked to the ball or they recognize runs off the ball and track players making runs away from the ball into the other half.
8. To lessen the workload and keep everyone involved, have players switch with targets and outside side players when they pass to them.
9. Elements of play the target game teaches:
   Attacking as Individuals and as Team
   a) **Creating Space** by running off the ball to receive or to help a teammate receive.
   b) Developing **quick support play**, working angles and distances and incorporating switching play using the side players.
   c) **Passing long and short** to targets and to teammates.
   d) Receiving and turning in **tight situations** and dribbling in **1v1 situations**.
   e) **Lots of touches** on the ball for the players in this practice.
   f) **Quick decision making** is required in this session because the numbers are small, the area tight and the transitions rapid.

Defending as Individuals and as a Team
a) **Pressurizing** players on the ball to regain possession.
b) **Supporting** pressuring players and tracking runners off the ball.
c) **High pressure** to regain possession in the attacking half to be able to go straight to the target to score.

We have transitions from defense to attack and attack to defense, quick decision making and improved concentration as the switch occurs. There are interchanges of positions between inside players, targets and side support players.

As a coach you can work in this session how to defend properly as individuals and a team or how to attack properly as individuals and a team.

Conditions to impose to change the focus of the game
1. No restriction on touches, then 3, 2 or 1 touch, but only if it is on to do so.
2. Introduce a neutral player for a 5v4 overload in the middle if possession isn't kept easily.
3. Interchanges of players outside to in, inside to out as they pass the ball, observing the quality of the pass and the first touch of the receiver.
4. Have one teammate at each end so you are attacking both ends, but once you have passed to one target you keep possession and must try to get to the other target. You can't go back unless the opposition win the ball and then you get it back, only then can you go back to the same target.
5. To lessen the workload and keep everyone involved, have players switch with targets and outside players when they pass to them. This causes a constant transition of players and focuses the players' concentration.
6. The team can only score if they get an overlap, crossover or 1 – 2 in during the build up.
7. No talking, so players have to rely on their vision to play.
8. Players move into the target zone to receive (timing of run and pass) so we don't play with actual targets. Different players can then become the target player.
9. Man Marking – Have the players man mark so they must track a player when they don't have the ball and they must lose their marker when they have the ball. This is a good test to see who is working hard and who isn't as they have a designated job to do. You can see who works to get free of their marker and who works hard to prevent the player they are marking from getting the ball.
10. This session is particularly good as a midfield play practice session as you can liken it to moving the ball from defense through midfield to the striker. Then the target player (striker) maintains possession and the team can go the other way, the target striker becoming a defender for the attacking team, starting the move, and the other target becomes the striker to pass the ball to. So it is consistent movement end to end with the attacking team from a defender into midfield to a striker.
11. To improve the speed of thought, reward a successful one touch pass with a goal or point. Scoring a goal by passing to the target player now is worth three goals or 3 points.
12. The team in possession can pass back to the opponent's target players to help keep possession of the ball. Liken this to passing back to the keeper in a game situation.

THREE TEAM TRANSITION DIRECTIONAL TARGET GAME WITH 15 PLAYERS

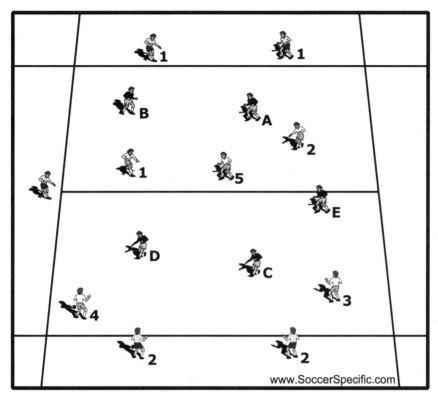

Diagram 228

1. Make it a 3 team game for 15 players. Each game lasts 10 minutes, the winning team stay on the field as a reward. You can vary the positions of the outside players, 2 target players at each end and one support player on one side or one support player on each side, one target player at one and end and two at the other and so on.

2. To make it technically a 10v5 game, have the team in possession play with the outside team. They are trying to score at one end, so these players are on their side but they are also able to work with the side player and the two target players of the other team, using them as support players also.

3. This encourages them to pass back and open the play up and not be focused on just playing forward all the time.

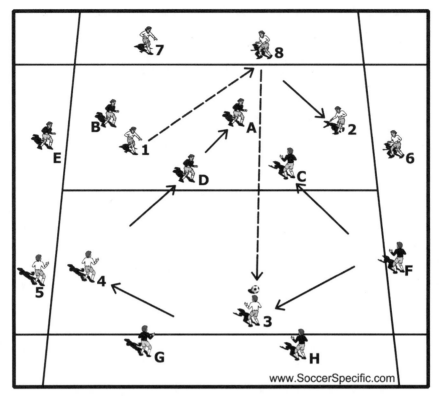

Diagram 229

1. This is an example of what to look for on the defending side of things.
2. Here the ball has been passed to the target (8) and a goal scored. The defenders are ball watching and not seeing the runs "off the ball" of their opponents.
3. The idea of getting the ball back into the other half before they can score again when in possession highlights these moments that players need to recognize in a game situation.
4. (1) plays the ball to target (8) to score. (2) supports the next pass short and at a wide angle, and (3) and (4) make runs into the other side of the field and off the ball to get free and receive a pass. Defenders are all ball watching and not looking at these runs, thus (3) and (4) get free. Poor defending, but the attackers get it right.
5. The coach has to identify these situations and stop the game to show the set up and ask the defending players what they need to do.

Problems to Identify and Coach:
Offensively
1. Lack of movement off the ball by players in both halves.
2. Poor quality of passing.
3. Correct decision making of when and where to pass.
4. Poor communication.
5. Poor angles and distance of support and lack of variation of these concepts (long, short and wide are needed so there are lots of options).
6. Mentally slow change from attack to defense when possession changes.

Defensively

1. Not seeing movements off the ball of the attacking players and not tracking these runs.
2. Ball watching, allowing players to get in behind.
3. Not pressing the ball quickly enough.
4. Working too much individually and not as a unit.
5. Mentally slow change from defense to attack when possession changes.

COACHING CLINIC SESSION PLAN 45

(For age 12 years and older)

OBJECTIVE: ENCOURAGING DRIBBLING AND TURNING THROUGH QUICK TRANSITION PLAY

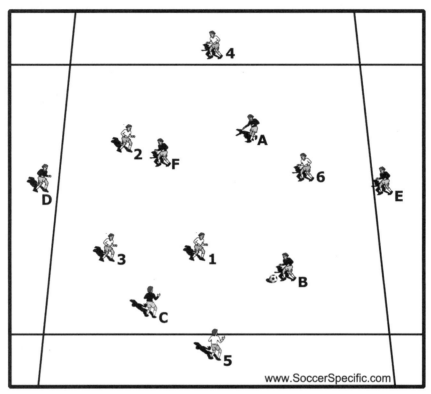

Diagram 230   **40 x 40**

1. **Rules:**
   a) Attacking different ends of the zone. Helps transition and dribbling and turning on the ball (a goal is scored by passing the ball to a target and keeping possession).
   b) Outside players change with inside players who pass to them.
   c) Once a goal has been scored at one end, the team has to score at the opposite end. They can go back to where they scored the goal and use this player as a support player only.
   If possession changes and then the team win it back, they then have the choice of going to either goal until they score one goal. Then they attack the opposite goal again.
2. **Observations:** Players get a rest by passing into the target and transitioning positions. This maintains speed of play because they don't get too tired.
3. **Coaching Points:**
   a) Quality of pass by inside player
   b) Quality of first touch by outside player to move into space quickly and set up a new attack.
   c) Players must change direction as they gain possession of the ball because they are defending one end then suddenly attacking at right angles to where they were defending. This helps quick decision making.
   d) Attitude to attack quickly is important, so players must be positive in mind and action.
   e) Individual 1v1's
   f) Team passing and support play.
   g) Everything done at pace.

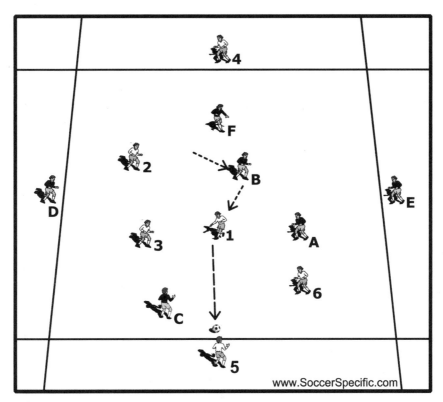

Diagram 231

1. (1) wins the ball off (B) and immediately must change direction to score a goal.
2. Two directions to go: to target player (4), or target player (5); here the choice is a pass to target player (5).
3. Defensively, the letters team now needs to focus on defending in a different direction to which they were attacking, thus defending two sides.

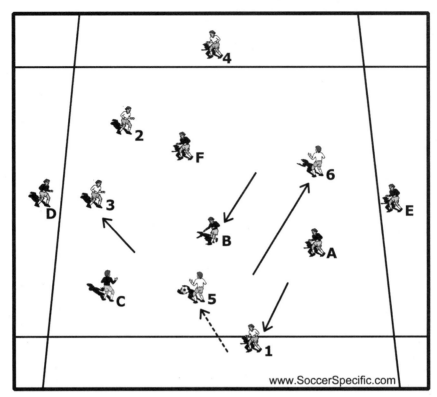

Diagram 232

1. (1) passes to (5) to score a goal and takes (5)'s place as a target. (5) brings the ball out and attacks the opposite goal.
2. If the pass to the outside target player is a long one and the run is very long for the passer, then the closest teammate to the target player can move out for efficiency and quickness.
3. Here (3) and (6) move off the ball to support (5). (2) is already in a good position to receive a pass.
4. Once a team gains possession they can score in either end goal of their own team.
5. Should (B) win possession then (5) win it back, (5) can pass to either of the outside target players to score a goal.
6. Players should try hard to keep possession and work the ball from one end to the other, scoring goals at both ends.

COACHING CLINIC SESSION PLAN 46

(For age 12 years and older)

OBJECTIVE: DEVELOPING AWARENESS USING QUICK TRANSITION DIRECTIONAL PLAY

Another session that can be used often with different points of emphasis. The focus of an individual session using this game could be:

1. Focusing on the 1v1 confrontation between players in the game; or:
2. Focusing on the "Quickness of transitional play" by making it two touch, focusing on the players "ON" the ball as they receive it and try to move it quickly forward; or:
3. Focusing on the players "OFF" the ball, emphasizing their movement and positioning OFF the ball to support the player ON the ball; or:
4. Focusing on the defending team and how they counter the opponents.

These are just four ideas you could use. While I try to cover all the possibilities in the Coaching Points section to this session, as the coach you can focus on each of these as one topic only in an individual session rather than try to get all the information covered in one session. Perhaps do four sessions developing each idea, then a fifth session bringing it all together.

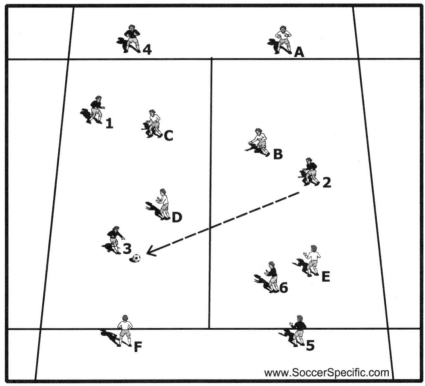

Diagram 233   **60 x 40**

1. Quick continuous attacking play, which is good for anaerobic fitness. Here the players are breaking one way, passing to an outside player and switching positions, inside player out, outside player in then attack the other side of the zone.

2. **Coaching Points:**

   a) Technical ability on the ball in 1v1 situations.

   b) Quick Transition in attack - As the transition between players happens, for example (3) changes with (5), the numbers team must get the ball to (4) as quickly as possible.

   c) Observe the movement of (1), (2) and (6) in terms of their support positions. As the directional change takes place, they must move in anticipation to find space to help the player on the ball as the switch occurs.

   d) Observe also, as the change occurs, the positions of the defending team. Has the decision been made quickly enough on who presses the ball? Are the other defensive players supporting and covering and especially tracking runners off the ball? The coach must learn to look away from the ball and observe what may happen next before it happens.

   e) This session improves quick decision making, tight control because the spaces are small to play in, and thinking in advance due to the switch in direction of the play. You can also work on the defending players.

   f) Progression: If a player beats an opponent in a 1v1 situation, the team gets an extra point or goal each time.

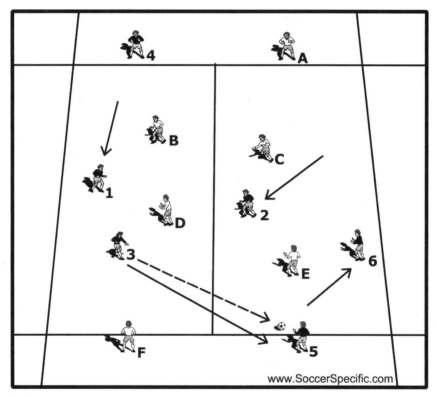

Diagram 234

1. Here (3) passes to (5) and (3) leaves the area. As the ball is traveling to (5), (1), (2) and (6) must get into a position to help (5) as early as possible. So in theory, (5) can make a one touch pass to any or all of them. Thus (5) already has three passing options.

2. Their movement is OFF THE BALL and away from their markers.

3. Of course the defenders will move to compensate but for the sake of what I am trying to show it is easier to get the point across by showing the movements of the attacking team only.

4. The attacking players in the actual practice may get free like this anyway if they time it correctly.

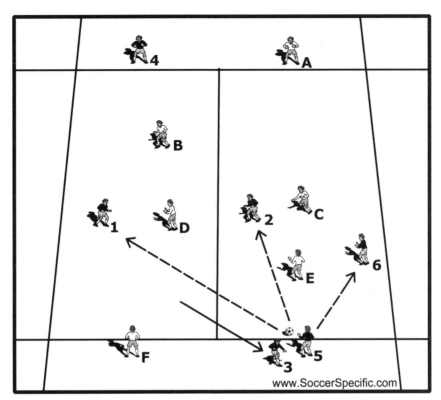

Diagram 235

1. The attacking players each help (5) by being open for a pass.
2. (5) may elect to run with the ball, but at least three are three options available for a pass if needed.
3. (5) may even elect to play a long pass straight to (4) on the other side of the field if the pressure from the closest defender is not fast enough. In this case, you may ask the closest player (in this case player 2), to be the switching player instead of (5).
4. You could even then work on defending in this game, but you should focus on defending totally or attacking totally in the session. It is better not to try to do both as it can be confusing for the players..

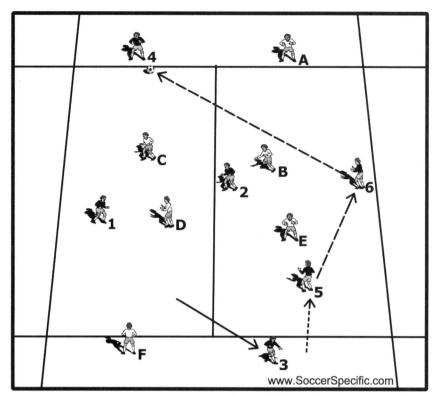

Diagram 236

1. Here (3) does pass to (5) and they switch positions. (3) then plays a quick pass to (6) who passes to target player (4) who scores another point and this player (4) has to quickly attack the other way again.

2. You could argue that the best place to dribble is in the opponent's half, but this being a small area, you could encourage players to do it all over the field. Be sure, though, to make them aware of the safety and risk factors if it were a game situation.

COACHING CLINIC SESSION PLAN 47

(For age 12 years and older)

OBJECTIVE: USING A PRESSURIZING GAME TO WORK ON ATTACKING TRANSITIONS

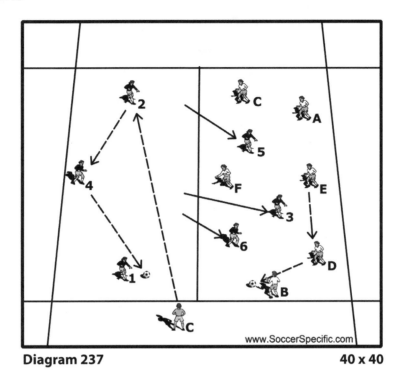

Diagram 237   **40 x 40**

www.SoccerSpecific.com

1. **Coaching Points for Attacking:**
   a) Creating Space to receive or draw opponents away from space for teammates
   b) Quality Passing (weight, accuracy, timing, short and long)
   c) Support Positions (angle, distance, communication)
   d) Switching Play (moving the ball around using the overload advantage)
   e) Maintaining possession
2. A Transition game creating 6v3 situations in both halves. If the three defenders win the ball back they work it back to their own half of the field. They then move back into their own half and three defenders from the other team go in to try to win it back (another 6v3).
3. While this is going on, the three players left alone have a ball to pass to each other to keep them working, passing and moving until their teammates win the ball back. They then pass the ball to the coach who gives it to the remaining three players from the other team. This is using the Awareness principles at all times, focusing on what is happening on the ball and away from the ball.
4. This also keeps the three players left from standing still or just standing close to the halfway line where, if they receive the ball, the other team don't have far to run to win it back. Even without the second ball these players should be spread out away from the action to give themselves time and space to receive the ball and keep it.
5. All players are working all of the time. The three players must observe what is happening in the other half while passing their own ball around so that when their teammates win possession and bring it back into their own half they are ready to receive and also they recognize the time to play their own ball to the coach.

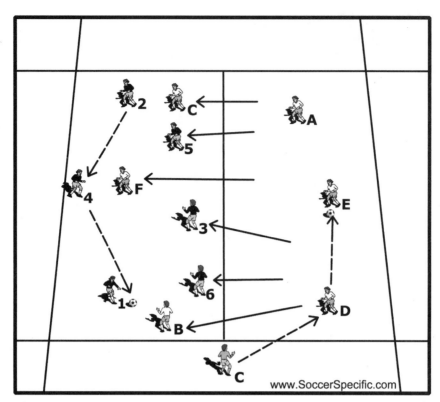

Diagram 238

1. Here the numbers team have won the ball back and (5) has passed it to (2). The numbered players now retreat back to their own area to try to keep the ball there; three lettered players raid the area to try to win it back.
2. It is always a 6v3, though the coach can change it to a 6v2 for example if the players are having trouble maintaining possession, or 6v4 if they are good at keeping the ball and need a bigger challenge.

TRANSITION FROM ONE SIDE TO THE OTHER

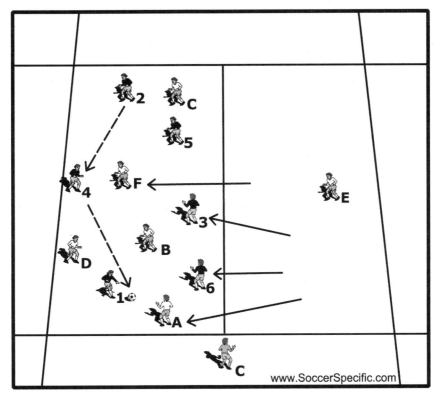

Diagram 239

1. Now it is a switching fields transition game. One player stays in the other side of the field and if that player's team wins possession they have to pass it long to this player (in this case player (E)) and all the players from both teams move into that side of the field except for one letters player.

2. The numbers team now have control of the ball and need to keep it, the letters team have to try to win it back, and they will leave the one player in their own half of the field for the long pass and transition if and / or when they win it back.

3. Therefore it is a 6v5 in each half of the field in favor of the attacking team in possession of the ball.

4. **Progression 1:** Leave 2 players out either side so it becomes a 6v4 game. If this makes it too difficult to win back the ball, make this a two touch game.

5. **Progression 2:** Now leave 3 players in the other half of the field so it becomes a 6v3 game and now make this one touch only. This is a real test but the overload of players should help.

COACHING CLINIC SESSION PLAN: 48

(For age 12 years and older)
OBJECTIVE: IMPROVING ONE AND TWO TOUCH PLAY USING THE AWARENESS
THREE TEAM GAME FOCUSING ON QUICK THINKING, QUICK AND EARLY FOOT
POSITIONING; SUPPORT AND FINISHING

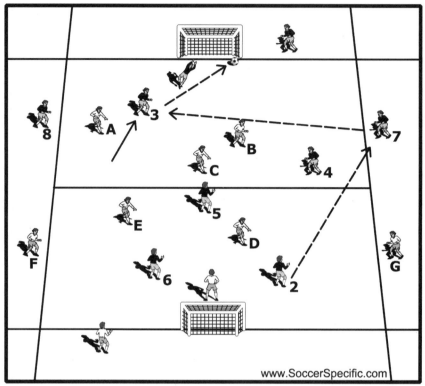

Diagram 240   **60 x 40**

1. **Coaching Points:**
   a) Thought processes on and off the ball
   b) Feet and Body positioning before receiving the ball
   c) Quality of Passing, especially weight of pass if a 1 or 2 touch condition
   d) Quality of Support and Movement "off the ball"
   e) Quality and Speed of Finishing
   f) Effective Team Play
2. Three team game with 17 players. When one team scores they stay on, the losing team go off and the winning team play the outside team.
3. Great if you have 2 keepers and 15 outfield players but you can arrange it based on the number of players you have at the practice, there are many variations on this theme. Size of field depends on the number of players. Here it is a 60 x 40 yard area. Coaches can be one touch players on the outside to help.
4. **Competitive:** Play the game over a certain time period and see which of the three teams scores the most goals in that time. In this set up it is best if the outside support players have only one touch to pass the ball back in, which will usually set up a one touch finish to goal. Alternatively the first team to score a goal stays on the field, the losing team goes off and the 3rd team comes on.

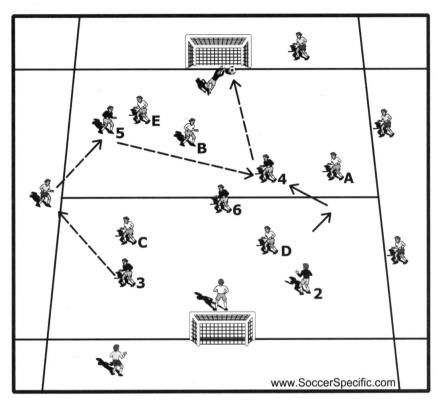

Diagram 241

1. Fifteen players to work with so place five on the outside, one of which will be a keeper for this outside team when they get into the game.
2. Here (C) blocks a pass to striker (5) from (3) so the outside player is used in a support position to get the ball to (5). (4) loses the defender (A) and gets a layoff pass from (5) to score. This is just one example of many situations that can be created by this game plan.

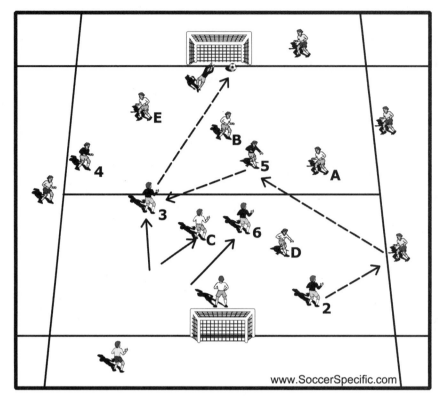

Diagram 242

1. Outside players have two touches to begin, then go to one touch only. Inside players begin with three touches, then go to two touches, then go to one and two touches (one touch is encouraged but only if it is on to do so).
2. As the outside player has only one touch, the inside players passing to them have to think, before they pass the ball, about weighting the pass and making it accurate so that the outside player can pass it back in successfully with one touch.
3. The outside player must, before receiving the ball, view the field and see where the players are (own players and opponents) to enable them to keep possession successfully with the correct one touch pass.
4. The player or players able to receive this next pass back inside from the outside player must make sure they are available to receive the next pass by getting into an open position to receive in front, behind and to the side to help the outside player, knowing the outside player has only one touch.
5. So, inside and outside players work together to ensure they are successful.

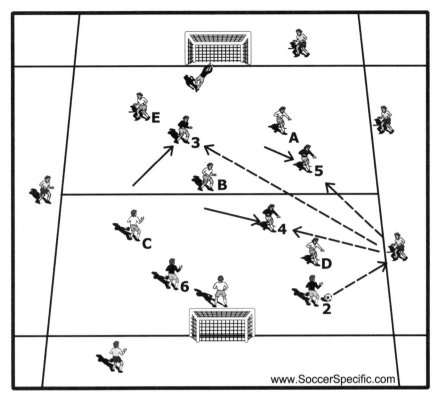

Diagram 243

1. Player (2) has two touches so must pass the ball quickly to the outside player who is available to receive the pass. The outside player has only one touch, so to make the next pass successful, three things have to happen:
   a) The pass has to be accurate, but more importantly the weight of the pass has to be such that it is easy for the player receiving the pass to make a one touch pass on;
   b) The player receiving the pass has to know his or her options of the next pass before receiving;
   c) The players in the team need to get open to help the player receiving the pass, knowing they only have one touch to move the ball on. So they need to be on the move to find space to receive before the outside player receives the pass.
2. Good communication is essential between the players here.
3. Here players (3), (4) and (5) have given the outside player three options. But also the passing player (2) can receive the pass back, so he must also be available. Alternatively (if allowed depending on the rules for the game you imposed) the outside player can pass directly to another outside player; though this for me makes it a little too easy.

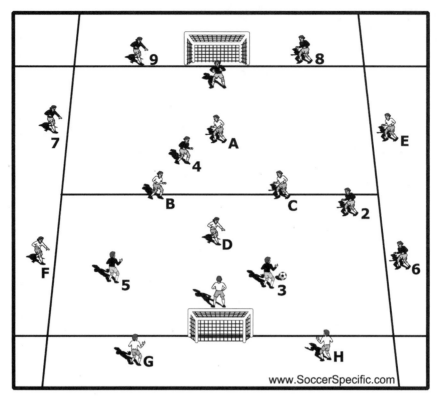

Diagram 244

1. Eighteen players and a 4 v 4 game with side players to support and goal line players for 1-2's to set up shooting chances. You can vary the number of players playing in the game.

2. Players are on the outside need to keep on their toes. Game lasts until players are beginning to be fatigued (or first team to score. losing team off). Rotate outside players in, inside players out.

3. **Progressions:**
   a) Outside players 1 or 2 touch restriction on the ball.
   b) Inside players touches restriction on the ball.
   c) Player passes to outside player and switches, gets the players thinking especially if it is when the player coming in has only 1 touch so must immediately find a player.
   d) Occasionally bring in all the players so it's a 9 v 9 with the keepers, this tests how they play in a restricted space with more players to deal with.
   e) Reduce the size of the area to 40 x 20, go 4 v 4, this gets more shots on goal.

COACHING CLINIC SESSION PLAN 49

(For age 12 years and older)

OBJECTIVE: USING AN 8v8 GAME WITH COMPOSURE ZONES TO AID TEAM PLAY AND INDIVIDUAL PLAYER DEVELOPMENT

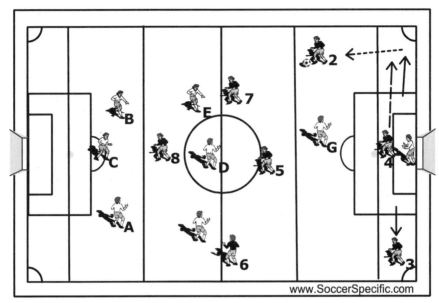

Diagram 245   **60 x 40**

1. Overload at the back. Striker can't encroach into the 5-yard composure zone. Defenders pass ball across under no pressure until one is free to run it out. Attackers can now try to win it back.
2. Players stay in their own zone to keep their shape. Support in front and behind.
3. Open it up so players can move between zones.
4. Defenders can take the ball back into the composure zone for safety. This encourages spreading out and playing from the back. Be patient, keep possession; go forward at the correct moment.
5. **Defenders** – spreading out, running with the ball, passing the ball, supporting the keeper, keep possession, decision making.
   Midfield – Receiving and turning, switching play, linking play, runs, keep possession, creating space, decision making.
   Forwards – As above, also supporting short and long, diagonal runs in front of the ball, holding the ball up, lay offs, dribbles \ shots, quick decision making.
6. As the ball advances, players at the back move up. Keep checking positions and shape of the team.
7. To get a full game started, have one team standing still and let the other team play through them to get a feel for how to build up the play.
8. Develop this by having both teams with a ball each playing through each other where they are not under the pressure of losing the ball.

PROGRESSIONS

1. Players interchange between zones one at a time, always returning to the original set-up. Check the balance of the team with and without the ball. We have created a 4v3 in the midfield zone with player (2) moving up.
2. If they lose possession, players either drop back in or you can develop the clinic to include pressing to regain the ball. e.g. If you are losing the game, go full high-pressure and leave three players in the attacking third, two in the midfield third and two in the defensive third.

PROGRESSION
3 – 3 – 1 system

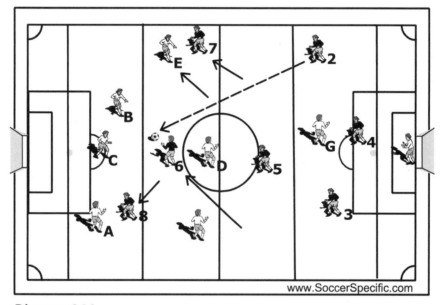

Diagram 246

3. **Condition:** Goals can only be scored if all players are over the defensive third line. This encourages keeping compact vertically.
4. Restrict the number of touches on the ball if they are able to do so to encourage quick passing and movement and to improve the speed of decision-making.
5. Vary play by encouraging defenders to pass directly to the forwards; midfield players can then support them facing the opponent's goal (easier to support rather than receiving and having to turn with the ball).
6. If you have problems making the session work with equal numbers then reduce the game to an 8v5 situation using one forward, one midfielder, two defenders and a keeper on the opponent's team until the players are comfortable, then go into the full workout.

POSSIBLE PASSING OPTIONS

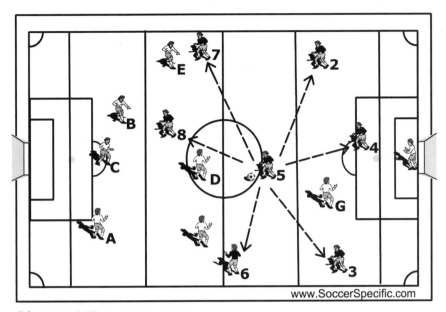

Diagram 247

1. Player (5) on the ball. Three possible options to pass forward e.g. to (6), (7) or (2) who continues the run. If forward is not an option because of pressure, the ball can go to the side to (8) or back to (3), (4) and the keeper to keep possession until the situation allows for a forward pass again (you won't obviously get all these options to pass but it shows how it can work).
   Caution – in attack, be aware of quick counter if opponents win the ball i.e. we have a 2v2 at the back.
2. **Discussion:** You can get so much work into this session, every time you look there may be a new situation. Choose a theme and stick with it and when you have established it with the players, only then should you move on to another theme (you can again use the same set-up, as it is so flexible).

COACHING CLINIC SESSION PLAN 50

(For age 12 years and older)

OBJECTIVE: USING TRANSITION GAMES TO MAINTAIN SHAPE AND BALANCE THROUGHOUT THE TEAM:

PLAYERS STAYING IN THEIR OWN THIRDS

7 v 7   3-2-1

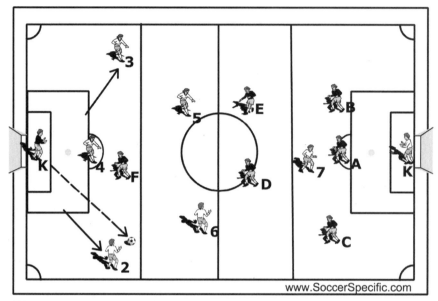

Diagram 248   **60 x 40**

1. To ensure the players have a chance to build up the play from the back, have a 3v1 overload at each defensive third to begin.
2. We are looking to be successful with offensive play building up from the back. This gives it a greater chance of success and thus positive reinforcement for the players.
3. As they get better at this and gain success you can change it to a 3v2 situation so it is more difficult to succeed. A 3v2 means an 8v8 situation with the players developing play but staying in their own third to emphasize team shape through the units.

8 v 8   **3-2-2**

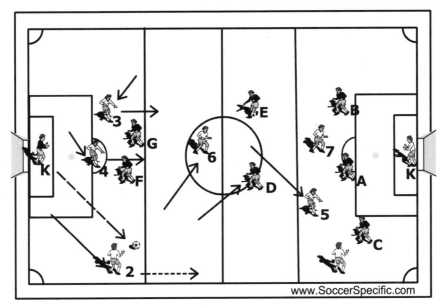

Diagram 249

1. Now we are transitioning between thirds and as a defender changes the balance in midfield from a 2v2 into a 3v2, a midfielder then moves into the attacking third to change the balance from a 2v3 into a 3v3.
2. (6) clears the space for (2) to bring the ball forward. (4) and (3) cover across behind the field to support and be in a good position to cover should the move break down. This is clearing the space in front of the ball and filling in behind the ball.
3. (5) makes a run into the attacking third to be another target for (2) to pass to.
4. If the player can't go forward and has to play it back, ensure the players behind the ball get in positions where they are free to receive it and able to support the player on the ball.

OVERLAP PLAY

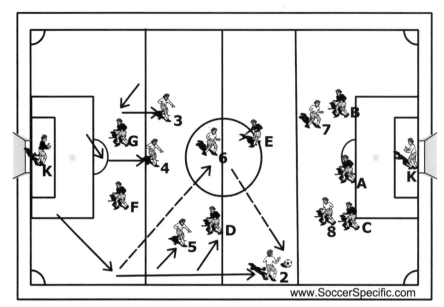

Diagram 250

1. Here a full back makes an overlap run to provide an option for (6) to pass to. (2) passes to (6), (5) clears the space wide to run into for (2) by taking defender (D) inside, and (2) runs onto the return pass from (6). This is a particular movement that can be practiced and developed in this set up as the run is difficult for the opposition to identify and counter.
2. The overlap can occur also from the middle third into the attacking third.
3. Wide defenders need to be constantly encouraged to get into good wide receiving positions to take the ball forward into attacking areas of the field.
4. The fact that (F) can't track the runner into the middle third yet during this progression helps highlight the importance of this kind of attacking run from a wide area.
5. Likewise, (6) may change the point of attack and (3) can make the overlap run from the other side and on the blind side of striker (G).

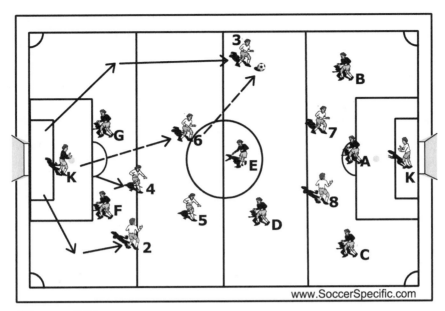

Diagram 251

1. **Develop:** Have offside from the defensive third of the field. (4) passes the ball forward and (4), (2) and the keeper push up. Strikers (F) and (G) are left offside.
   Player (4) passes the ball into the middle zone to (5), (3) moves up from the defensive zone to the middle zone to support. This type of transition movement is important because it allows players to move freely between the zones knowing they will have a team mate covering for them.
2. In terms of the opposition, this rapid movement and transition makes it difficult for them to pick players up, to read what your team is doing. Usually (E) would be marking (6) (who can cover) but now has to think about marking (3). Or (B) who was marking striker (7) has to leave that player and defend against (3), leaving (7) free.
3. This means defenders aren't just defenders, midfielders aren't just midfielders and attackers aren't just attackers. They work to help each other through the three units of the team and are free to mix the game up. This is total soccer, played to encourage the free movement of players throughout the teams.

OVERLOAD IN ATTACK TO MAINTAIN POSSESSION

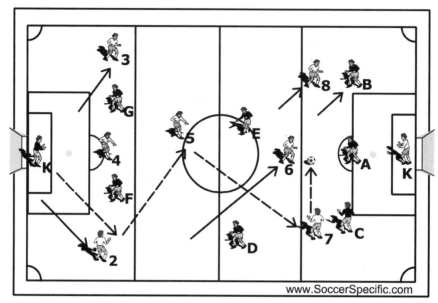

Diagram 252

1. Here (5) plays the ball to (7) and (6) makes a run off the ball to support in the attacking third. (8) moves (B) away to help (6) find space to shoot. You can practice this session with different numbers of players to get the same effect, building up to an 11v11 game.

2. Transitions can depend on the stage of the game; if your team is chasing the game to score being a goal down then (6) would probably stay in the attacking third, not immediately return to help (5) in the middle third but keep an overload in the attacking third situation there but the basis of the session is to show how to maintain a balanced shape in your team.

3. Practice movement (switching) of strikers and midfield players to move defenders around (especially if they man mark), so play isn't in straight lines all the time. For example in another situation (8) and (7) may switch sides to create space for one another (see over).

SWITCHING POSITIONS

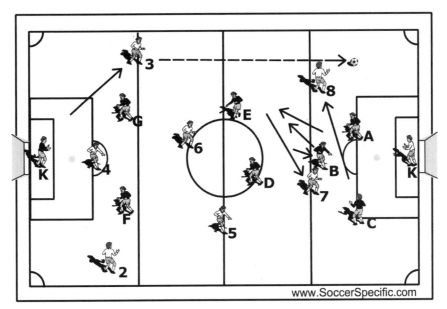

Diagram 253

1. Here (7) checks to the ball then checks away creating space for (8) to come in to receive the pass. (8)'s movement should be late and fast to get away from (B) or (C). If (8) goes too early he / she closes down their own space and allows (B) or (C) to track and get there early to stop the move.
2. Another option could be (5) making a diagonal forward run into the space created by (8)'s movement or even (6) moving into the space. The best move of these two would be (5) as the run is harder to pick up and is from an angle not in a straight line as (6)'s run would be. In this situation (8) could also make a run away from where the ball is going to take (B) away from the area (3) is playing the ball into.

TRANSITIONS BETWEEN THIRDS FOR DEFENDING TEAM ALSO

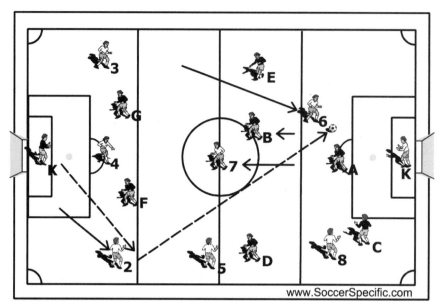

Diagram 254

1. **Progression:** Players can transition back into zones from the attacking third to the midfield third and the midfield third to the defensive third. Defenders still cannot move between zones.

2. **Example:** A striker moves back into the midfield third (to receive to feet or free space for someone else to move into) and a midfielder moves forward into the attacking third.

3. **Develop:** Allow defending players (as above) to track attacking players into the other zones. Above, the defender follows the striker going short, creating space behind for another striker to move into or a midfielder to break forward into (in this case 6). Ultimately open the game up so the players have no boundaries to use for focus and see if they can work out how to keep that balance and shape on an open field of play.

WORKING WITH FOUR ZONES

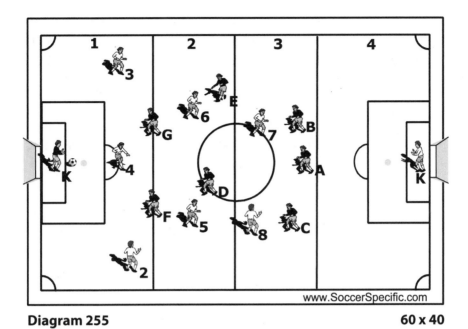

Diagram 255   **60 x 40**

1. We have essentially four zones to play in. The players can only play in three of the four zones at any one time.
2. This ensures movement up and down the field, maintaining distances between units.
3. Players cannot enter zone 4 until the ball goes into zone 4.

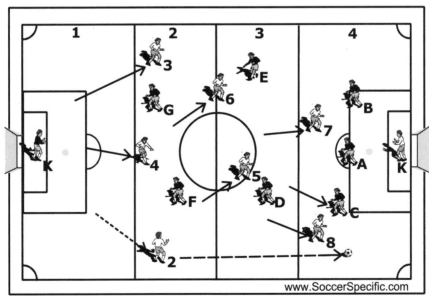

Diagram 256

1. The ball has been played into zone 4. Here the numbers team has moved forward out of zone 1 and into zone 2 and the whole team has moved forward one zone. This helps them maintain distances between the units and does not allow the team to get too spread out when either attacking or defending.

PROGRESSIONAL DEVELOPMENT FROM START TO FINISH

Set up is as follows; the field is arranged in thirds: defending, midfield and attacking. In the set up here we have a 3v2, a 2v2 and a 3v2. If you have problems getting the movement going from the back in a 3v2 then have a 3v1 at each end to begin (to make it easier to find space) and a 3v3 in the middle.

1. STAY IN OWN THIRD.
   Players stay in their own thirds to get a feel for how to maintain shape and how to use width in attack. Spread out in possession in a 3v2 overload at the back in the defending third to create a situation where the players are available to receive the ball in space and pass it forward.
2. TRANSITON BETWEEN THIRDS
   Players are allowed to transition between thirds but only one at a time. The defending team cannot move between thirds to track the attacking players. When the attacking team loses possession they then become defenders and must immediately drop back into the third they started in. The reason for dropping back and not trying to win it back immediately is because we are working on offensive play and want both teams to practice build up play. You can run the ball in, pass it in, or pass it in to a runner from your own third.
3. OVERLAP PLAY FROM WIDE DEFENDERS
   This particular type of movement is very important in this session and the opportunities presented to do so will be numerous.
4. OFFSIDE FROM THE DEFENDING THIRD
   Introduce offside in the final thirds at both ends of the field. This encourages teams to move up as the ball is played forward.
5. OVERLOAD IN ATTACK MAINTAINING POSSESSION
   Here we have worked the ball into the attacking third and we leave an overload in this third to regain possession should it be lost. This strategy would be useful in particular game situations. For instance, if we are a goal down and have to take chances.
6. SWITCHING POSITIONS
   Work on movement of midfielders and strikers in terms of play not always being in straight lines. For example, movement across the field where two midfielders switch positions or likewise up front where strikers can switch about, moving defenders around.
7. TRANSITION BACKWARDS BETWEEN THIRDS
   Allow players to transition between thirds coming back as the initial movement, for example a striker may drop back into the middle third to receive. A midfielder may push on into the space the striker created by the movement.
8. TRANSITIONS OF DEFENDING PLAYERS
   Allow defenders to track players into the other thirds they venture into. Now all players can move between thirds but still have it only one at a time. This helps highlight how to create space for someone else by the movement of players; a striker comes short, pulls a defender with them and space is created in the area they came from for another striker or a midfielder to move into to receive the pass.
9. FREE PLAY
   Open the game up. See if players can maintain their shape without the help of the thirds.. They should be able to transition between units but also keep their balance.
10. NUMBER OF TOUCHES RESTRICTION
    Introduce a three, two then one touch restriction to see if the players can work more quickly and still gain success. This speeds up decision making. When it is one touch,

condition it so they can take more than one touch (a pass may be so heavy they need two touches) but emphasize they use one touch if it is on to do so. This keeps it realistic.

11. CONCLUSION

We have developed the clinic from working in thirds (or quarters), introduced many progressions to work up to letting the game go free and observing if the players can incorporate into the free game situation, all they have learnt. I would recommend using this clinic on a regular basis and set it up for the scrimmage that is usually done at the end of a coaching clinic session.

COACHING CLINIC SESSION PLAN 51
(For age 12 years and older)
OBJECTIVE: DEVELOPING A TRANSITION GAME TO ENSURE MOVEMENT OFF THE BALL IN QUICK PASSING BUILDING TO AWARENESS IN ONE TOUCH PLAY

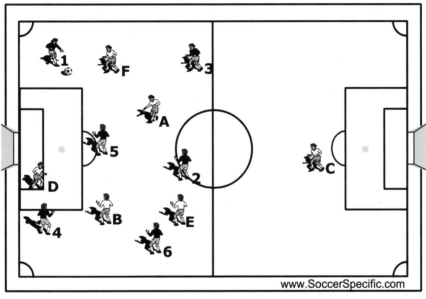

www.SoccerSpecific.com

Diagram 257   **60 x 40**

1. An important aspect of One Touch Play is the ability of the players to move off the ball and support the player on the ball by doing so and for them to find space between and around defenders.

2. A 6v5 in one half and a target player in the other half to get the ball to when the defenders win the ball. Play free to allow the players to get comfortable on the ball so as many touches on the ball as they need.

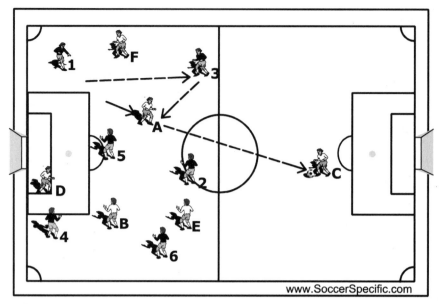

Diagram 258

1. Here defender (A) intercepts the pass and passes to target player (C).

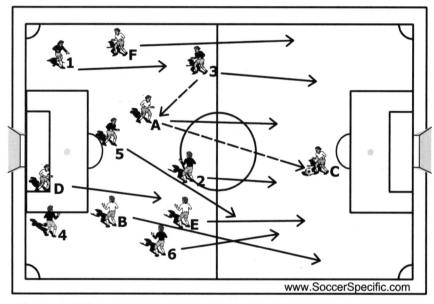

Diagram 259

1. All players must follow into the other half except one defending player, in this case player (4).
2. The numbers team is now the defending team and must try to win possession and get the ball back into their half of the field to their own target player (4).

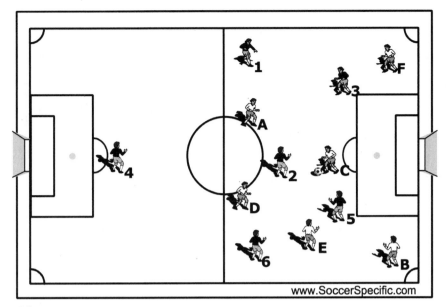

Diagram 260

1. Here we have a 6v5 in the other half. The game is still free play to begin. This is a great conditioning game too. The players have to work very hard to make it work and the movement between halves ensures lots of quick transition and running off the ball and emphasizes the importance of movement off the ball.
2. **Coaching Points for the Attacking team:**
   a) Maintaining possession
   b) Passing and Support play
   c) Quick plays where possible to make it difficult for the defenders using the one player overload advantage
3. **Coaching Points for the Defending team:**
   a) Defensive pressing
   b) Quick transition of the ball on winning possession into the other half of the field

PLAYING TWO TOUCH

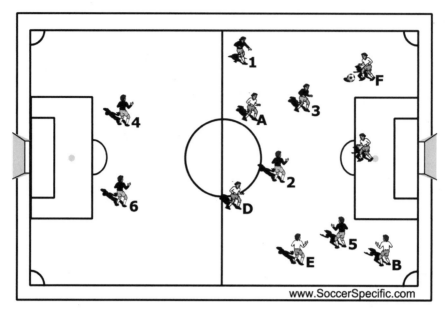

Diagram 261

1. Have two target players, so now we play with a 6v4 overload. The players can now move to two touch play as it is easier to maintain possession against one fewer defender.
2. With fewer touches, players need to work even harder off the ball to help the player on the ball as decisions need to be quicker.

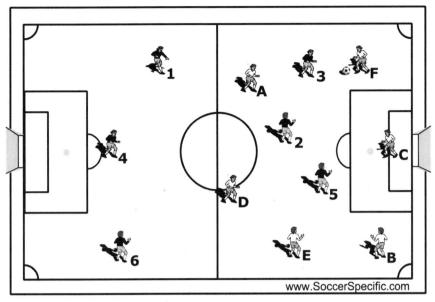

Diagram 262

1. Now we have 3 target players to pass to and a 6v3 over-load which makes it even easier for the attacking team to maintain possession of the ball, so we now play 1 touch only. Obviously this will mean the players are really tested in their awareness.
2. The target player receiving the pass initially has two touches because it is a long pass and likely with pace, but as they get good at it insist on a one touch transfer, which means the other two target players need to be ready to help.
3. **Coaching Points:**
    a) Awareness of all players' positions before receiving the ball (own players and opponents) plus where the spaces are to pass to.
    b) Correct foot preparation to receive the ball, having then to make a one touch pass
    c) Correct body position, open stance in the way you are going to make the pass, unless you are using a fake then pass to fool the defender. Body position should be such that it helps you make a successful next pass.
    d) Correct pace / weight of the pass to help the next player when receiving it, that player having to move it on one touch as well.
    e) Movement off the ball by all the other players to help the player on the ball, but do it before the player receives the pass, not after.
    f) Asking players to position between defenders and into spaces to help the player about to receive the ball to move it on one touch.
    g) Finally when you think the players are ready have them play a 6v6 one touch only scrimmage.
    h) Test them in a proper scrimmage game against opponents now; you can play 2 touches only in the first half and one touch only in the 2nd half. Or; play one touch in the first half and free play the second and see its overall effect. Prepare for ugly play initially when playing one touch only (or maybe not); depending on how well the players have developed the skill.

COACHING CLINIC SESSION PLAN 52

(For age 12 years and older)

OBJECTIVE: DEVELOPING AWARENESS IN MOVEMENTS "OFF" THE BALL BETWEEN THE UNITS IN OVERLOAD SITUATIONS

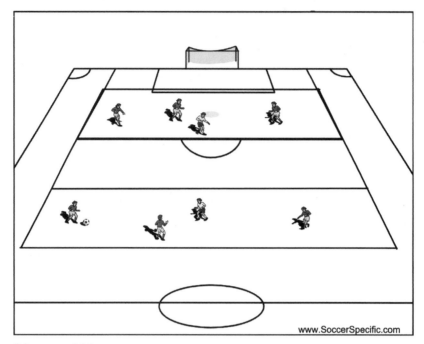

Diagram 263

THIS IS A GOOD WARM UP FOR THIS SESSION

1. A 3 v 3 in each end zone
2. A Ball each team passing and moving but teams are not playing against each other yet.
3. The central zone is the shadow striker zone known as zone 14 and usually where the number 10 plays.
4. **Coaching Points:**
   a) An Awareness of the passing player of when and where the player drops into the free zone
   b) An awareness of the receiving player as to when the passer is ready to pass
   c) Good communication via visual cues through eye contact or aural cues through speaking makes this work
   d) Movement OFF the ball by the player to get free and into open space
   e) Timing and angle of the run
   f) Timing; accuracy and pace of the pass
   g) Good receiving and turning skills with an awareness of what is behind before receiving it
   h) Receive or be a decoy for someone else; depending on where the defender is.

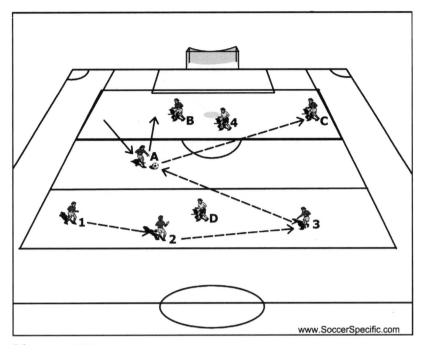

Diagram 264

1. Passing and moving, (4) drops in to receive as does (C) going the other way.
2. Movement OFF THE BALL to receive in the middle zone (zone 14)
3. (4) Takes the ball back into his own end zone, as does (C) in the other end zone and play continues. All players are moving finding space to receive the ball. The two teams pass between each other but cannot tackle each other.

   a) Timing of the pass
   b) Timing of the run
   c) Angle of the run
   d) Timing of each has to be exact for it to work.

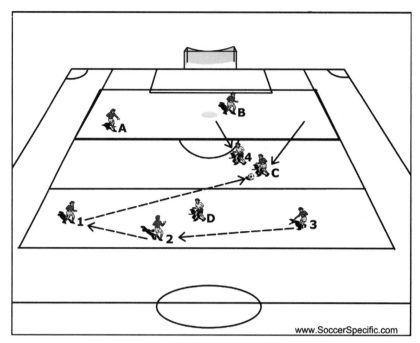

Diagram 265

1. **Development:**
   a) Now 2 players come to meet the ball in opposite halves of zone 14 and at different angles and depth to each other.
   b) Still no opposition so it is free flowing movements linking the two front players now. Do this going both ways with both teams so there is congestion in the middle.
2. **Coaching Points:**
   a) Timing of the run, timing of the pass
   b) Angles of support of each player in terms of each other's position.
   c) Looking before receiving as the ball is travelling; assessing the next move
   d) Make it a one touch pass in the middle zone (Zone 14) from (6) to (4) to (5) therefore testing the player's awareness
   e) Development: Passing to opposite colors
3. It is always a 2v1 in the middle now, with the neutral player always on the attacking team.
4. Again color coordination and recognition plays a role in the play as the overloaded yellows have to pass to a yellow or neutral player in the middle and then these players actually pass to the overloaded red players in the other side. Here we now have competitive small sided games in three separate areas on the field.

Progression 1: Have the players miss out the middle third players and pass from the back to the front. Players in the middle then support behind in a receiving capacity but now going the other way.

If the defender wins the ball in an outside third (3v1 against) he has to pass to his own color (or pass to the neutral player) in the middle; who then passes to his corresponding color in the other outside third.

MOVEMENT OFF THE BALL BETWEEN THE UNITS THROUGH THE SHADOW STRIKER

1. I have reduced this to 3v1's as opposed to 3v3's in each zone to add success. You can do the same session and build it up making it a 3v2 in each zone then ultimately a 3v3 and eventually one touch.
2. So; Two 3v1's in the outside areas, the middle area is free and open.

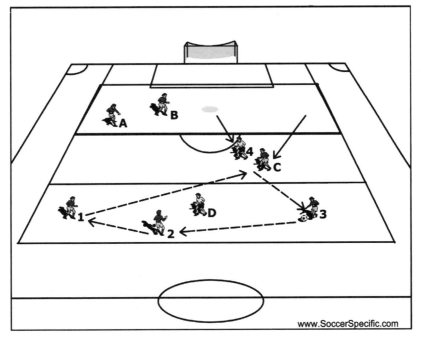

Diagram 266

3. Players are passing and maintaining possession then a player from the other side drops into the middle free zone to be free to receive and turn and pass into the other zone. They then continue there with a 3 v 1 keep away. Can condition it to 1 or 2 touches on the ball to challenge the players
4. Color coordination and recognition is important here because when the reds pass the ball in they are passing to a yellow and not a red; and vice versa.

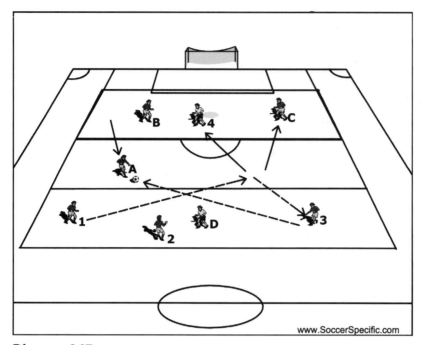

Diagram 267

1. Players are looking at the teammates in their own zone to pass to but also into the other zone for a player to drop into and support and hence they can switch the direction of play. No pressure to start and the defender must stay in the same zone so the receiving player is always free.
2. Looking for good angles of support at all times; avoid straight line support as it limits vision behind the play. Players try to support in a sideways on stance to open up their field of vision.
3. Passing can be at an angle; as can the support position of the receiver. So a player on the right tries to pass to a player on the left dropping into the middle; and vice versa.
4. So the cue is more specific now, if a player receives the ball on the right of the grid and has their head up looking to pass, this is the cue for a player on the opposite gird on the left side of it to drop into the middle to receive and turn.
5. **Development 1:**
   a) Once the receiving player who has checked to the middle receives the ball (on their first touch); that is the cue for the defender to close them down and pressure.
   b) This should still give the receiver long enough to receive and turn and pass without losing the ball but we are building up the pressure on that player. It is almost a passive movement because the defender has so far to make up to get close.
6. **Development Two:**
   a) The defender can close the ball down as the passer moves so now they do not need to wait for the first touch. This changes the options considerably depending on how good the defender is.

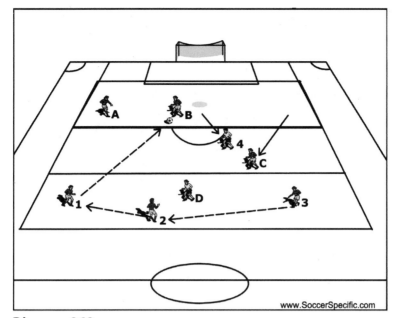

Diagram 268

Here we show the defender (4) closing (C) coming short at the same time.

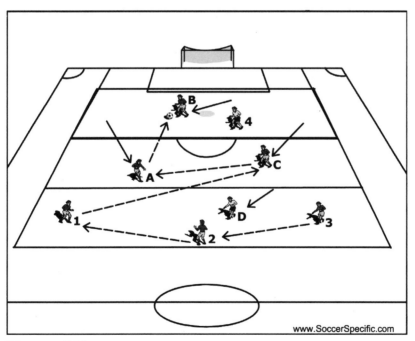

Diagram 269

Here we show (C) still receiving the ball under pressure but can't turn so lays the ball off into the same zone it came from to another player (3) in that zone.

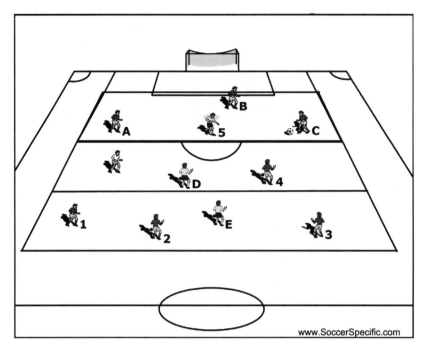

Diagram 270

1. Here (C) has laid off the ball and checked back into their own zone taking the defender (4) with them and another player (A) becomes the new receiver and gets it to feet in a free area to turn and pass and the 3 v 1 begins again.
2. You can also liken this situation to a midfield player dropping off the marker and receiving from the back four.
3. Rotate the defenders.

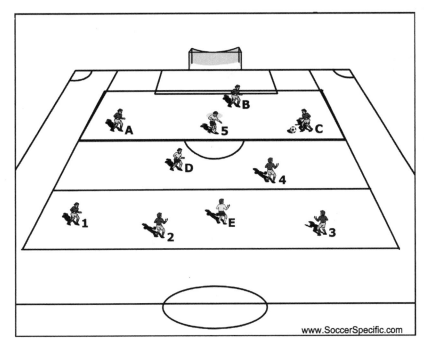

Diagram 271

1. Another option for the passer (1) now is to avoid (C) who is tightly marked now and whose movement has changed the position of the defender (4) and so has opened up a pass to the other players in their other third of the field. Here is the end product above. Two players may go short at the same time; don't worry about this as it may happen in a game anyway.

2. **Coaching Points:**
   a) An Awareness of the passing player of when and where the shadow striker drops into the free zone
   b) An awareness of the receiving player as to when the passer is ready to pass
   c) Good communication via visual cues through eye contact or aural cues through speaking makes this work
   d) Movement OFF the ball by the shadow striker to get free and into open space
   e) Timing and angle of the run
   f) Timing ; accuracy and pace of the pass
   g) Good receiving and turning skills with an awareness of what is behind before receiving it
   h) Receive or be a decoy for someone else; depending on where the defender is.

Important points with regards to awareness:
The cue for the receiver is seeing; the passer on them getting the ball; having their head up; and seeing the free space and even making eye contact with the receiver.
If the receiver (Shadow Striker) goes to early and the passer is not ready to pass (for example if they have the ball but have their head down looking at it and hence have not seen the potential run, or their body position limits their peripheral vision and prevents them from passing early) then they can check back out, and open up the space for the next shadow striker having taken their marking defender away from the space; in order to leave it free for the next player. By then the passer may have their head up and be ready to pass or; maybe even have passed the ball off in their own grid and the next player to get it has seen the 2nd run into the free middle area and they make the pass.

The cue for the 2nd shadow striker to make their run can be the check back of the first shadow striker.

Two come short to receive and combine

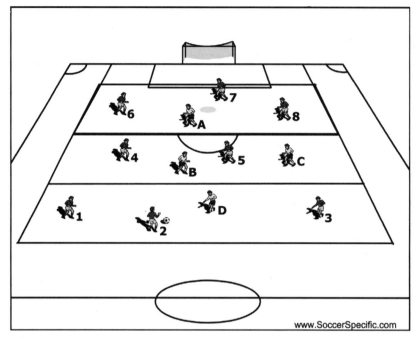

Diagram 272

1. No defenders again. Now the first player (C) and the passing player (1) have to mentally combine to connect with the run and the pass, so the timing of each match, and the cue for the 2nd striker (A) to make their run is off the run of the first striker (C) so again correct timing of the support run is important.
2. Players need to arrive as the ball arrives, too early and in a game they can be marked and will tend to stand still (certainly in this practice), too late and a defender may intercept in a game situation). If they are in two early then need to check back again and someone else can take their place.
3. Ensure we maintain the ratio of attackers to defenders in each third of the area; always working to get back immediately to the 3 v 1 and 3 v 1 in each outside third.

A 4 v 1 IN EACH SIDE

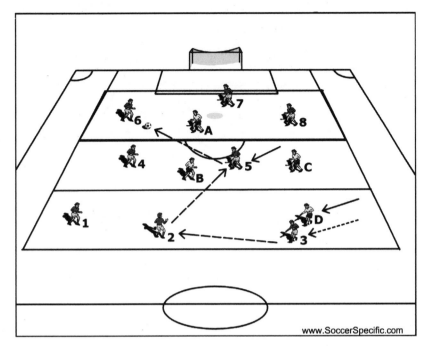

Diagram 273

The same idea but it is a 4 v 1 in each third now. You can vary the numbers in each outside third based on the ability of the players and / or based on the number of players you have training, 2 v 1, 3 v 1, 3 v 2, 4 v 2 and so on.

3 v 1; 1 v 1 v 1 and 3 v 1

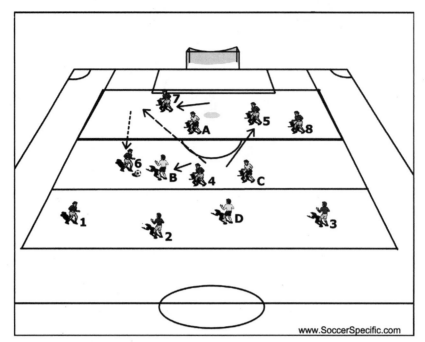

Diagram 274

1. It is always a 2 v 1 in the middle now, with the neutral player always on the attacking team.
2. **Progression 1:** Have the players miss out the middle third players and pass from the back to the front, players in the middle then support behind in a shadow striker capacity but now going the other way. We are looking at long passing practice now also.
3. You can vary this session now with different set ups, use your imagination to make this work, for example, 3 v 1; 1 v 1 and 3 v 1; or 3 v 1, 2 v 2, and 3 v 1.

3 v 1; 1 v 1 v 1 and 3 v 1

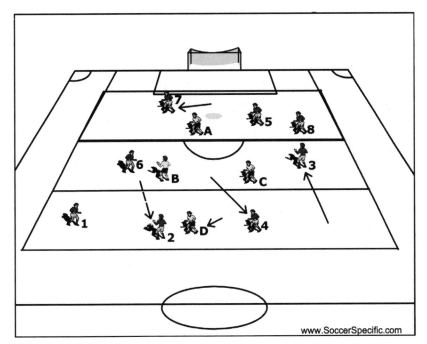

Diagram 275

It is more difficult to get the ball across the thirds now because the numbers are equal in the middle.

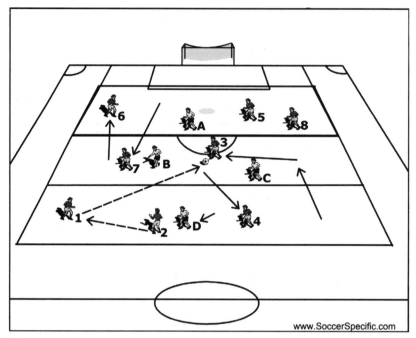

Diagram 276

1. If the defending team wins it they have to get it to their own color in the next grid. The attacking team in that grid; then try immediately to win it back and pass through the thirds again. As before we are looking to maintain the same attacker to defender ratio's in each third.

2. **Progression 2:** Make the overloads in each outside third smaller so it is now a 2 v 1 at each end. Use free play still then perhaps go to a 3 v 3 in each end zone.

3. **Progression 3:** Change the number of touches allowed in each grid, make it a one (ultimately), two or three touch limit (based on the ability of the players).

4. **Progression 4:** Different touch limits in each third, free play in the middle and the 2 v 2, 3 touches in one outside third, 2 touches in the other outside third or at best one touch to REALLY test them.

5. To advance it even more for quick thinking have a 4 v 1 in one end so it is easier to succeed with a bigger overload of players; and have a one touch pass limit to counter this.

6. So, easier with more players, more difficult with fewer touches on the ball, you can play around with this idea and try many variations.

7. With one touch the communication between the outside third players and the middle third players has to be very acute from either player, that is, both the passer and the receiver.

2 v 2, 2 v 2 and 2 v 2

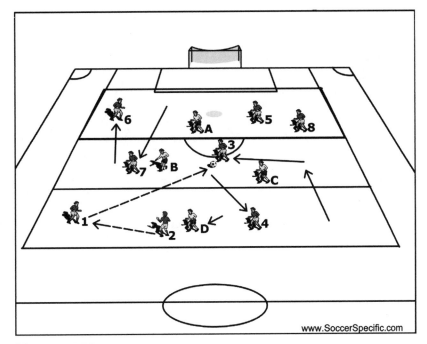

Diagram 277

8. Equal numbers in each zone makes it more difficult.

9. **Progression 5:** Interchange of players between the thirds.

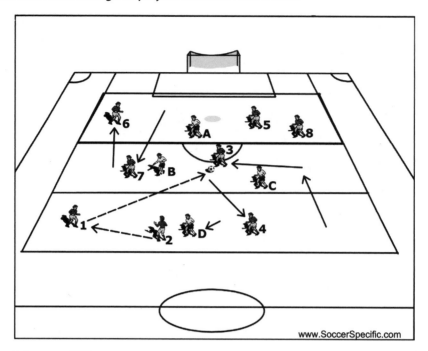

Diagram 278

10. (4) checks out and (6) checks in and takes his place. This is an interchange of players between units now as the receiver (6) now can pass the ball into the opposite end zone in this case to player (5).

11. **Progression 6:** The player on the ball (5) above can go into the middle third directly either through passing or dribbling; or either end third player can go instead and exchange positions. Players must watch each other's body language and movements to determine who does what.

12. **Progression7:** Here we have an interchange in the opposite side of the field now with (5) and (6).
13. Good communication is a must in this practice, and the emphasis now is really "off the ball movements" of players resulting in interchanges between the units.

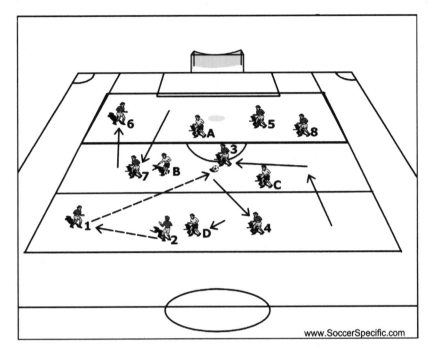

Diagram 279

14. **Progression 8:** Players can now run between all the thirds, which would equate in game situation to a fullback overlapping from their defending third into the attacking third, other players exchange areas around them to maintain the ratio of attackers to defenders in each third of the area.
15. There are many variations here and this is a fitting way to end this book with the emphasis on coaches being able to look at a session plan and change it to suit their own needs.
16. This particular set up totally allows for this and even encourages them to do so.

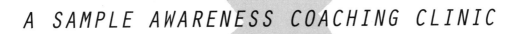

A SAMPLE AWARENESS COACHING CLINIC

Soccer Awareness Coaching Clinic presented by Wayne Harrison at the following important soccer coaching education events:

- NSCAA National Soccer Coaches Convention: Indianapolis - Jan 2007
- World Class Coaching: International Coaching Seminar; Kansas City - Feb 2007
- Coaches' Super Clinic: Atlantic City - Feb 2009

THE AWARENESS COACHING METHOD FOR SOCCER

A PSYCHOLOGICAL APPROACH TO THE GAME
Developing Anticipation, Imagination, and "Awareness" in Your Players using the Awareness Coaching Method

"Graphics are courtesy of SoccerSpecific.com; the best graphics I have come across for presenting sports session plans". Thanks to Soccer Specific for allowing me to use their work.

AREAS OF AWARENESS
The Awareness process is having an awareness (an understanding) of all options available "before you get the ball" and looking ahead of the ball (and getting the feet right to receive the ball), and once you get it to make the correct decisions based on this prior and ongoing information. This is designed to help the player keep possession more easily and not get caught and lose it.

Possession of it can then be broken down into "possession with few touches" (which is epitomized by the way Arsenal in England plays the game using lots of one and two touch plays) and possession with many touches (such as dribbling or running with the ball). This awareness before possession of the ball includes keeping the head up whilst about to control the ball, knowing where team mates are, where opponents are, where the spaces are, but at the same time keeping an eye on and possession of the ball.

On the other hand once the player has the ball, if they decide the right option is to dribble or run with this and thus maintain possession of it themselves with more touches, then that brings in another type of awareness which is that of what to do during possession and the ensuing maintenance of the ball, as opposed to an awareness of what to do with it before receiving and as they receive it. Learning all types of awareness takes a lot of work, practice and training.

We can further break down awareness to that "On the Ball" and also that "Off the Ball":

"On the Ball" signifies the player about to receive it or who has just received it, "Off the Ball" refers to all the other players who are not directly involved in possession of the ball, yet, basically the other 10 players on the field but particularly those around and close to the ball who may be in the best positions to help the player on the ball. They need to be moving into good open space to help the player about to receive the ball to help them keep possession by moving it on quickly if that is the required decision.

So 4 areas of awareness; On the Ball Awareness before receiving, On the Ball awareness as the player receives it and moves it on quickly using 1 or 2 touches only; On the Ball awareness if the player keeps it using several touches; and "Off the Ball", awareness of players getting open early to help the player On the Ball.

This works if all players are in synch and thinking ahead of the ball and not just the player on the ball.

Our focus here in this clinic is mainly Awareness On the Ball with few touches (the beautiful way Arsenal in England play for example), moving the ball on quickly with one or two touches and being able to psychologically think ahead and identify the next correct pass to keep possession. We will finish the clinic by combining "Awareness On the ball with few touches" and Awareness "Off the ball" with two fast moving themed games to link the two.

We are trying to establish the following in the players make up:
A. WHAT they do? (The technique or skill used; and what are the options to move or pass the ball depending on the position on the field of play).
B. WHERE they do it? (Position on the field can dictate this in the decision making process).
C. WHEN they do it? (The timing of the technique or skill used)
D. HOW they do it? (The selection of the technique or skill used)
E. WHY they do it? (The tactical objective)
F. What is the END PRODUCT? A pass, a shot, a cross, a dribble, or a turn
G. What do they do next once the ball has left them?
(Likely move to support in the next phase or a later phase of play, getting free from a marker to be able to be a part of the development of play again)

Coaching Style: The Coaching Style will be of a Command Nature due to the clinic situation with new players and a limited time to do the clinic, but Question and Answer and Guided Discovery styles will be used where we are able.

Introduction
I first got the idea of this type of training when playing with Alan Ball at Blackpool Football Club in England when he joined us as player – head coach as he was winding down his career. Alan Ball was a World Cup winner with England in 1966 playing 72 times for his country and who had a distinguished career in England. He epitomized the one touch play this type of training develops, rather like Paul Scholes of Manchester United, Fabregas of Arsenal, and Alonso of Liverpool do today. Bally actually used to say he only needed HALF A TOUCH!! I believe him having seen him play (if there is such a thing)!! The fact that even at age 37 no one could get near him (because by the time you had closed him down the ball had gone) and he rarely lost possession in games or in training proved that. Alan Ball was my inspiration for this method of play, as was Eric Harrison who is referenced later.

It has never been more important in soccer to be good at this type of play. The game continues to get faster and faster at all levels of play, requiring quicker and quicker decision making.

So, based on their simple concepts, I have developed the idea further that had lead to a book on the topic (Recognizing the Moment to Play) and this coaching clinic.

PROGRESSION 1

DEVELOPING AWARENESS IN POSSESSION OF THE BALL THROUGH A FUN POSSESSION GAME WITH A BALL EACH

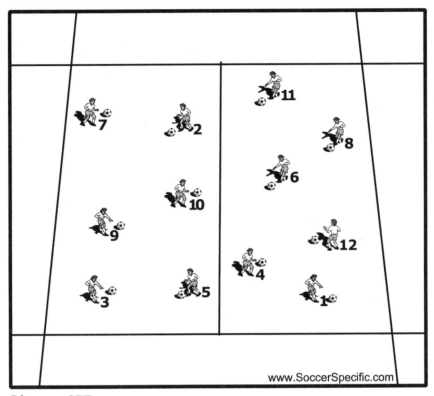

Diagram 277

This is a good Warm Up

1. Each of the 12 players has a ball. They must protect their own ball but at the same time try to kick someone else's ball out of the area. Once your ball is kicked out you cannot kick anyone else's ball out. You can vary the game by allowing chances, maybe up to three each before they are ultimately out of the game. When they are out have them juggle the ball to keep practicing skills.
2. Play until the last player is left with his own ball and everyone else's ball has been kicked out. This player is the winner.
3. Variations can be you have three areas of play. When a player is kicked out he goes to the next area and so on. This way they get two chances but also you can have two winners in each group with an overall winner at the end. Or you can just decrease the area they are playing in to make it harder as there is less space to work in.
4. **Coaching Points:**
   a) Awareness of where other players are while maintaining possession of the ball, ensuring players are looking around away from their own ball.
   b) Dribbling and Turning,
   c) Shielding,
   d) Tackling,
   e) Anaerobic Fitness work.
This is a practice that is fun but ensures relevant skills are practiced by the players.

PROGRESSION 2
A GAME WORKING ON AWARENESS IN POSSESSION OF THE BALL

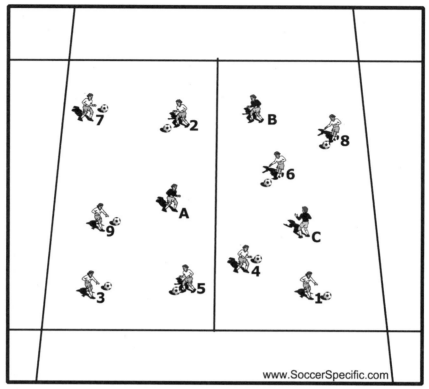

Diagram 278

1. There are 12 players in this clinic (it can be any number). 9 with a ball, 3 without. The 3 players without a ball have to win a ball and pass it to the coach. If a player loses his ball he can join in with the other players, helping them keep possession through passing and support play. EMPHASIZE LOOKING AROUND, LOOKING OVER THE SHOULDER.

2. To make this competitive, rotate the players so different groups of 3 work together. Time each group to see who does this in the quickest time.

3. This represents winning the ball and keeping possession in a game, rather than kicking it out of play and losing possession again.

4. The session develops from an individual 1v1 attacking / defending workout to a passing and support situation. You can work on the defenders by encouraging them to work as a team, maybe in 2's for instance to have a better chance of winning the balls. The defenders can pass the ball around until one can find the coach with a pass. Attackers during this time can try to win it back before it goes out the area and keep possession.

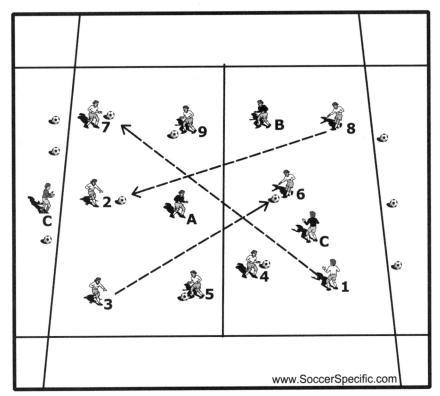

Diagram 279

1. This is showing the progression of the session where the defenders have won 6 balls and passed 3 to the coach.
2. Coaches should move around so the players have to monitor their position using their peripheral vision
3. **Coaching Points:**
   Attackers with the ball –
   a) Dribbling and turning practice,
   b) Shielding the ball,
   c) Moving and support play,
   d) Quality of passing, players keep possession by passing between each other once one or more lose their ball.
   e) Awareness of positions of both sets of players and where the spaces are.

   Defenders without the ball –
   a) Practicing defensive pressurizing skills,
   b) Team work (in 2's or more) to win the ball using supporting defensive skills –
   Angle / Distance / Communication,
   c) Maintaining possession after winning the ball,
   d) Awareness of the player to pass to (the coach or a teammate to get it to the coach),
   e) Quality of the pass once they win the ball.
4. This game is fun and competitive for the players but it also provides a situation where they are learning important skills.
5. Every ball won by a defender must be passed to the coach to show they have won the ball but also kept possession of the ball. This teaches the players the importance of not just winning possession of the ball but also trying to maintain possession after winning it. If the

defending player passes the ball to the coach and it is not accurate and does not get to the coach's feet then the attacker who had the ball gets it back to continue in possession. This ensures quality of passing from the defender who has won back the ball in the first place.

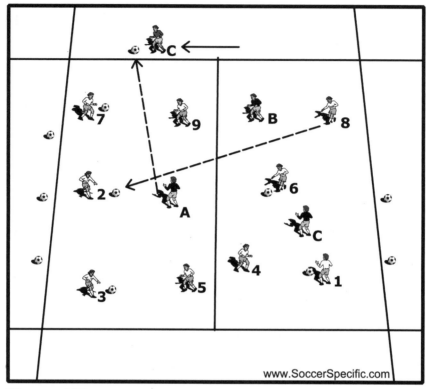

Diagram 280

6. **Develop:** Make it a two team game, one defends, one attacks. Time each team to see how long it takes for them to win possession of each ball and make a successful pass to the coach. The clock stops when all 6 balls have been passed successfully to the coach.
7. Now defenders need to have awareness too. When they win the ball they need to know quickly where the coach is to pass the ball to and consequently be successful. So, while they are defending trying to win the ball they are also watching the coach in their peripheral vision.

PROGRESSION 3:

OBJECTIVE: IMPROVING ONE AND TWO TOUCH PASSING WHILE MAINTAINING AN AWARENESS OF WHAT IS "BEYOND THE BALL"

Another very simple way to develop peripheral vision is with hand signals from the coach. The coach holds his hand up periodically and shows a certain number of fingers for the players to see and to call out. Developing this awareness off the ball is essential for the players to learn to "see the field" in a peripheral sense. This is a very simple way of aiding this development.

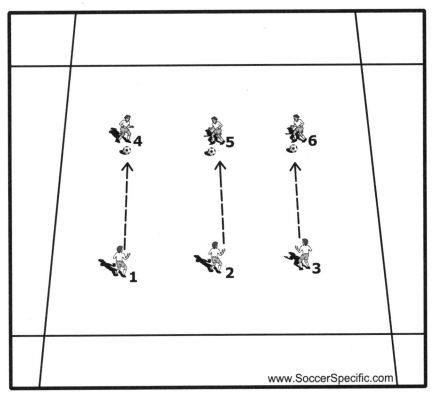

Diagram 281

1. Simple passing in two's back and forth. Begin with two touches, then one touch where possible. Coach can dictate the distance between them.
2. Ask the players to look into "each other's eyes" as they pass and NOT at the ball to see if they can keep possession between them.
3. This will be difficult at first but in time players will look up and not down at the ball during games, a basic step in "Awareness" development.
4. They should be able to see their ball in their "peripheral vision".
5. Encourage using both feet to pass the ball.
6. **Competitive:** Count how many passes they can get in during a given time.
7. **Coaching Points:**
   a) Head Up (looking into the other player's eyes)
   b) Ability to look at the player AND see the ball also in their peripheral vision
   c) Good first touch to set up the second touch / pass
   d) Technique of Passing

PROGRESSION 4:
OBJECTIVE: BASIC THEN PROGRESSED AWARENESS TRAINING IN THREES

This is a very simple idea with players in three's passing the ball back and forth, focusing on good passing but also starting to train the middle player to look over his shoulders before receiving the pass to see where the player he is going to pass to is positioned. So he looks away from the ball as it is traveling to him or as the passer is about to pass the ball. The conditions added ensure the middle player does actually look to see where the next pass is going before receiving the initial pass, otherwise he will get caught making the wrong decision.

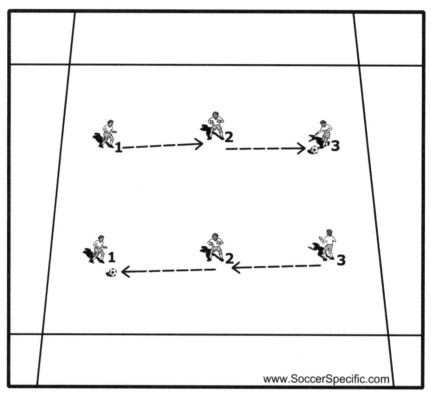

Diagram 282

1. **Coaching Points:**
   a) Look over shoulder "before receiving" (where you are passing to).
   b) Body Stance – half turned (can see behind).
   c) Support at an angle.
   d) Save a touch – let weight of ball determine this- let it run across the body and move one touch.
   e) Always looking around developing your Awareness of other players' positioning before, during and after receiving the pass
1. **Progression and Conditions:** Opposite player stays or closes the middle player down.
2. If closed down by the outside opposite player, the middle player passes back to the same player.
3. If not closed down the middle player turns and passes to the opposite player.
4. This identifies if the middle player has looked to see where the player behind him is, "before" receiving the ball.

5. If (3) closes down on (2) as (2) receives the ball, and (3) then determines to turn and to pass the ball to (2), this then shows that (3) has not looked to see where (2) is because (3) has turned to pass which is the wrong decision. If (3) had looked first then the correct result would be (3) passing back to (1) if (2) closes (3) down.

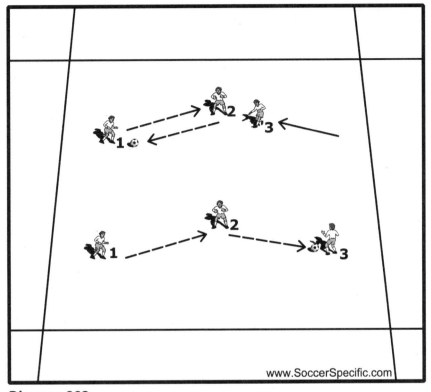

Diagram 283

PROGRESSION 5:
TWO TEAM SET UP

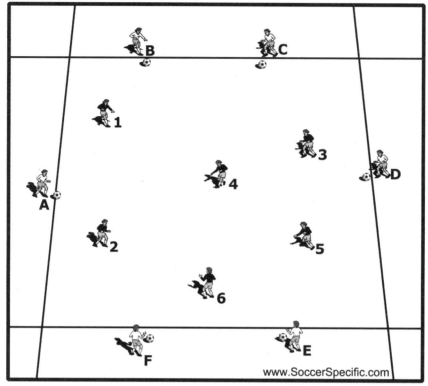

Diagram 284

1. **Coaching Points:**
   a) Head up (awareness of the space and the players in it).
   b) Looking before receiving to receive and turn; to see who is free, to see where other players in the area are, to see where the space is to take the ball.
   c) Body position open to receive,
   d) Focus on the first touch and where to take the ball; for more touches or maybe a one touch pass if it is available.
   e) Concentrate on the quality of the pass to the outside receiver.
2. One team inside, one team outside. A ball is with each outside player to begin.
3. Pass to an inside player who receives and turns and finds another outside free player with a pass. Then look to receive from another outside player.
4. The outside player receives and moves the ball side to side until another inside player is free to receive a pass. This ensures all the players are working both inside and outside the grid.
5. **Competitive:** Have each player count the number of successful passes he makes in a given time. Observe and comment on those who try to do it too quickly and lose control of the ball and disrupt the momentum of the session (for example they rush the pass, it is not accurate and the receiver ends up running away retrieving the ball which wastes precious time).
6. Change the practice to all balls starting with the inside players. These players now look to pass and receive a give and go from an outside player.
7. Rotate the players so both teams have the chance to play in the middle of the grid.
8. Move both teams to the middle; divide the grid into two with each team passing to their own team within their own grid area keeping teams separate to begin.

AWARENESS CHANGEOVER SESSION

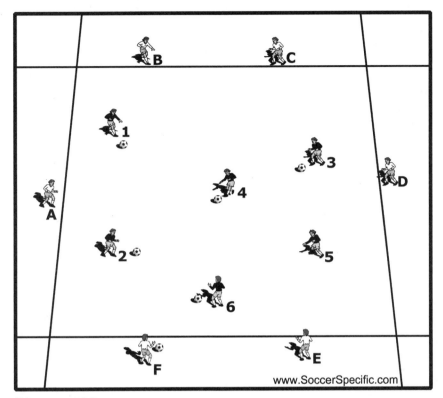

Diagram 285

1. Inside team a ball each, look to find a free outside team player and pass to him. Outside player brings the ball back in, inside player moves outside the zone waiting to receive a pass from someone else.
2. Set up second touch with a good first touch. Awareness of whom is free to receive the pass.
3. **Coaching Points:**
   a) Quality first touch of outside player.
   b) Decision making of inside player in terms of when and where to pass and technique (quality) of pass.
4. **The Coach can create conditions:**
   a) Get a turn in or dribble before passing.
   b) All in (many) touches, 3 then 2 touches.
   c) Play 1- 2 with inside player then go outside.
   d) Do a crossover with outside player rather than make a pass.
5. Inside player passes to outside player and closes down quickly, simulating a defensive movement. The receiver has to make a good first touch away from the pressure i.e. to either side of the pressuring player.
6. It's a good session because everyone is working but they get short intermittent rests, so quality is maintained.
7. **Develop:** Start with one ball per team then go to two balls each team, players on the outside have one touch but can take two if needed if players on the inside have not made an angle for them to receive the ball back inside the area. Two touches on the inside. This speeds up the decision making on the inside and outside particularly as previously the outside players could control it and wait until an inside player was available; now they can't.

Now the inside players need better awareness to help the outside players too. As one is passing to the outside, another inside player must be looking to support the next pass back inside.

8. Competitive: Have each player count the number of successful passes he makes in a given time.

PROGRESSION 6
DEVELOPING AWARENESS "BEFORE" RECEIVING THE BALL: TWO TEAMS PLAYING "THROUGH" EACH OTHER

Divide the players into two teams, a ball each team, passing and moving in the same area passing through each other, but not playing against each other.

This is an incredibly simple exercise but one I watched a famous Youth coach, Eric Harrison at Manchester United do many years ago at an FA Symposium with Beckham, Scholes, the Nevilles and Ryan Giggs to name a few famous players he developed through the youth academy. He told us he used this for his warm up every day to develop his player's awareness on and off the ball.

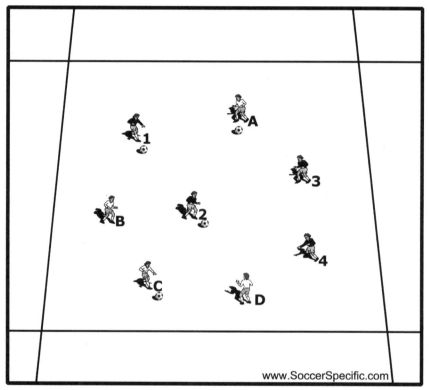

Diagram 286

Technical/Tactical Design
Lots of touches on the ball are achieved in this practice.
a) The players must play with their heads up (so they see what is around).
b) Look over the shoulder before receiving the ball.
c) Body stance open to receive the ball.

d) Move the ball on the 1st touch away from pressure and into space or towards where you are passing it or one touch transfer if that pass is on.

e) Awareness of teammates positions on the field in advance.

f) Awareness of opponents positions on the field in advance.

g) Passing to space to move players into a better position on the field

h) Passing to feet.

i) Turns / dribbles / 1 touch / 2 touch / free play.

j) Communication (key words).

k) Support Angles / distances to help the player on the ball.

Develop:

a) Increase the number of balls per team.

b) Pass to opposite colors. Below we have several balls being passed.

c) Progress to an overload game, for example 3v3v3, before going to an equal numbers two team game of possession.

PROGRESSION 7

IMPROVING AWARENESS "BEFORE" RECEIVING THE BALL THROUGH A SIMPLE NUMBERS CONDITIONED GAME

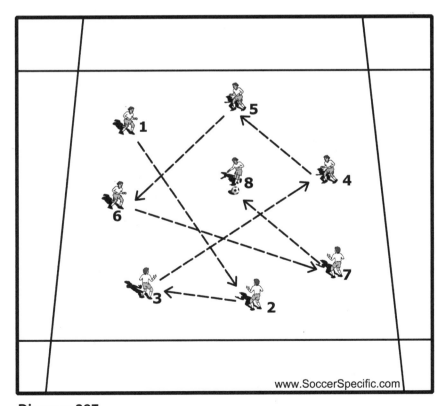

Diagram 287

1. The numbers game FORCES the players to look before they receive by the very condition placed on them. There are 6 Players and only 1 ball to begin. Players must pass in sequence i.e. 1 passes to 2; 2 passes to 3; 3 to 4 and so on to 6 who passes to 1 and we begin again. You can have player's static to begin as easy introductions to the theme then have them passing and moving. In a roster of 12 players 2 groups of 6 can do this in different areas separately to begin.

2. Players receive from the same person and pass to the same person each time. This develops great awareness of time, space and player positions. This is continuous work on and off the ball. Awareness of: the position of the player you receive from as well as the player you pass to. Because of this players begin to anticipate the pass to them and where it is coming from.

3. We are trying to create a situation where players are looking two moves ahead, not just one. For instance, as (1) is about to pass to (2), (3) should be looking to support (2) for the next pass already, looking two moves ahead before the ball leaves (1). Likewise, (2) should already know where (3) is.

4. This exercise helps to develop peripheral vision.

5. **Develop:** Use two balls then three balls at the same time. Start with a ball at (1) and (5) then at (1), (4) and (6). To keep the sequence going players must move the balls quickly with few touches, hence their peripheral vision improves dramatically. As soon as they have passed one ball off the next one is arriving, so quick thinking is needed to make the correct decisions.

6. **Coaching Points:**
   a) Awareness of where the player to receive from is before receiving the pass
   b) Getting into position to help the passer make a successful pass
   c) Awareness of where the player to pass to is before receiving the pass
   d) Open Body position to receive the pass to enable a resulting one touch pass if necessary

PROGRESSION 8:
SEMI – COMPETITIVE AWARENESS NUMBERS GAME: PASSING IN SEQUENCE

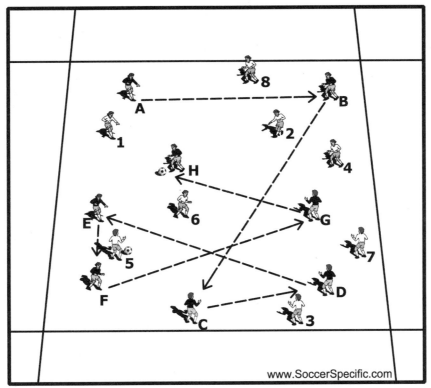

Diagram 288

1. Now have 2 teams passing separately 1 to 6 in "each team", with a ball each team in the same area. The example shows the passing of the numbers team only for simplicity.

2. **Develop:**
   Count the number of passes each team gets in a certain time frame to add a competitive element to the game. Who can get the highest number of passes made in a given time frame?

3. **Emphasize:**
   a) Movement "off" the ball to open up angles for passes between other players.
   b) Verbal communication between players to help them identify where they are; passing player can call who they are passing to, receiving player can ask for the pass.
   c) Ensure players spread out throughout the area to have them playing both long and short passes.
   d) Encourage fewer touches on the ball at each reception to move it around the field more quickly, helping players develop good transitional play.

PROGRESSION 9:
WORKING ON PERIPHERAL VISION "BEFORE" RECEIVING THE BALL THROUGH THE SPECIFIC PERIPHERAL VISION COACHING GAME

A 40x30 area is organized as shown in the Diagram below. Six players are used within the activity. Repeat the setup to accommodate the entire team.

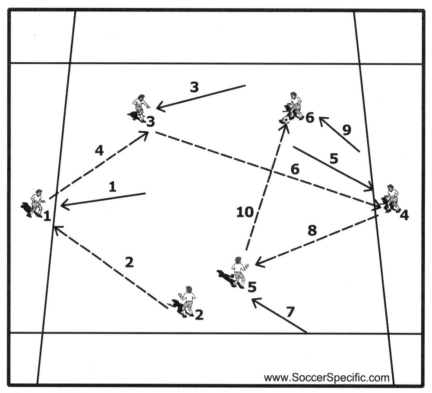

Diagram 289

This is a simplified set up to get initial understanding. Increase numbers as previously e.g. two teams of six. We started earlier with one ball and six players so each person on the ball had five passing options.

Now we must identify one and only one pass and try to make it. That pass is to the person who runs outside the zone. This player is the free player (unmarked). The session goes as follows and numbers are used only as a reference. The players can pass to anyone, in any order, but always looking for that vital run by a player to the outside area:

1. Player (1) runs outside the area (perhaps after several passes within the zone).
2. Player (2) on the ball sees the run and must pass to (1).
3. As (1) is about to receive (as the ball is traveling to him) (3) moves into a position to support (1), showing anticipation and awareness.
4 (3) has already seen the run by (4) and passes. (4) brings the ball back in and the game continues. (4) passes to (5) who has moved into position in anticipation and (5) passes to (6) who also has done the same. This is an indicator of how quickly players recognize the run and consequently make the pass.

5. Hence players are beginning to look one and two moves ahead of the ball. It doesn't need to happen so quickly in terms of the next player running outside but it serves as an example. The run can be likened to a penetrating run into the attacking third where the player hasn't been picked up or tracked and is in a great position to attack and score if the passer sees him and makes the pass.

6. **Coaching Points:**
   a) Decision: Movement of the player running out of the area to initiate the move
   b) Observation of this movement or run by the other players
   c) Observation by the one player receiving the pass as this movement of a run outside the area is taking place
   d) Decision by this player to make the quick pass to the outside player
   e) Quality of Passing: A one or two touch pass to the outside player for speed of action to show the run was spotted
   f) Weight of pass to the next passing player so he has the choice of making a one touch pass if he has seen the run
   g) Observation of the receiving player on the outside of the runs of others to receive the next pass
   h) Support Positions: Other players already making movements to give the receiving outside player options to move the ball quickly with good support in terms of angles, distances and timing.

SPECIFIC PERIPHERAL VISION COACHING SESSION

Further development, ideas and ideals of this practice leading to the introduction of defenders as opposition but in an attacking overload situation.

1. Within the zone there are many passing options, but as soon as a player makes the run outside that is the pass to make. Coach can determine the tempo of the game e.g. to avoid too many running out at the same time the coach can signal to an individual player to move out without the others knowing so only one at a time goes out.

2. Once the free player is outside and waiting for a pass, see how many passes are made inside the zone before someone sees the right pass i.e. to the outside player. This is an indication of which players play with their heads up (and hence have good peripheral vision) and which don't, (hence have poor peripheral vision or even none at all).

3. The fewer touches on the ball the player needs to get the ball there the greater his anticipation of the run. One touch is the ultimate objective.

4. More touches means more reaction time needed and in a game situation this may mean a player being caught in possession before he can make the pass.

5. Initially the coach may see several passes made within the area while a player stands and waits outside. This will happen less and less as the players improve their peripheral vision.

6. The exciting part is when the coach sees one of the players make the right pass quickly in a game situation due to the work they have done in this session.

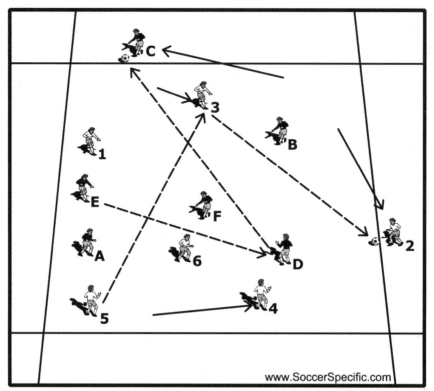

Diagram 290

1. Here we have two teams playing in the same area, player (5) passes to player (3). Player (2) as the ball is traveling runs outside the area, player (3) has to see this movement and make the next pass to that player. If (3) makes it with a one touch pass that is excellent as it shows he has seen the run as the ball is arriving and made the quickest pass possible to get the ball to (2). Player (2) then brings the ball back into play and the passing sequence starts again.

2. Likewise player (E) on the other team passes to player (D), player (C) runs out of the area and the set up continues.

PROGRESSION 10:
GAME SITUATION (WE WILL USE A 2 TEAM GAME HERE FOR EASE OF TRANSITION BUT AN OVERLOAD THREE TEAM GAME CAN OFTEN BE A BETTER STARTING POINT, MOVING TO THE TWO TEAM GAME EVENTUALLY).

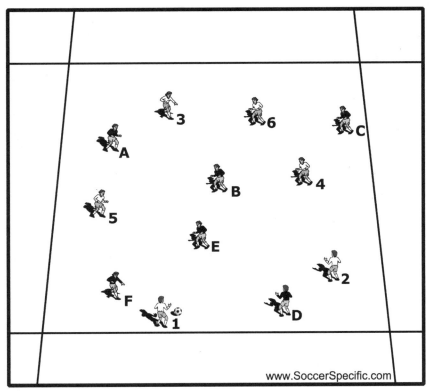

Diagram 291

1. A two team game for ease of transition with limited time (you can use neutral players to make it easier to work initially it is always best to begin with an overload situation to help them make it work). Five passes a goal.
2. The winner is the team who scores the most 5 pass - goals, you may do the first to score ten goals.
3. **Develop:** Include running out of the area in the game and if a player does this and receives a pass successfully they get three goals for it. Defending players can't track them outside the area.
4. This will encourage players to make outside runs as there is a reward and it will also test the players on the ball as to their peripheral vision and how quickly they identify that particular run. This must happen in less than 6 seconds though and if after a short time the player does not receive a pass then they come back into the game.

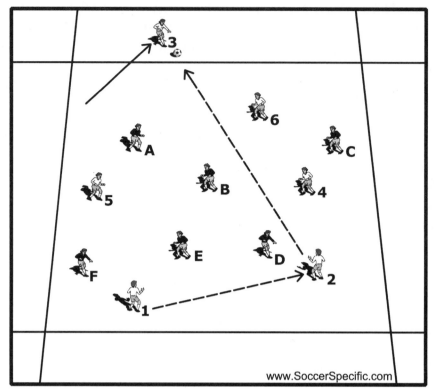

Diagram 292

5. Player (3) makes a run out of the area as (1) passes to (2). (2) sees the run and passes and scores 3 goals. (3) brings the ball back in and the game continues.
6. You are looking for players to anticipate where (3) needs support and move into position to help.
7. Other players need to move off the ball to get into open positions for the first pass or in anticipation of the next ones.
8. You can also reward a one touch pass with a goal to encourage quick play.

PROGRESSION 11: QUICK TRANSITION DIRECTIONAL PLAY
OBJECTIVE: DEVELOPING AWARENESS USING QUICK TRANSITION DIRECTIONAL PLAY

Another session that can be used often with change of focus. The focus of an individual session using this game could be:

1. Focusing on the 1v1 confrontations in the game; or:
2. Focusing on the "Quickness of transitional play" by making it two touch, focusing on the players "ON" the ball as they receive it and try to move it quickly forward; or:
3. Focusing on the players "OFF" the ball, emphasizing their movement and positioning OFF the ball to support the player ON the ball; or:
4. Focusing on the defending team and how they counter the opponents.

These are just four ideas. While I try to cover all the possibilities in the Coaching Points section, you can focus on each of these as one topic only in an individual session rather than try to get all the information covered in one session. Perhaps do four sessions developing each idea then a fifth session bringing it all together.

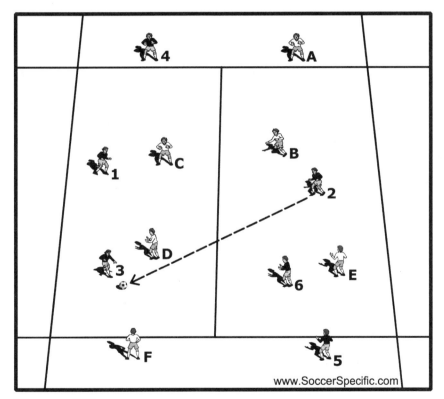

Diagram 293

1. Quick continuous attacking play which is good for anaerobic fitness. Here the players are breaking one way, passing to an outside player and switching positions, inside player out, outside player in, then attack the other side of the zone.
2. **Coaching Points:**
   a) Technical ability on the ball in 1v1 situations.
   b) Quick Transition in attack - As the transition between players happens, for example (3) changes with (5), the numbers team must get the ball to (4) as quickly as possible.

c) Observe the movement of (1), (2) and (6) in terms of their support positions as the directional change takes place. They must move in anticipation to find space to help the player on the ball as the switch occurs.

d) Also observe the positions of the defending team as the change occurs. Has the decision been made quickly enough who presses the ball? Are the other defensive players supporting and covering and especially tracking runners off the ball? The coach must learn to look away from the ball and observe what may happen next before it happens.

e) This session improves quick decision making and tight control because of the limited space. You can also work on the defending players.

f) **Progression:** If a player beats an opponent in a 1v1 situation the team gets an extra point or goal each time.

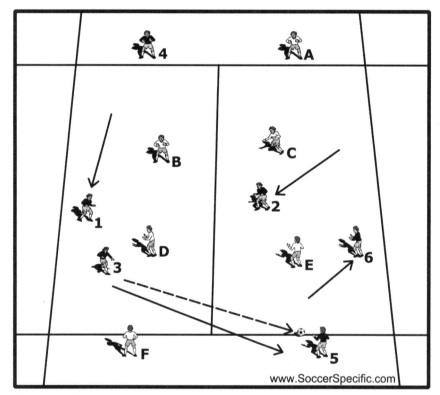

Diagram 294

1. Here (3) passes to (5) and (3) leaves the area. As the ball is traveling to (5), (1), (2) and (6) must get into a position to help (5) as early as possible so that (5) can make a one touch pass to any or all of them. Thus (5) already has three passing options.

2. Their movement is OFF THE BALL and away from their markers.

3. Of course the defenders will move to compensate but for the sake of what I am trying to show it is easier to get the point across by showing the movements of the attacking team only.

4. The attacking players in the actual practice may get free like this anyway if they time it correctly.

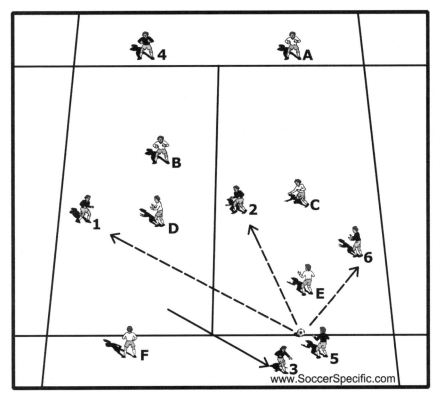

Diagram 295

1. The attacking players each being free to help (5) by being open for a pass.
2. (5) may elect to run with the ball but at least three are three options available for a pass if needed.
3. (5) may even elect to play a long pass straight to (4) on the other side of the field if the pressure from the closest defender is not fast enough. You may then ask the closest player (in this case player 2), not necessarily the passing player (5) to be the switching player instead if (5) passes it directly to (4).
4. You could even then work on defending. It's important, though, to only focus on one phase at a time, either defending or attacking. Trying to work on both phases at once can be confusing for the players.

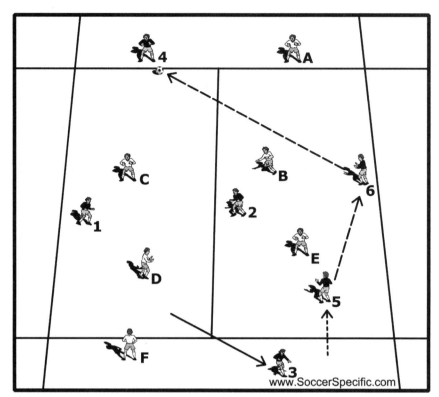

Diagram 296

1. Here (3) does pass to (5) and they switch positions. (5) plays a quick pass to (6) who passes to target player (4) who scores another point and this player (4) has to quickly attack the other way again.

2. You could argue that the best place to dribble is in the opponent's half but this being a small area you could encourage players to do it all over the field while making them aware of the safety and risk facts if it were a game situation.

PROGRESSION 12:

TEACHING AWARENESS AND MOVEMENT "OFF THE BALL" THROUGH THE TRANSITION DIRECTIONAL TARGET GAME

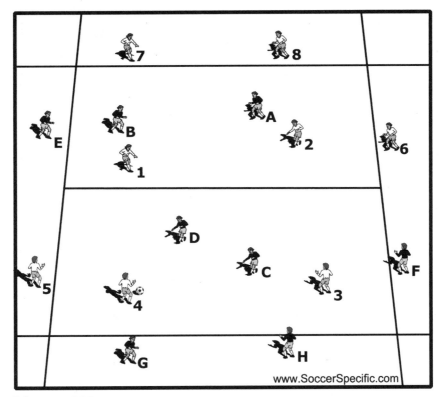

Diagram 297

1. **Rules:**
   a) Players must pass the ball to their target players to score. To score again they have to work the ball back into their own half of the field to be able to return.
   b) Target players have two touches as do side players.
2. **Coaching Points:**
   a) Creating space by running off the ball to receive or to help a teammate receive.
   b) Quality of passing; long and short to targets and to teammates.
   c) Support play: working angles and distances incorporating switching play using the side players.
   d) Receiving and Turning in tight situations and dribbling in 1v1 situations.
   e) Quick decision making is required in this session because the numbers are small, the area tight and the transitions rapid.
3. **Develop:**
   a) No restriction on touches then 3, 2 or 1 touch, but only if it is on to do one touch.
   b) All outside and target players have one touch only where possible
   c) switch with target players as they receive the ball.
   d) Switch with outside players

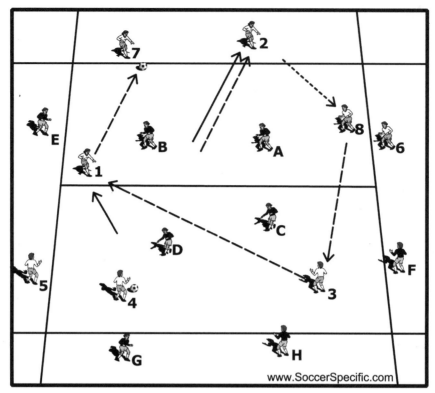

Diagram 298

1. Here is an example of the transition and movement off the ball to make it happen.
2. (2) passes to target player (8) who brings the ball back into the playing area.
3. (3) makes a run into the other half of the field on the blind side of (C) to receive the next pass. They need to get the ball into that half to be able to score.
4. (1) makes a forward run into space to receive the next pass off (3) and passes to target player (7) who can start the play again.
5. (1) switches with (7) and becomes a target player for the next phase of play.
6. **Observe the Attacking Team** – Recognize their movement off the ball. For example, to work the ball into their own half, see if the players make runs early as soon as the ball is at a target. Some should support short and some long so the target has choices.
7. **Observe the Defending Team** – See if they are sucked to the ball or they recognize runs off the ball and track players making runs away from the ball into the other half.
8. To lessen the workload and keep everyone involved, have players switch with targets and outside players when they pass to them.

9. Elements of play the target game teaches:
   Attacking as Individuals and as a Team
   a) Creating space by running off the ball to receive or to help a teammate receive.
   b) Developing quick support play by working angles and distances, incorporating switching play using the side players.
   c) Passing long and short to targets and teammates.
   d) Receiving and turning in tight situations and dribbling in 1v1 situations.
   e) Lots of touches on the ball for the players in this practice.
   f) Quick decision making is required in this session because the numbers are small, the area tight and the transitions rapid.

Defending as Individuals and as a Team
a) Pressurizing players on the ball to regain possession.
b) Supporting pressuring players and tracking runners off the ball.
c) High pressure to regain possession in the attacking half to be able to go straight to the target to score.

We have transitions from defense to attack and attack to defense, quick decision making and improved concentration as the switch occurs. We have interchanges of positions between inside players, targets and side support players. As a coach you can work in this session how to defend properly as individuals and a team or how to attack properly as individuals and a team.

Conditions to impose to change the focus of the game
1. No restriction on touches, then three, two or one touch, but only if it is on to do so.
2. Introduce neutral player to form a 5v4 overload in the middle if possession isn't kept easily.
3. Interchanges of players outside to in, inside to out as they pass the ball, observing the quality of the pass and the first touch of the receiver.
4. Have one teammate at each end so you are attacking both ends, but once you have passed to one target you keep possession and must try to get to the other target. You can't go back unless the opposition win the ball and then you get it back, only then can you go back to the same target.
5. To lessen the workload and keep everyone involved, have players switch with targets and outside players when they pass to them. This causes a constant transition of players and focuses the players' concentration.
6. The team can only score if they get an overlap, crossover or 1 – 2 in during the build up.
7. No talking, so players have to rely on their own vision to play.
8. Players move into the target zone to receive (timing of run and pass) so we don't play with actual targets and different players can then become the target player.
9. Man-marking – Have the players man mark so they must track a player when they don't have the ball and they must lose their marker when they have the ball. This is a good test to see who is working hard and who isn't as they have a designated job to do. You as a coach can see who works to get free of their marker and who works hard to prevent the player they are marking from getting the ball.
10. This session is particularly good as a midfield play practice session as you can liken the start when the ball is at a target to a defender passing it to the other side through midfield to the other target who is now a striker. Then this target player maintains possession and the team can go the other way. The target striker then becomes a defender for the attacking team starting the move and the other target becomes the striker to pass the ball to. So it is consistent movement end to end with the attacking team from a defender into midfield to a striker.
11. To improve the speed of thought, reward a successful one touch pass with a goal or point. A goal scored by passing to the target player is worth three goals or 3 points.
12. The team in possession can pass back to the opponent's target players to help keep possession of the ball. Liken this to passing back to the keeper in a game situation.

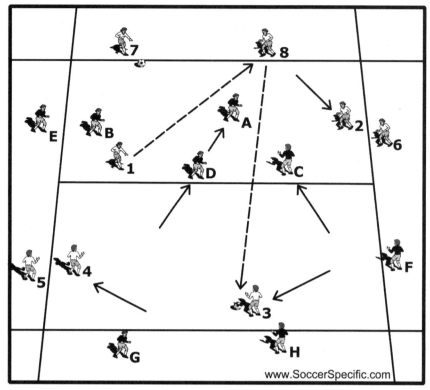

Diagram 299

1. This is an example of what to look for on the defending side of things.
2. Here the ball has been passed to the target (8) and a goal scored. The defenders are ball watching and not seeing the runs "off the ball" of their opponents.
3. The idea of getting the ball back into the other half before they can score again when in possession highlights the kinds of moments you need to identify in a game situation.
4. (1) plays the ball to target (8) to score. (2) supports the next pass short and at a wide angle, and (3) and (4) make runs into the other side of the field and off the ball to get free and receive a pass. Defenders are all ball watching and not looking at these runs and so (3) and (4) get free. At the same time you can say the numbers team got it right offensively.
5. The coach has to identify these situations and stop the game and show the set up and ask the defending players what they need to do.

Things to Identify and Coach
Offensively
1. Lack of movement off the ball of the players in both halves of the field.
2. Poor quality of passing.
3. Awareness of the players identifying correct decision making of when and where to pass.
4. Poor communication to help each other.
5. Poor angles and distance of support and lack of variation of these concepts (long; short and wide are needed)
6. Mentally slow change from attack to defense when possession changes.

Defensively

1. Not seeing movements off the ball of the players on the team in possession of the ball and not tracking these runs.
2. Ball watching, allowing players to get in behind them.
3. Not pressing the ball quickly enough.
4. Working too much individually and not as a unit.
5. Mentally slow change from defense to attack when possession changes.

PROGRESSION 13:
DEVELOPING TEAM PLAY THROUGH A DIRECTIONAL TWO TEAM AWARENESS GAME

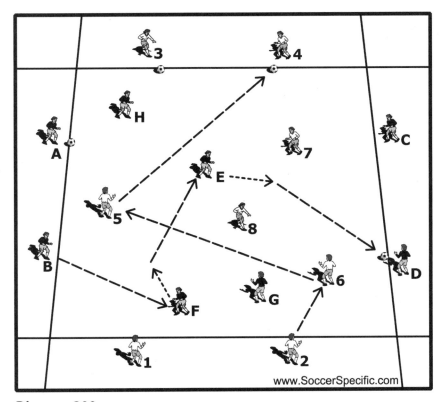

Diagram 300

1. **Coaching Points:**
    a) Awareness of where teammates and opposing players are before you get the ball
    b) Awareness of where the spaces are to move into before you get the ball.
    c) Quality of the First Touch: First touch into the path you are taking to get the ball to the outside player or one touch transfer if possible
    d) Support positions of teammates off the ball
    e) Playing through the other team in the opposite direction, testing positional ability
    f) Directional movement as in a game
    g) Everything done at pace.
2. Example above of playing through the midfield with another inside player to reach one of the targets.
3. Each player takes one touch to take the ball in the direction they want to go and the second touch is a pass to the next player.

4. It may be a one touch pass that is needed, depending on the distances involved. It may be they need more touches on the ball because no one is immediately available to receive a pass. Or you may condition it so they need to do a dribble of some sort in the middle before they pass to the next player. There are many variables you can introduce to suit your needs.

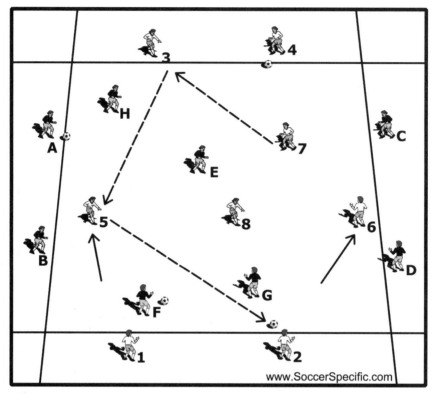

Diagram 301

1. Encouraging players to look ahead of the play. Here (7) passes to outside player (3) and another player (5) is supporting (3) for the next pass, working a triangle of support.
2. (3) needs someone to pass to. To help (3) make a one touch pass quickly, (5) has already moved as shown and gotten into position to receive.
3. As (5), who is receiving the pass from (3), gets into an angled support position ensuring his body is open, he has to have these things in mind before receiving the pass:

    a) Where is the space to go to in order to receive the pass from (3)?
    b) Who is free at the other end to make the next pass to?
    c) Where is the space to take my next touch, or can I pass it one touch to (1) or (2) on the other side? Here (5) decides to pass to (2) and (6) is already in a position to support (2).

SWITCHING POSITIONS WITH THE OUTSIDE PLAYER

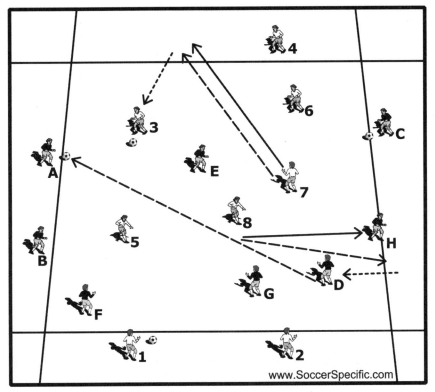

Diagram 302

1. Now, to involve everyone in the middle, have the players switch positions when they Pass to an outside player. (7) Passes to (3), and (3) then takes the ball back in with a good first touch to then look to pass to another player and get the ball to the other side.
2. Likewise (D) receives from (H) and runs the ball into the middle to continue the movement, and (H) runs out of the area to be an outside receiver. (D) then passes to (A) and switches with him.

PROGRESSION 14:
GAME SITUATION

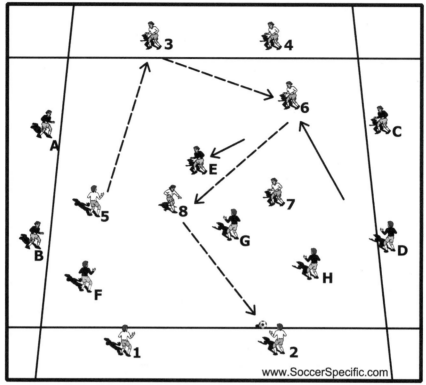

Diagram 303

1. Now we take the session into a game of 4v4.
2. The inside numbered players work with outside numbered players and score by completing a pass to the outside players. They then have to get the ball to the other side to score again. Inside letters players work with the outside letters players so teams play in opposite directions.
3. **Game:** Play to 10 goals then rotate the players so all players get the chance to play.
4. Rotate the teams.
5. Here the numbers team have scored a goal at one end then switched the play to the other end by quick and accurate passing to score another goal.

GAME SITUATION SWITCHING WITH OUTSIDE PLAYERS

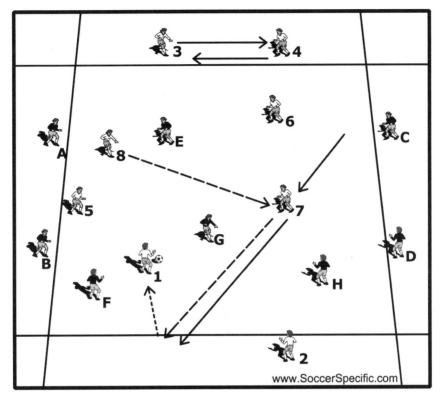

Diagram 304

1. Developing the idea with outside players switching with inside players on scoring a goal with a pass.
2. **Progression:** Introduce scoring a goal by making a successful one touch pass within the game to encourage the players to think quickly and make instant decisions when they receive the ball.
3. Have outside players switching positions so when they receive the pass it is to a moving player . This is more passing to space than to feet.

PROGRESSION 15: COOL DOWN:
OBJECTIVE: DEVELOPING PASSING AND SUPPORT THROUGH THE DIRECTIONAL PASSING AND SUPPORT THREE ZONE GAME
RUNNING WITH AND WITHOUT THE BALL
LONG PASSING

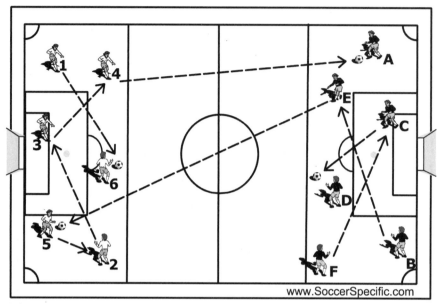

Diagram 305

1. You can use various numbers of players at each end of the grid in this sequence.
2. Players pass and move in their own grid until one player makes eye contact with a player in the other grid (or a call) and plays a long pass to that player. Balls are constantly changing grids; players have to have awareness in their own grid to receive but also awareness of when a pass is on from the other grid (must have head up and be constantly looking around to see this). If they don't observe where their own teammates are or those in the other grid, they won't be successful with this so they must play with their head up and have the ability to look away from the ball as well as at it, observing all the options that are on both in their own grid and the other one.
3. Conditions – Ball can't bounce between grids for chipped or lofted passes, or must be driven along the ground with pace for quick passing.
4. Develop running with the ball across the grids. Pass and move within own grid then a player picks a moment to run and takes it.
5. Keep balance of balls in each grid. Start with one in each, trying to avoid two in one grid at once. Then increase to two balls per grid.
6. Long pass then follow the ball (supporting the pass) into the other grid. So not only balls are being transferred but also players. Players must move as quickly as possible to support in the other grid.
7. **Coaching Points:**
   a) Awareness of the positions of players in both grids, thus ensuring the players have their heads up to see the pass when it is on to do it.
   b) Movement off the ball to make themselves available in both grids to receive a pass.

c) Quality of short passing in one grid and long passing into the other grid.

d) Depending on the theme, the development of awareness of when and where to pass, to run with the ball, to make a movement off the ball (third man run for example), to receive and turn with the ball, and so on.

RUNNING WITH THE BALL

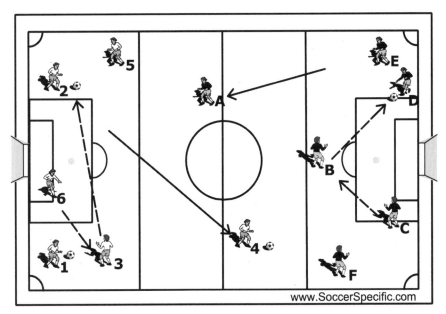

Diagram 306

8. The skill practiced here is specifically running with the ball, still identifying passing and moving options but also looking to make a run when the time is right.

9. **Coaching Points:**

a) Head Up – look forward

b) Good first touch out of feet, 3-4 touches maximum, not dribbling.

c) Run in a straight line, the quickest route.

d) Running Style - use the front foot to control the ball using the laces.

PASSING THEN SUPPORTING THE PASS

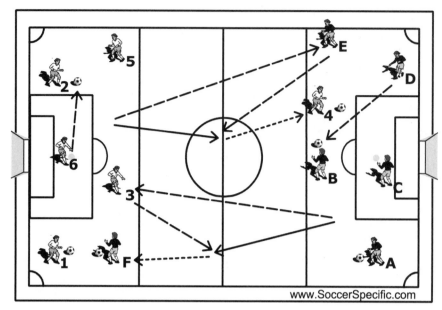

Diagram 307

This is like a player passing into a striker and receiving the pass back (one touch if possible for quickness of transition) and then running the ball forward into the attacking third.

THIRD MAN RUN DEVELOPMENT

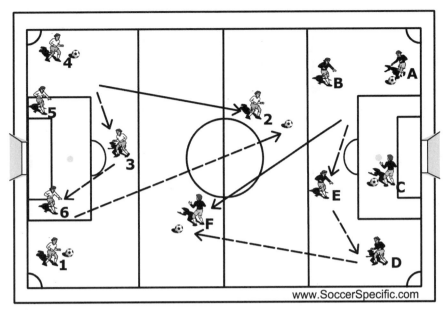

Diagram 308

1. Third man run development – A player makes a run into the neutral area between the grids; a player on the ball must see this quickly and pass to the player making the run. Try to drop the ball in front of the player to run onto. The running player then takes ball into other grid. At the same time another player goes the opposite way. Start with one ball in each grid and build up.

2. **Progression:** Vary the type of runs to be made, straight or diagonal. Diagonal passes and straight runs, and diagonal runs and straight passes as above or diagonal runs and diagonal passes. In a game, this type of movement makes life difficult for defenders. Above, (F) Passes to (E) but continues the run forward, (E) passes back to (D) who passes into the path of (F) continuing the forward run.

3. If a player makes a run and doesn't receive a pass then he works his way back into his own grid. Relate the move to a player making a forward run, not receiving the pass, working back and drawing a defender, which allows another player to make the run into the space left to receive a through ball.

4. Receiving and Turning – a player moves out of the area and positions side on at an angle to receive and turn (looking before receiving) and take the ball to the other grid. The same happens on the other side.

5. **Coaching Points:**
   a) Timing of the 3rd man run off the ball into space
   b) Observation of the run by the player on the ball
   c) Pace, accuracy and timing of the pass in front of the receiving player

PLAYING GIVE AND GO'S

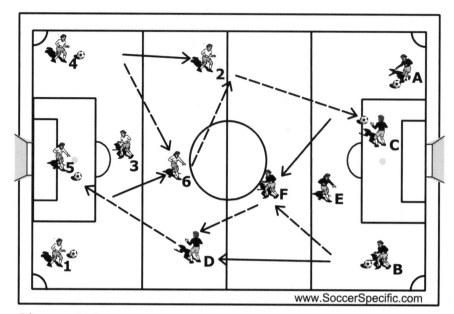

Diagram 309

1. Give and Go's (Movement in two's) - A player moves into the neutral zone (with a third man run off the ball) and another player on the ball passes to him. The passer then follows and receives a pass back (a 1– 2 move) and then passes the ball into the other grid. Both players move into the other grid and join in. On entering, the existing players in this grid must balance things up and look to break in twos the other way as soon as possible.
2. **Progression:** Introduce a defender in each grid. This is now a 4v1 and only one ball per grid.
3. As the number of players involved increases, increase the number of balls used so at times two players can be making moves across the free space from the same grid at the same time, hence there is constant movement between grids. The players will get good at passing and moving and being able to look beyond the ball.

INTRODUCING DEFENDERS

Up to now there have been mainly NO OPPOSITION GAMES or SHADOW PLAYS to allow players to develop anticipation, awareness, vision and imagination regarding passing, receiving,
support and composure on the ball to name just a few of the many aspects of play this helps
develop. We can now introduce DEFENDERS to add pressurizing situations to test the players.

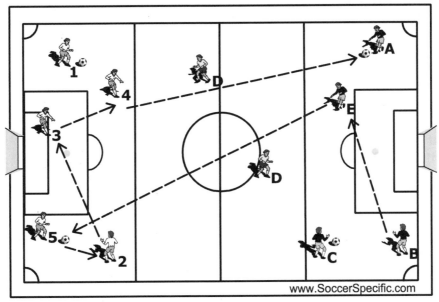

Diagram 310

1. Introduce defenders to put the players under pressure when they pass or run the ball across
   the middle of the field.
2. It can begin with 2 defenders, then 3 defenders to make it more difficult where defenders
   can intercept passes or tackle players with the ball.
3. Use this at every stage of the workout as the players improve. This would include:
   a) passing across the area,
   b) running the ball across the area,
   c) third man runs,
   d) passing then supporting the pass,
   e) playing give and go's,
   f) receiving and turning, and so on.
4. This is taking the session to a more competitive level with defenders included. Now the
   players not only have to focus on passing, running and supporting in their own zone, and
   into the other zone, they have to see where the defenders are to get past them.
5. If a defender intercepts the ball he switches quickly with the player whose pass was
   intercepted.

IMPORTANT EVENTS WHERE THE AWARENESS COACHING METHOD HAS BEEN PRESENTED:

2009:

MINNESOTA STATE YOUTH SOCCER ASSOCIATION:
AWARENESS TRAINING AND THE PSYCHOLOGICAL LINK BETWEEN DEVELOPING FAST FEET AND A QUICK MIND IN DECISION MAKING

2009:

REEDSWAIN SUPER CLINIC IN ATLANTIC CITY:
AWARENESS TRAINING AND THE PSYCHOLOGICAL LINK BETWEEN DEVELOPING FAST FEET AND A QUICK MIND IN DECISION MAKING

2009:

NEW JERSEY STATE SOCCER ASSOCIATION:
AWARENESS TRAINING AND THE PSYCHOLOGICAL LINK BETWEEN DEVELOPING FAST FEET AND A QUICK MIND IN DECISION MAKING

2007:

NSCAA NATIONAL CONVENTION IN INDIANAPOLIS:
"RECOGNIZING THE MOMENT TO PLAY"

2007:

WORLD CLASS COACHING IN KANSAS:
AWARENESS TRAINING AND THE PSYCHOLOGICAL LINK BETWEEN DEVELOPING FAST FEET AND A QUICK MIND IN DECISION MAKING

2005:

REEDSWAIN SUPER CLINIC IN ATLANTIC CITY:
1. AWARENESS TRAINING AND SHADOW DEFENDING

2004:

MINNESOTA STATE YOUTH SOCCER ASSOCIATION:
TEACHING AWARENESS IN SOCCER PLAYERS

2003:

MARYLAND WINTER SOCCER SYMPOSIUM IN BALTIMORE:
RECOGNIZING THE MOMENT TO PLAY AWARENESS TRAINING

2001:

MINNESOTA STATE HIGH SCHOOL SOCCER COACHES ASSOCIATION:
THE IMPORTANCE OF ANTICIPATION IN SOCCER

2000:

STATE FAIR FOR THE MYSA:
ANTICIPATION / IMAGINATION / AWARENESS; A PSYCHOLOGICAL APPROACH TO SOCCER

CONCLUSION AND DISCUSSION

My aim for the second edition was to present the awareness coaching method in coaching clinic session plan form to have a continuous, logical and progressive training program on the Awareness Concept. I hope I have achieved this. This book is more than twice the size of the previous edition and there are of course many new ideas included here.

With this version the coach now has all the progressions in awareness training put into a logical order of session plans, so it is easier to move from one idea onto the next in the correct sequence.

Simplified coaching clinic session plans focusing on technical skill training are important aspects of training to cover and are a prerequisite to awareness training. Once players are proficient in the basic techniques of the game, they are ready for the awareness training in this book. Session plans become more competitively based as you move through the book.

The main theme running through all these practices is quite simply teaching the players to LOOK BEFORE THEY RECEIVE THE BALL, to identify every option in advance depending on where their teammates and the opposition players are positioned.

This is the raw ingredient we are trying to establish in the players' minds above all else. All the other aspects related to this requirement fall into place as you go through the program. Everything I am attempting to show you in this book stems from this simple basic philosophy.

Added onto this is the need to have an awareness ON THE BALL. That is, when the player has and maintains possession of the ball. This type of awareness is with potentially many touches on the ball as opposed to few touches of the ball; but the principles are the same and equally important for both aspects.

I hope this has given you some insight into the thought processes that a player must go through in order to assimilate all that goes with playing soccer successfully.

It must be clear that this isn't a book that covers many different topics but it is focused on the basic fundamentals of performance in soccer, to enable the players to have a preparation standpoint from which future development of their game can take place. It hasn't been my intention to cover the technique of shooting or heading, but to develop the link between the mind and the body in terms of the development of awareness on the pitch.

Most of the work is done in small-sided games where the players get lots of touches on the ball and are able to have concentrated practice on the fundamentals they need to learn. The majority of the exercises have the players spending considerable time touching and manipulating the ball and it is advisable that the coaches allow this to happen and not spend too much time explaining and thus stopping the momentum of the exercises. Show the players what you want then let them get on with it, stepping in to make coaching points only where and when it is appropriate.

Where you can use small sided groups, do so. If you have a squad of twenty players, for example, it is best to split them in two and have each group perform the exercise in question. Numbers don't always allow for the best way to develop any particular exercise but it is up to the individual coach to use his imagination and experience to set it up to allow the players to use the exercise in the best way possible. Always include a soccer ball or several soccer balls in the exercises so players always have the opportunity to practice their skills.

This book has been a journey of discovery for me as I hope it has been for you the reader in its content and focus. It is a different approach that I have taken from conventional soccer coaching books but one that I think is important to explore in terms of the requirements needed to become a soccer player.

The coach can develop from this book with a little imagination new ideas on how to progress players on the principles of the Awareness program. I do not have the exclusive rights of thought on this. I want this book to be the catalyst to encourage coaches to aid the further development of coaching by producing their own ideas and views on the topic and helping to take its development even further.

This is the beauty of the game. People embracing an idea and improving its content, its effectiveness, being inspired to take it to the next level. Have the confidence to read it, use it, break it down and change it to suit your own needs and those of your players. Value your own perspective and use this insight to help your players become the best they can and in turn you will be on the road to be the best coach you can.

On reading this book and using it's methods of coaching, if you believe it has helped you become a better coach, helped your understanding of the thought processes a player has to go through and ultimately guided you into producing better players, then I have achieved my goal.

Thank you for taking the time to share with me the love and enthusiasm I have for this wonderful game. We never stop learning and improving our knowledge and must strive to be the best we can be. We owe this not just to ourselves, but more importantly to all the players we coach over the many years we are involved in the game.

E-mail: wayneharrison@soccerawareness.com
Web Site: www.SoccerAwareness.com